Anthropology of Contemporary Issues

A SERIES EDITED BY

ROGER SANJEK

Accommodation without Assimilation

SIKH IMMIGRANTS IN AN AMERICAN HIGH SCHOOL

Margaret A. Gibson

Cornell University Press

Ithaca and London

First published 1988 by Cornell University Press.

International Standard Book Number (cloth) 0–8014–2122–5
International Standard Book Number (paper) 0–8014–9503–2
Library of Congress Catalog Number 87–47861

Printed in the United States of America
*Librarians: Library of Congress cataloging information
appears on the last page of the book.*

*The paper in this book is acid-free and meets the guidelines
for permanence and durability of the Committee on Production
Guidelines for Book Longevity of the Council on Library Resources.*

To Lynn
with love

Contents

Preface

This book is the outgrowth of a study carried out between 1980 and 1983 on home-school-community linkages and the forces that promote and impede success in school for immigrant youths. It focuses on one group of immigrants, the Punjabi Sikhs from northwest India, and their experiences in an American public high school. The setting for the study is a rural California town I call Valleyside, located in the Sacramento Valley about one hundred miles from San Francisco. I learned of Valleyside and its growing Punjabi population from local educators, who were concerned about mounting interethnic tensions both within the schools and in the community at large. "There has been some really nasty backlash against the Punjabis in recent months, nasty poems circulating about them, people refusing to sit next to them," one school administrator explained. "We have a problem and we need guidance," said another. With funding from the National Institute of Education and with the support and cooperation of district officials and Punjabi Sikh community leaders, a research project was launched to investigate the problems Punjabis faced in school. I served as principal investigator and project director. Dr. Amarjit Singh Bal, himself an emigrant from the Indian state of Punjab, served as coinvestigator and president of the community organization that administered the research grant.

As I carried out background research for the project, it became readily apparent that there was little published material on South Asian Americans in general and less yet about Punjabi Americans. There was a similar dearth of material on the school experiences of immigrant youth. In recent years the need for such materials has become increasingly apparent as the number of immigrants attending American schools continues to rise and the problems of the Indian Punjab continue to make headlines. Most Americans know about the Indian army's invasion of the Golden Temple and Indira Gandhi's subsequent assassination by her Sikh bodyguards, but few know anything about the growing Punjabi Sikh community in America. Most Americans know that immigrant children may encounter difficulties in school, but few know anything specific about their difficulties. This book addresses the joint need for materials on South Asian Americans and on immigrants in our schools.

The book deals with other general themes as well: minority-majority relations, the processes of Americanization and assimilation, mediocrity in American high school education, parental involvement in schooling, and Asian American and immigrant achievement. It explores the economic-adaptation patterns of the Punjabi immigrants as well as their school-adaptation patterns. For comparison, it also treats the school performance of majority-group students.

During the planning phase of the project, Punjabi parents asserted quite explicitly that their children's difficulties in school stemmed not from their home culture and its differences from the dominant culture in this society but from the expectations of "whites," as the Punjabis call them, that the children replace Punjabi ways with those of the larger society. Fieldwork revealed a sharp difference in perspective between the minority and majority groups. In formal interviews and informal conversation, majority-group parents, students, and teachers expressed their belief that the Punjabis needed to give up their Indian ways and to become Americanized. Teachers and administrators assumed, moreover, that schools could and should play a major role in helping to assimilate these newcomers. As used by educators, *assimilation* and *Americanization* meant much the same thing, the absorption of the immigrant group into the American fold. What was implied, also, was that immigrants must shed their distinctive identities and conform to the dominant culture if they are to be accepted. The concept of cultural assimilation was viewed positively by members of the majority group, but it had unmistakably negative connotations for most Punjabis. Like many other minorities in America, Valleyside Punjabis wanted to preserve their separate identity and culture. They admonished their children to withstand conformist pressures, to maintain the symbols of their distinctiveness, and to cultivate their roots within their native community. At the same time, however, they encouraged their young to accommodate themselves to the official rules of the school and to adopt the "good" ways of "the Americans." This book explores this strategy of accommodation and acculturation without assimilation. Although the actual research site will be familiar to many, I have chosen a pseudonym for the town, in hopes that the reader's attention will focus on the generalizable issues that arise from the study rather than a specific town and high school. Many American communities are now feeling the impact of a new wave of immigration, and the experience of Valleyside is in essence that of the whole United States. In using a pseudonym I wish also to deflect attention from the particular school district that hosted the research. Most of the problems described herein are by no means peculiar to any single school setting but are, I would suggest, deeply embedded in the fabric of American society and its system of schooling.

The school district and local community opened their doors to a team of outside researchers because they hoped the insights gleaned would aid their efforts to strengthen educational programs and improve social relations among the different groups served by the Valleyside schools. Although I alone am responsible for the interpretations presented here, I know that the other research team members join me in expressing our gratitude to all the parents, students, and educators who participated in the study and our hope that research findings will contribute to our common goal of improving educational opportunities for young people in Valleyside and elsewhere in the nation. My special thanks go to Andros Karperos, superintendent of schools, and George Zerkovich, high school principal, for facilitating all aspects of the research. Without their support, there could have been no project.

I also acknowledge my enduring gratitude to those who joined with me in carrying out the fieldwork for this study. Amarjit Bal sparked my initial interest in Punjabi Americans and during our two years of collaborative work contributed greatly to my understanding of Sikhs, Sikhism, and the Punjab. Gurdip Dhillon and Beth McIntosh, project research assistants, who must often have wondered if the fieldwork phase would ever end, were always willing to contribute in ways that far exceeded their job descriptions. I am indebted, too, to Amarjit Aujla, Davinder Deol, and Rajinder Singh for a wide variety of assistance, including the interviewing of Punjabi parents, and to Hari Singh Everest, Neelam Agarwal, Bidya Pradhan, and Bob Singh, who served as project advisers and consultants.

The project was administered by the South Asian American Education Association, an organization dedicated to the goals of improving educational opportunities for South Asian Americans and promoting understanding and appreciation of the cultural heritage of the South Asian American people. I extend my thanks to Major Gurcharn Singh Sandhu for staunchly backing the research and to all members of the association's board of directors who supported the project. Grateful thanks go also to the National Institute of Education for funding the fieldwork and for its support of research on the sociocultural context of schooling.

I owe a special debt to those whose ideas and previous research have most directly affected my own. John Ogbu's work on the role of community forces in shaping school performance patterns is reflected throughout this volume. I was fortunate, too, in being able to draw upon Bruce La Brack's extensive research on the Sikhs of northern California. Both served as project consultants and have provided intellectual support in the preparation of this book.

From project inception to manuscript completion, my husband, Lynn Marshall, has stimulated and supported the research. His enthusiasm for the study and personal interest in Sikh history have sparked and sustained my own. As an outgrowth of the Valleyside study, Lynn and I spent the 1983–1984 academic year in Punjab, largely in Pakistan, but traveling in India when opportunity arose. We visited Amritsar, Chandigarh, and the Doaba region of Punjab, the area from which most Valleyside Sikhs have emigrated. In the small village of Salala we were treated to Punjabi hospitality by the families of Sardar Genda Singh Dhillon and Sardar Jagjit Singh Dhillon. Their photographs appear in this book.

My thanks to Kathryn King, Rosalind Van Auker, and Lauretta Wilson at the California State University, Sacramento, library for their assistance in locating reference materials. I am also indebted to Roger Ballard, Christina Paulston, Adrienne Rudge, and Jane Singh for their helpful comments on draft chapters. Finally, I extend my thanks to Roger Sanjek, general editor of the Anthropology of Contemporary Issues Series in which this book appears.

Portions of Chapters 3 and 4 appear, in slightly different form, in *International Migration Review* 22 (Spring 1988) published by the Center for Migration Studies.

MARGARET A. GIBSON

Berkeley, California

Accommodation
without Assimilation

[1]

Introduction:
The Punjabi Sikh Case

The difference between an educated and an uneducated person is
the difference between earth and sky.

Punjabi folk saying

Our schools are filling once more with immigrant children, yet we
know comparatively little about their experiences in school. What
problems do they encounter? How successful are they in overcoming
these problems? How are they and their families fitting into American
society? What can schools do to improve educational opportunities for
immigrant students? This book looks at the schooling of one immigrant
group, the Punjabi Sikhs from northwest India. It focuses both on
barriers to opportunity for Punjabi immigrants and on the Punjabis'
resourcefulness in dealing with the barriers.

The setting for the study is an agricultural community in the Central
Valley of California and the area's only comprehensive high school. I
call the site Valleyside. Like many American communities in recent
years, Valleyside has experienced a rapid influx of immigrants. Between 1965 and 1980 the number of Asian Indians living in and around
Valleyside increased tenfold, to more than six thousand by local estimates. School district records show a growth in Asian enrollment for
grades kindergarten through twelve, from only 2.4 percent in 1972 to
nearly 13 percent by 1981. The overwhelming majority of the new
students are Asian Indians.

The first Indians to settle in Valleyside arrived in the United States
around the turn of the century. Most, however, have come since the
passage of the 1965 Immigration Act, and today they form one of the
fastest growing immigrant communities in America. Between 1965 and

[1]

1985 the number of Asian Indians residing in the United States grew from fewer than 15,000 to more than 500,000. About two-thirds of the recent arrivals were born in India, the remainder in other countries where Indians have established overseas settlements. They come, as they themselves say, because of economic opportunities. Many come also because they have relatives already residing in the United States.

Close to 90 percent of those who settle in Valleyside are Sikhs, members of a religion initiated in Punjab in the latter part of the fifteenth century. Punjab continues to be the homeland for Sikhs and Punjabi is their mother tongue. Most Valleyside Sikhs have migrated directly from Punjab to the United States, but even those few who had previously settled in Britain, Fiji, or East Africa continue to consider themselves Punjabis. Punjab is also home to many Hindus and Muslims, including some few families who have settled in Valleyside. While differing in religious beliefs, Sikh, Hindu and Muslim Punjabis, particularly those from the rural areas, share many elements of a common regional culture and identity.

When India won independence in 1947 Punjab was partioned between India and Pakistan (see Map 1)). The wave of communal violence that followed this partition forced Muslims living in eastern Punjab to move west and, similarly, Sikhs and Hindus living in western Punjab to move east. Many of the Sikh families now living in Valleyside were forced to abandon their farms in Pakistani Punjab and begin life anew in Indian Punjab. The portion of Punjab falling within India was further divided in 1966, again primarily for religious reasons, to create the Indian states of Punjab, Haryana, and Himachal Pradesh. Sikhs are the numerical majority in Punjab, Hindus in Haryana and Himachal Pradesh (see Map 2).

Throughout this book I use both *Punjabis* and *Sikhs* to refer to the Valleyside Sikhs. In discussing school performance I use the more inclusive *Punjabi* to refer specifically to the full group of South Asian students attending Valleyside High—Sikh, Hindu, and Muslim.[1] In a few cases I also distinguish Sikhs from non-Sikhs, primarily in my discussion of which immigrants have taken up orchard farming in Valleyside. This is actually less a matter of religious affiliation than of caste.[2]

The overwhelming majority of Valleyside Punjabis are agriculturalists by tradition. Most have been born into the Jat landowning group in northern India, historically a group of tribes, but now commonly regarded as a caste within the Indian social system. Jats are a proud,

[2]

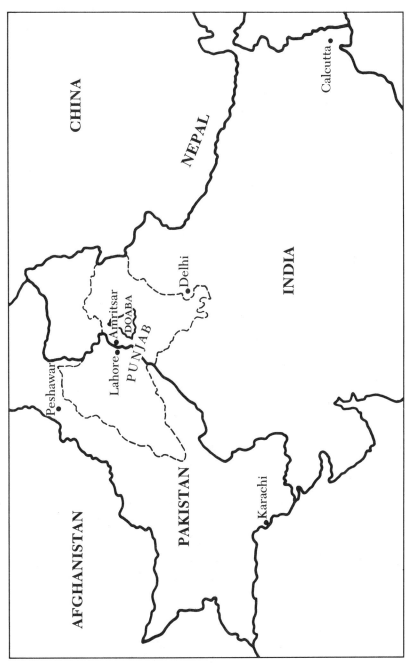

Map 1. The Partition of Punjab in 1947

Map 2. Indian Punjab after 1966

independent, and self-reliant people, dominant in both numbers and power in most Punjabi villages. Although those who have emigrated to Valleyside had only small to moderate-size landholdings in Punjab, they considered themselves, and were considered by others, to be members of the highest-ranking group within the social structure of their villages. They come to the United States not so much to flee either low status or poverty as to maintain or improve their family's economic condition.

[4]

In Valleyside, Punjabi children encounter many difficulties when they first enter school. Many of the obstacles to their success are those faced by any group that has to adapt to a new language and a new way of life. For some youngsters the transition is made swiftly. For others the difficulties prove more lasting. In either case, the problems they experience raise important educational issues. For example, why do some language-minority students become fluent in English while others remain limited-English-proficient throughout their school careers? What can and should the schools do to facilitate the transition process? How can schools help the newcomers acquire the requisite skills to become fully competitive academically and in their search for jobs?

Other problems stem from the adaptation process itself. Immigrant students, for example, must accept standards of behavior at school which are quite different from those that govern them at home. They may even acquire values that are in conflict with those of their parents. If such conflicts arise out of the educational process, what approach should the schools take either to avoid or to deal with them? A third type of problem grows out of majority-group beliefs about Americanization and American culture. How is the national culture represented by the schools or by majority-group students? What is the appropriate role of the school in helping newcomers adapt to life in America? While my discussion of these and related issues treats a relatively small rural town in California and a small, little-studied group of South Asian immigrants, the issues addressed touch most communities and school districts across the nation.

Although this book centers on patterns of school performance, my analysis focuses not on the students themselves but on the family and community forces that influence their performance. To understand these patterns we need to know something of the history and culture of Punjabi Sikhs in India and why they choose to come to America and to Valleyside. We need to know their current situation, their strategies for getting ahead, and the nature of their relationships with members of the dominant white majority in American society. We also need to know their previous educational background and their attitudes about the education of their children. This study of schooling thus becomes a rather broader story of a set of Punjabi Sikh farm families.

The Academic Achievements of Asian Americans

Students whose cultural and linguistic backgrounds differ from those of the dominant group in this society do not yet enjoy equal educational

[5]

opportunities. All minority students face special problems in school. In spite of the barriers, some groups of minority students do comparatively well in school. There is increasing evidence, for example, that students of Asian ancestry, both immigrants and U.S. born, complete more years of education than any other segment of the population (Coleman et al., 1966; Peng et al. 1984; U.S. Commission on Civil Rights 1980; U.S. Bureau of the Census 1984b; see also Hirschman and Wong 1986). In California, nearly 40 percent of all Asian American students graduate in the top 12.5 percent of their high school class, compared with 16.5 percent of white graduates, 5 percent of black Americans, and 4.7 percent of those of Hispanic origin (Turner 1981). A higher proportion of Asian American students, furthermore, today complete four years of college than do students in the population at large, and Asian Americans are overrepresented at some of the most prestigious universities.[3] In California, 15.6 percent of the Asian American high school graduates attend the University of California, compared to 5.5 percent of white graduates and only 1.6 percent of black and Hispanic graduates.[4]

Much of the literature on Asian American academic success refers specifically to students of Chinese and Japanese ancestry, but the 1980 Census data reveal similar patterns of educational achievement for Filipinos, Koreans, Asian Indians, and Vietnamese. Although there is clear variation within and among these groups, in each case they attend school for more years than majority-group age-mates. In the case of Asian Indians, for example, 72 percent of all those aged eighteen to nineteen were attending school in 1980, compared to 53 percent of all non-Hispanic whites of the same age. Of those twenty-two to twenty-four years old, fully 39 percent of the Indians were attending school compared to only 17 percent of the whites (U.S. Bureau of the Census 1983c).

Statistical evidence regarding the school success of immigrant groups must be interpreted with care. Many of the more recently arrived Asian immigrants are highly educated, affluent professionals and the fact that their children do well academically may simply be further evidence of how schools help to reproduce class status from one generation to the next.[5] For example, nearly two-thirds (63.1 percent) of all recent Asian Indian immigrants, twenty-five years old and over, have completed four years of college, and the majority hold managerial, professional, and technical positions (U.S. Bureau of the Census 1984b). As we shall see, however, the statistics on academic persistence seem to apply not only to the offspring of well-educated Asian Indian professionals but also to children of Punjabi Indian agricultural laborers, factory workers, and small orchard farmers.

Various explanations, sometimes contradictory, have been offered for the educational achievements of Asian American youths, including a "culturally advantaged" home environment (Schwartz 1971), interaction between genetic and cultural factors (Vernon 1982), and compatibility between Asian cultural traditions and those of the Euro-American middle class (Caudill and De Vos 1956). None of these explanations, however, adequately attends to the variation in backgrounds and experiences among groups of Asian Americans or within a single group.

The popular image of Asian Americans as a "successful" minority stems also from their patterns of economic achievement. Contrary to popular opinion, however, the income levels of Asian Americans continue to lag behind those of white Americans with comparable education (Hirschman and Wong 1984; Nee and Sanders 1985; U.S. Commission on Civil Rights 1980:12). Although United States census data appear to indicate that the median family income for some Asian groups now surpasses that of white Americans, the summary statistics fail to reflect the number of workers per family, their education, or their residential location. The summary statistics, moreover, fail to represent the diversity of experiences within and among the various groups or to set the groups' achievements in proper context.

Asian Indians provide a case in point.[6] The median income for all Asian Indian families residing in the United States in 1979 was $24,993, or approximately 20 percent more than that for all white American families (U.S. Bureau of the Census 1983c). Yet the median income for Indian families in Valleyside was approximately $15,000, including children's earnings. Newer arrivals, especially those with no teenage children to supplement the family income, lived at or near the official poverty level.

The statistical indicators of Asian American success, reported out of context, encourage neglect of the serious problems many people of Asian descent continue to face in this country (see Chun 1980; Kim and Hurh 1983; Suzuki 1977; Wong 1985; Yoshiwara 1983). Of particular concern in this book are the problems faced in school by Asian American students, those born in this country as well as newer arrivals.[7]

For example, the popular image of academic success places unfair expectations for high achievement on all Asian American young peo-

[7]

ple. The success stereotype, moreover, draws attention away from the pressures on Asian American children to conform to the dominant culture and the impact of such pressures on their social and emotional development. It implies, furthermore, that racism is no longer a problem for Asian Americans and, as an extension, that Asian Americans no longer need assistance from programs directed toward the special needs of minority students. Asian Americans are, thus, "declassified as legitimate minorities" (Wong 1985:65). Yet, as we shall presently see, the Valleyside Punjabis have very special needs, not only associated with the requirements of learning a new language and culture but also resulting directly from the racial hostility and conformist pressures that permeate their school experience. Finally, and most perniciously, there is the danger that statistics on Asian American academic success may be used against other academically less successful minority groups in this society to blame them for their persistent failure and to imply that they need only emulate Asian American strategies to become academically successful (see Suzuki 1983).

To guard against these dangers we need to examine the diversity of experiences among the various groups of Asian Americans as well as within each group. We also need to understand the nature of the success strategies employed by Asian Americans and to explore whether these strategies are characteristic of other groups of academically successful students. At the same time, we need to analyze the barriers to educational success faced by Asian American youths and to ask how these barriers differ from those encountered by other minority students. It is the aim of this book to provide one such analysis.

Immigrant Educational Performance

There is increasing evidence in this country and abroad that the children of immigrants, of whatever ethnic background, often stay in school longer than their majority-group age-mates. Foreign-born children who immigrate at an early age and receive all their schooling in the new country also tend to do comparatively well academically. In the United States, for example, 1980 census data indicate that young people of Cuban ancestry remain in school longer than majority-group peers (U.S. Bureau of the Census 1983c).[8] Smaller-scale ethnographic research indicates similar patterns of school persistence and success for West Indian immigrants (Foner 1983; Fordham 1984; Gibson 1983c)

[8]

and for immigrants from Mexico (Matute-Bianchi 1986; Valverde 1987) and Central America (Suarez-Orozco 1986).

Comparable patterns of minority-group academic success exist in other countries. In Australia, the children of non-English-speaking immigrants, notably Greeks, Yugoslavs, and Italians, have been found to stay in school longer, to like school more, and to have higher educational aspirations than Anglo-Australian youths of similar class background (Marjoribanks 1980; Martin and Meade 1979; Taft and Cahill 1981). Canadian studies also show higher educational and occupational aspirations and better school performance among language-minority immigrants of low socioeconomic background than among either the French-Canadian minority or the English-Canadian majority (Anisef 1975; Masemann 1975; Wolfgang 1975). Canadian-born children of non-English-speaking immigrants tend to be overrepresented in college-preparatory classes, compared to students whose first language is English (Cummins 1984).

In Britain we find a similar pattern. In spite of highly competitive university admissions, a higher percentage of Indian-born males entered British universities in 1979 than males born in the United Kingdom. In addition, significantly more of the Indians were sons of manual workers than were the British-born (Ballard and Vellins 1985). The data suggest not only that Asian Indian students are highly successful academically but also that they have, in the words of British social anthropologist Roger Ballard, a "much greater capacity than do white children to overcome the well-known obstacles of class in the British educational system" (263).[9]

Not all immigrant minority groups do equally well in school, and some, like their nonimmigrant minority counterparts, do significantly less well than the majority. Similar variations exist within each group, with some subgroups performing far less well than others. In spite of these variations, the overall pattern of immigrant academic persistence and achievement is strong and merits serious research attention.

A Comparative Approach

The Punjabi Sikh case is only one among a number of possible examples of immigrant school performance. Although necessarily unique, as is every individual case, it provides the opportunity to go beyond the Asian American success stereotype and place the achievements of one group of recent immigrants within their proper context. It also helps to meet the need for studies that control for such variables as students' prior educational preparation, length of residence in this country, age on arrival, English language proficiency, and parents' socioeconomic backgrounds (Steinberg, Blinde, and Chan 1984; Tsang and Wing 1985).

This book brings to light characteristics of what may be called an immigrant school-adaptation pattern. To illuminate this pattern, I devote substantial attention to "Valleysiders" (my term for the non-Hispanic white population) as a point of comparison to the Punjabis. The experience of the minority is measured against the base line of the majority, and the educational performance of majority students may then also be seen in a new light. Valleysiders, it will be shown, take the academic aspects of their schooling less seriously than the immigrant minority. They accord far greater importance than the Punjabis to extracurricular activities, work experience, and an active social life for teenagers. In a number of respects Punjabi academic performance makes that of the Valleysiders look mediocre.

Fieldwork for this study was carried out over a two-year period (1980–1982) by a team of researchers, Punjabi and non-Punjabi, male and female, insiders and outsiders to the Valleyside setting. The major research methods were those of participant observation and interviewing, both formal and informal. In addition, we analyzed school performance data for all twenty-one hundred students attending Valleyside High School, grades nine through twelve.

Much of the material presented is drawn from comparative interviews with forty-two Punjabi families and forty-two Valleysider families. The Punjabi group included every family that had a child in the senior class at Valleyside High School in October 1980. Since three Punjabi families had two children apiece in the twelfth grade, the group included forty-five students. The Valleysider group was a random sample of all non-Hispanic, non-Punjabi families with children attending twelfth grade in the fall of 1980. [10] These groups of parents and high school seniors, both Valleysider and Punjabi, make up what I refer to as *core samples*, to distinguish them from other samples used herein.

The selection of these samples for intensive study was based on a number of assumptions. First, we wanted a set of students, male and female, newcomer and more established, who were far enough along in high school that we might determine their performance profiles. Seniors, we believed, would best meet this objective and, in addition, would have some plan for what they hoped to do upon graduating from high school.

Second, since few Punjabi students drop out of high school and since Valleyside High is the only comprehensive high school in the area, we assumed that this group of seniors would give us a cross section of the larger Valleyside Punjabi community. Not all subsections of the population were equally well represented, of course, and some were not included at all, but this group of forty-two families yielded clearly defined patterns of adaptation among both parents and students. It also provided insights into the diversity within the Punjabi population at large. The interviews with Valleysiders offered a point of comparison, enabling us to see more clearly the similarities and differences between the school-adaptation patterns of the minority and majority groups.

Members of the research team participated in a broad range of community activities. Our research focus, however, was always schools and family involvement in schooling, rather than the neighborhood, the workplace, or the total Valleyside community as such. The analysis draws from our observations both within and outside the high school, as well as from the full set of comparative interviews with the seniors and their parents.

In addition to the Punjabis and the Valleysiders, there are a significant number of Mexican American students attending Valleyside schools. At the time of fieldwork Mexican Americans made up some 13 percent of the total Valleyside school population and 10 percent of the high school population. Although full analysis of Mexican American school-adaptation patterns lies beyond the scope of this study, I have included comparative statistics on the performance of Mexican American students attending Valleyside High. In formal academics the Mexican Americans, *as a group*, perform less well than either the majority group or the Punjabis. A subgroup of Mexican American high school students are performing extremely well, however. In the concluding chapter I return to these intergroup and intragroup variations.

A casual visitor to the Valleyside High campus would note that about a quarter of the student population is darker in hair and complexion than the rest. About half of these are Mexican Americans, and half Punjabis. All have definite pride of bearing. The visitor sees no glaring differences in dress or grooming between these groups or between minority and nonminority students. Everyone, in fact, is casually dressed and generally well groomed, in relaxed California fashion, quite in keeping with the campus itself. The buildings have a rather

Between classes at Valleyside High School.

suburban style, informal, single-story, and sprawling in a well-trimmed landscape. The physical setting, all open and sunshiny, perfectly expresses the easy informality of the students.

Among the Valleysider students—that is to say, the three-quarters of the student population who are non-Hispanic white—there is perhaps greater diversity in clothes than between the majority and the minorities. Valleysiders may range from the very neatly and somewhat more expensively outfitted "Quaddie" to the somewhat more scruffy "Burn-outs," "Cowboys," and "Back-parking-lotters." These differences might seem insignificant to an outsider, but they are very strong and very important to the students themselves. To recognize differences between Punjabis and Mexican Americans the visitor would likely need a student informant. Both groups are well groomed, al-

[12]

though in different styles. Punjabis tend to dress closer to the Valleysider norm. The Mexican American style tends to darker colors, often black and white, with sharply ironed pleats. An occasional Punjabi boy will have a topknot of long hair tied into a handkerchief or turban, and most Punjabi girls will have long, luxuriant, braided hair. A practiced eye might recognize that Punjabi girls differ from other groups by trying to look inconspicuous. It is most difficult to read in this seemingly relaxed and homogeneous mass of teenage students the wide differences in school performance which actually exist both between and within these groups.

This book describes school performance patterns and home-school-community linkages for males and females, rich and poor. Among the Punjabi students it also distinguishes the performance of recent arrivals from that of those raised from childhood in Valleyside. Because only a small number of second-generation Punjabis attend Valleyside High—in our sample of forty-two Punjabi families only one parent and six students were American-born—the focus is necessarily on the first generation. Background materials on Sikhs in their native India contribute to the analysis. In the concluding chapter I return to the more general issue of why immigrant minorities frequently do better in school than their nonimmigrant counterparts.

Sikhs and Sikhism

The Sikh faith was founded by Guru Nanak (1469–1539), the son of a Hindu record keeper who lived in a village some fifty miles west of Lahore.[11] Guru Nanak opposed both ritualism and hierarchy in religion and was critical of the formalism and ritualism of both the Hindu and Muslim priestly classes. Most especially, he believed that there is one Truth and only one and that all persons should have direct and individual access to the deity, each finding his or her own understanding. Following from this tenet, he preached a message of egalitarianism in which divisions between castes and between Hindus and Muslims made no sense. To help break the rituals of the Hindu caste system Guru Nanak instituted *langars*, communal kitchens where all ate together without regard to birth-ascribed status and Hindu barriers against commensality.

Nanak's teachings were elaborated by nine successors, who, as they gathered more and more of a following, became increasingly powerful politically. Their growing strength brought them into conflict with the local Mughal authorities. Arjun (1563–1606), the fifth Sikh Guru, completed the building of the Sikh temple in Amritsar, the holiest of Sikh shrines. In addition, he was responsible for compiling the writings of his predecessors, along with his own, into a holy book known as the *Granth Sahib*, which also includes writings of Hindu and Muslim poet-saints from throughout northern India.

The Mughal emperor, first impressed by the work of Guru Arjun, eventually grew jealous of him and his following and found an excuse to have him executed. In the period of Sikh persecution that followed, the sect began to change its character. This change was symbolized by Guru Hargobind (1595–1644), Arjun's son, who assumed his father's seat with two swords strapped around his waist, the one to symbolize temporal power and the other spiritual power. More and more Punjabis were drawn to Sikhism and to Hargobind's call for them to defend themselves against Mughal hostilities. The situation came to a head in the time of Guru Gobind Singh (1666–1708), the last of the ten Sikh Gurus, whose father had also been executed by the Mughal authorities.

The Sikhism of Nanak and the other early Gurus was spiritual and nonpolitical, but Sikhism under Gobind Singh became increasingly political and militant. Gobind Singh gave this change its philosophical justification, writing, "When all other means have failed, it is righteous to draw the sword" (as quoted in Singh 1953:44). Khushwant Singh describes this turbulent period in Indian history and its impact on Sikhs:

> The decaying Mughal Empire took to making scapegoats of minorities to explain away its failures. There were pogroms of unprecedented savagery in which the small community of the Sikhs was almost exterminated. Coincident with persecutions within the country came new Muslim invasions from the north, which destroyed any people or institution which they deemed un-Islamic. In such circumstances, martial traditions were forged which became an integral part of Sikh life and gave the Sikhs the reputation of being a fighting people. [1953:45]

Guru Gobind Singh turned the Sikhs into a formally corporate community by baptizing his followers into the Khalsa, a community of "the pure." Those who were baptized, women as well as men, pledged to observe five symbols of their faith, known as the "Five Ks": unshorn hair and beard (*kes*), a comb (*kangha*) worn in the hair to keep it tidy, a

Village elders having tea in Punjab.

steel band or bracelet (*kara*) worn on the wrist, a dagger or sword (*kirpan*), and a pair of shorts (*kach*) designed to allow free movement during fighting. It is likely, writes Khushwant Singh, "that by having his followers wear emblems which made them easily recognisable, the Guru wanted to raise a body of men [and women] who would not be able to deny their faith when questioned, but whose external appearance would invite persecution and breed courage to resist it" (1953:31). Guru Gobind also called upon all Sikhs to drop their Hindu caste names and, in their place, for men to adopt the name Singh ("lion") and women the name Kaur ("princess"). The Khalsa was thus to be a community of equals in which hereditary caste divisions were indistinguishable.

Guru Gobind Singh's vision of the Sikhs was as soldier-saints whose distinctive marks were simultaneously symbolic of the ascetic, the householder, and the militant soldier. With Guru Gobind the succes-

[15]

sion of Sikh Gurus came to an end. Upon his own initiation into the Khalsa, Gobind Singh announced that he would have no physical successors, that the *Guru Granth Sahib* would take over his role as the spiritual teacher and the Khalsa would assume his temporal role.

Sikhs since Gobind Singh

In the century following Gobind Singh, roughly the eighteenth century, the Sikhs had need of his warrior doctrine. Two Muslim groups competed for power in Punjab, Mughal emperors to the east and south, their power on the wane, and Afghans to the northwest, seeking to seize control. The Sikhs had to fend for themselves not only in raising their crops, tending to their families, and honoring their Gurus but in resisting great political powers feuding over control. They had also, of course, to define themselves as a distinct group in the larger mass of Hindu and Muslim peoples in South Asia. The experience forged a long-lived set of values and institutions, inspired by the teachings of the Sikh Gurus but tempered in the fire of life-and-death struggle and upheld despite constant contact with other religions.

In the eighteenth century the Sikhs were often forced into hiding, their only recourse to struggle individually or in small groups using something resembling guerrilla tactics. There were periods when Sikh shrines were desecrated and many Sikhs took refuge outside of Punjab. Sikhs were slaughtered by the thousands, and they responded by slaughtering their enemies when the occasion offered. In time they restored their holy shrines and reestablished themselves in Punjab. They carefully maintained their history, moreover, and especially the record of their martyrs.

Under Maharajah Ranjit Singh, in the nineteenth century, the Sikhs established a nation in which they were preeminent. There, they proved their economic productivity, administrative competence, military prowess, and especially their adaptability to modern "Western" technology and administration. Ranjit's Punjab, rich and strong, proved irresistible to the British, who seized the Punjab in two bloody and difficult military campaigns. Sikhs, thereafter, with their agricultural productivity in both older areas and new irrigated "canal colonies" and their military utility in the British Indian army, became mainstays in the British Raj.

When Sikhs revolted against British rule in a long series of bloody uprisings in the 1920s, in the name of protecting and purifying their temples and shrines, it shook the empire to its roots. Even earlier, at the time of World War I, overseas Sikhs returned to British India in order to foment revolution and died in the cause. The memory of those who gave their lives to these efforts are carefully preserved, both in formal written histories and in family traditions. Families obtain honor and reputation not only by hard work and material success, which then must be shared with the community, at least in part, but in courageous devotion and sacrifice to Sikh causes. Thus did Sikhs become the empire's most dangerous revolutionaries, largely for the same reasons that they had seemed to serve the empire so well, and thus did they produce in the twentieth century a series of courageous martyrs who resisted oppression and gave their lives for the maintenance of Sikhism, and for the independence of India itself.

Out of this historical experience there emerged a set of Sikh values and institutions—some of them common to other Punjabis—which have proved their viability and have been reinforced by subsequent social experience. Much of this culture has been embodied in folk sayings and traditional customs. There arose quite early on, for example, a special Sikh usage of the term *sardar*, which can mean something roughly equivalent to "sir" in American usage but with entirely different connotations. The word in Punjabi means "local leader," but it may be used in reference to any Sikh man, for example, as a form of polite greeting or as the subject of a folksy joke about a seemingly simple rustic from village Punjab turning the tables on an adversary. The principal connotation of this folk tradition is that every Sikh is a leader. There are similarly defined traditions and customs of friendship and brotherhood.

The egalitarian precepts of the Gurus were worked into tradition and language in a way that made every individual a venturer. Likewise, the Gurus' precept demanding hard and honest labor was worked into the texture of daily life. An exceedingly strong value was placed on family and the upholding of family honor, so that a Sikh man might go off to distant places and his ties with kin back home remain intact. Sikhs have developed toughness and resiliency as conscious community values. In India or abroad, they know they can rely upon those with whom they share close emotional ties. Sikhs, furthermore, rally around their community institutions. Service to the community, *seva*, is integral to gaining and maintaining honor and prestige, *izzat*.

Sikhs can succeed at intensely entrepreneurial activities and yet

[17]

readily unite for social and political action. In addition, they have always been riven by factionalism, usually intense, often acrimonious, occasionally violent. Sikhs contend with one another, even while loudly insisting on unity. This contradiction seems partly a product of their independence but likewise of their willingness, when challenged, fearlessly to stand their ground. They are not quick to fight, but as the British and Indira Gandhi have discovered in their turn, they are tough and deadly when pushed beyond forbearance.

The Current Crisis in Punjab

Full analysis of the issues leading up to the current crisis in Punjab lies beyond the scope of this book. The research here described took place several years before Gandhi's assault on the Golden Temple and her subsequent assassination. Most of those we interviewed had left Punjab well before the situation began to take on its current proportions. Because almost all media coverage of Punjab and Sikhs emphasizes the terrorism of Sikh radicals, however, and the call by these radicals, and indeed a growing number of moderates as well, for an independent Sikh nation, it is necessary to offer some discussion of the present situation so that the adaptation patterns of Valleyside Sikhs can be understood in proper context.

Sikhs account for only 2 percent of India's total population, but 8 percent of all central government employees and more than 6 percent of the officers in the governmental administrative services. Sikhs have also distinguished themselves in industry, trade, medicine, sports, and, of course, the military and agriculture. More than 7 percent of the army today is Sikh, and their proportion once was higher still. The "green revolution" in Punjab has not only brought prosperity to the state but has made India self-sufficient in the production of grain. Since 1951 Punjab's crop production has increased sixfold and much of the country is dependent on the rice and wheat produced by Punjabi farmers. Punjab today enjoys the highest per capita income of all Indian states (Akbar 1985).

The green revolution has brought overall prosperity, but it has also contributed to the present crisis. Many of the provisions of Indira Gandhi's governments—both from 1971–1977 and again from 1980 until her death in 1984—discriminated against the interests of the Indian farmers and the rights of states to govern their own internal

Sikh farmer crushing sugarcane in Punjab.

affairs.[12] Far from feeling they were being rewarded for their productivity, Punjabi farmers interpreted many of Gandhi's measures as deliberate intrusions into internal state affairs designed to weaken political opposition and to impose her rule. While the state governments in India control agriculture, the central government controls both industry and commerce. Because of central government interference, Punjab has not been able to develop its industrial base as rapidly as some other states, and therefore many educated Sikhs have been forced to search for work outside of Punjab.

The central government under Gandhi's leadership also held down the price it would pay for rice and wheat, for years imposing support levels far below the actual rise in production costs. At the same time, it barred farmers from selling their produce privately. These factors,

[19]

combined with many others, give Punjabi farmers the feeling that they are being exploited by the central government.

Other serious and legitimate issues involve water rights, the sharing of the state capital, Chandigarh, with the neighboring state of Haryana, restrictions on the size of family farms, and Gandhi's disfranchisement of Punjab's political mainstream. This last proved the most dangerous and ultimately brought on the present tragic state of affairs. Not only did Gandhi initially provide covert support to the Sikh fundamentalist leader, Sant Jarnail Singh Bhindranwale, as a means of destabilizing Sikh opposition to herself and her Congress party, but she also suppressed the voices of moderate Punjabi politicians and used her control over the media to characterize all Sikhs who spoke out against her as religious fanatics, terrorists, and separatists. The results of these and her other more explicit policies for suppressing responsible Punjabi leadership were the rise in power of Bhindranwale—who quickly became a threat to Gandhi's influence—and a growing conviction on the part of many reasonable and responsible Sikhs that Gandhi was indeed deliberately punishing them for daring to stand up for what they perceived to be their interests.

In the end, Gandhi ordered the Indian army to invade the Golden Temple in order to rout Bhindranwale and his band of followers, who had made their headquarters there. Other means might well have been used, and sooner, to deal with the dissidents. Instead, the army's attack, which heavily damaged the Golden Temple complex, totally destroyed Sikh archives, and killed more than one thousand innocent Sikh pilgrims, was perceived by Sikhs everywhere as an attack on Sikhism itself.[13] This, and the massacre of thousands of Sikhs by angry Hindu mobs after Gandhi was assassinated so outraged the Sikh community throughout the world that many Sikhs today feel there is no means, save independence, to protect themselves. Many others, and within India they may be the majority, see a separate Sikh nation as unworkable and hope there can be some other peaceful solution to the present crisis.

Although news of day-to-day life in Punjab is hard to come by—the state has almost continuously been off-limits to foreigners, including overseas Indians, since Gandhi's assassination—it seems that village life continues apace, largely unaffected by communal tensions. Even in cities friendships are maintained across sectarian boundaries. The underlying causes for the present troubles were largely political and economic, not religious. "Religious differences as such," as Murray

Leaf points out, "are not a threat to national integration, but religious intolerance incorporated into political conflicts certainly would be" (1985:496).

Roger Ballard toured Punjab in the summer of 1985 and filed this report:

> Away from [the] obvious centres of tension, everyone was at pains to stress the normality of everyday life, and that close personal relationships are still sustained between Hindus and Sikhs.
>
> Among economically active Sikhs, farmers, industrialists and business-men, the idea of Khalistan—a separatist state—was almost universally rejected. . . . Those who sought extreme solutions, I was frequently told, were a very small minority, almost all were either students or unem-ployed. But other, more bitter undercurrents are also present. Sikhs remain deeply distrustful of Delhi and all its works, and are strong supporters of greater regional autonomy. [1985:406][14]

The residents of Punjab, Hindu as well as Sikh, have nothing to gain by fighting among themselves. Prior to Gandhi's ill-advised assault on the Golden Temple and some fifty other *gurdwaras* throughout Pun-jab, Bhindranwale's militant stance was not widely supported by Sikhs in India. Even after the desecration of the Golden Temple, there was no widespread Sikh revenge. Similarly, after the massacre of thousands of Sikhs in Delhi following Gandhi's assassination, law and order was maintained in Punjab and no revenge was taken by the Sikh commu-nity at large.[15] Most Punjabis, Sikhs and Hindus alike, have responded to the current tragic course of events with great forbearance.

Although the current history of Punjab has little direct bearing on the story told here, these events are deeply felt by Valleyside Punjabis. The emotional tie to Punjab and to Sikh holy places is strong. Current events in India, moreover, have great bearing on the continuity of Punjab as the Sikh homeland and the symbol to Sikhs worldwide of their faith and their persistence as a separate people.[16]

The next chapter offers a theoretical framework for understanding the school performance of Punjabi Sikhs and other immigrant minor-ities. Chapter 3 provides a brief history of Asian Indian immigration into the United States, focusing on the impact of American immigration laws on Punjabi adaptation patterns prior to 1965. Chapters 4 and 5 describe the Valleyside case, first looking at the economic adaptations of the forty-two Punjabi families in the core sample and then at their relationships with the Valleysider majority. In Chapter 6 the discussion shifts to schooling and the academic performance of the various groups of students. Chapter 7 examines home-school linkages and the role of family and community forces in shaping school-adaptation patterns. Chapter 8 turns to barriers to school achievement, focusing on the tracking system at the high school and the pressures on minority students to conform to the ways of the majority group. The concluding chapter centers on the implications of the study for both theory and practice.

[2]

An Emerging Theory of
Minority School Performance

> We have come to this country, and we have to learn from them
> [white Americans], but we also have to keep the advice of our
> country. . . . If the children will just take up their good values and
> leave the rest, then we will keep our standards. If we leave every-
> thing and do as they do, we will go downwards.
>
> Punjabi farmer, Valleyside

Punjabi Sikhs say of themselves, "Wherever we go, we are successful." Success, however, is a relative term and a subjective one. A
freshly arrived immigrant judges economic success differently from an
old-timer. For both wealth is a primary means of gaining honor for the
individual, the family, and the community, but Sikh perceptions regarding wealth and the attainment of it are shaped by their prior
experiences in Punjab as well as by the opportunity structure in America. Thus, a newcomer to America views a minimum hourly wage of
$3.35 in an entirely different light from one who has lived here many
years. Throughout this study I provide both objective and subjective
data on "success." I show how Punjabis are doing economically and
educationally in comparison to Indians back in Punjab and to the
Valleysider majority. I also explore Punjabi perspectives on success
and show how their comparative sense of satisfaction with life in America influences their adaptation patterns.

The Sikhs of Valleyside, no less than those in India, are justly proud
of their accomplishments, achieved in many cases in the face of severe
adversity. They are also justly proud of their success in maintaining a
separate identity. Within India and wherever they have immigrated, in
Britain, East Africa, Canada, and the United States, Sikhs have re-

sisted absorption into the majority group. Endogamous marriage practices, together with a shared sense of peoplehood arising out of their unique historical experience (Castile 1981; Spicer 1971, 1980), help Sikhs, wherever they settle, to persist as a minority enclave. Most readily distinguished by their unshorn hair, their beards, their steel bangles and their brightly colored turbans, they are also known everywhere for their rugged independence, their proud demeanor, and their insistence that fellow Sikhs adhere to cultural norms. Sikhs are especially concerned that their children grow up within the fold and place considerable pressure on their young to uphold Punjabi Sikh values and customs.

At the same time—and this has been an important factor in their adaptation—Sikhs have proved themselves receptive to change and adept at learning new ways from other groups with whom they come in contact. Sikh migrants consciously and explicitly advocate a strategy of accommodation to their new environment. The nature of their accommodations varies according to the social system of the host society and their specific situation within it.[1] In general, however, Sikh parents encourage their children to become skilled in the ways of the dominant group. Just as explicitly they counsel their young to resist complete assimilation and to maintain strong roots within the Sikh community.

So it is with the Punjabi Sikhs of Valleyside. Their strategy of *accommodation and acculturation without assimilation* is a major theme of this book. I use the term *assimilation* to describe the process whereby individuals of one society or ethnic group are incorporated or absorbed culturally into another. At the individual level, cultural assimilation implies loss of identification with one's former group. Although proud to become Americans, most Punjabi Sikh immigrants openly and actively reject the notion that Americanization means giving up their separate identity.

In the present case, rejection of assimilation by no means indicates a rejection of all aspects of the dominant or mainstream American culture. Quite the reverse. Valleyside Punjabis encourage their children to adopt the "good" ways of "the Americans." And the children, for their part, rapidly and readily embrace many more aspects of the dominant culture than most of their parents would prefer. Acculturation occurs for all Punjabi immigrants and their children in their new Valleyside setting. By *acculturation* I mean a process of culture change and adaptation which results when groups with different cultures come into contact. The end result need not be the rejection of old traits or

[24]

their replacement. Acculturation may be an additive process or one in which old and new traits are blended (Haviland 1985:628–29). Valleyside Punjabis adopt many aspects of the dominant American culture while also maintaining their Punjabi culture. In the process of acculturation their Punjabi culture is itself transformed.

In some areas, such as those pertaining to family honor, sex roles, and marriage, Punjabis actively resist the influence of the dominant culture, fearing that such influence will erode values they perceive as fundamental to the persistence of the Punjabi identity. Their resistance to conformist pressures leads, at times, to situations of conflict between themselves and white Americans. Punjabis respond to such tensions by keeping themselves socially separate, by demanding the right to maintain their ways and protect their interests, with force if necessary, or by accommodating themselves only in public to the norms of the larger society and, in private, observing a Punjabi way of life.

In overseas settings, Punjabis frequently make an effort to conform publicly to requirements of the larger society in order to avoid or reduce conflict between themselves and other groups. In other words, Punjabis choose in certain situations to subordinate their ways to those of the dominant group when they believe this to be in their best interests or those of their children. They may adopt such an approach even though they consider their own ways superior to those of the majority. It is in this sense that I use the term *accommodation*. For example, most Punjabi parents urge their children to accommodate themselves to the official rules and standards of the public schools in this country—such as the one that has adolescent males and females attend school together—even when they may personally disagree with these rules.

Although the concept of accommodation in the social science literature generally implies the response of a minority group to situations of racial conflict and inequality, and does so in the present case as well, the term also refers to a process of mutual adaptation between persons or groups for the purposes of reducing conflict and allowing separate group identities and cultures to be maintained. I return to this notion of mutual adaptation and accommodation in the concluding chapter.

Not all Valleyside Sikhs pursue a common strategy of accommodation and acculturation without assimilation. Some embrace far fewer aspects of the dominant culture than others; some are far less willing than others to subordinate their Punjabi ways to the will of the majority. A few advocate full assimilation, at least for their children, arguing

[25]

that it is in their children's best interests to become incorporated into the mainstream. In general, the older generation—the parents of high school students—tends more toward accommodation and the younger generation—the students themselves—tends more toward acculturation. Both agree, however, on the desirability of resisting full assimilation. My focus is on this predominant pattern.

Valleyside Punjabis differ sharply from the urbanized and highly educated Asian Indians, including many Sikh professionals, who have settled since 1965 in metropolitan areas throughout the United States.[2] Most of those who settle in Valleyside come directly from small villages in Punjab and have had little previous contact with Western life-styles and values. They arrive with few salable skills, speak little English, if any, and, in the case of women in particular, have had little formal education. Most must work, at least initially, in back-breaking, low-paid jobs as farm laborers in Valleyside fruit orchards. They are viewed with hostility by many Valleysiders and encounter prejudice and discrimination in their daily lives and in their search for jobs.

In spite of these difficulties, a substantial proportion of the Punjabis who arrived in Valleyside before 1970 had become farm owners by 1980. Punjabis today own approximately half the peach acreage in the tri-county area surrounding Valleyside, an area that includes some of the richest and most productive orchard land in California and produces about a third of the state's canned peaches.[3] A few Punjabi old-timers have become large landowners, but most have only small holdings. More recent arrivals, moreover, who in 1980 comprised about three-quarters of the Valleyside Punjabis, work either as agricultural laborers or as factory workers in nearby cities. Nonetheless, in spite of their modest occupations, most Punjabi families manage to save sizable sums of money for such expenses as a child's wedding, a return trip to India, or the down payment on a home. Their children, furthermore, armed with American educational credentials, are entering white-collar and solidly middle-class occupations such as engineering and computer science. Although most maintain a strong Punjabi identity, they move easily in the larger American society and enjoy many aspects of middle-class American life, such as family outings to Disneyland, a honeymoon in Hawaii, and a vacation in Europe.

Most of the Punjabi parents we interviewed believed themselves to be better off financially than would have been the case had they remained in India, and many Valleysiders also view them as economically successful. To say, however, that these Valleyside Punjabi Sikhs are successful, as I do in certain contexts and as they do themselves, is not to say that they have achieved parity with the white majority or that prejudice and discrimination have ceased to have a negative impact on their lives or livelihood. *Success*, according to *Webster's*, means "the gaining of wealth or position" or "something having a favorable or satisfactory result." It is in this sense that I use the term.

In order to explain the accomplishments of these Indian rustics, Valleysiders have devised a folk explanation, which maintains that the Punjabis are able to borrow money at discounted rates from special banks available only to Indians. The loan money, it is insisted, is actually American tax dollars, sent originally to India and somehow recycled to the overseas Indians. The myth of the "cheap bank loan" expresses the dominant group's more generalized animosity toward the minority and helps promote a sense of righteous hostility toward the Punjabi Sikhs. Unwilling to accept the economic successes of a group of culturally distinctive, non-English-speaking and largely uneducated Asian immigrants or to place their accomplishments within proper context, Valleysiders prefer to believe that they themselves are victims of unfair economic competition.

Punjabi School-Performance Patterns

Punjabi students raised in the United States are about as likely as majority-group classmates to be placed in "fast track," college-preparatory classes on entering high school, even though most enter elementary school knowing little or no English. While in high school they take, on average, somewhat more math and science classes than nonminority classmates and almost as many English classes. Gender differences emerge, however. Punjabi boys take far more science and math than Punjabi girls.

There are sharper differences between the American-educated Punjabis and newer arrivals. Those who arrive in this country after fourth grade fare far less well in school than those raised from early childhood in America. Although most persist in school through twelfth grade, many never break out of a remedial track in high school and are destined to be at a competitive disadvantage in their subsequent search for employment. For these students the combination of barriers simply proves too great, despite a home culture that is similar in most respects

[27]

to that of Punjabi classmates who entered American schools at an earlier age.

These patterns will be explored in the pages that follow. We shall see how the home culture contributes to the positive school-adaptation patterns of Punjabi children even though there are few books in the home and parents, by and large, have limited formal education. An immigrant perspective on the American opportunity structure, together with folk theories of success passed on from parents to children, help account for academic accomplishments, even in the face of major obstacles. Within school, these barriers relate to the structure of school programs and the prejudiced attitudes of many white youngsters. They relate also to differing definitions of what is appropriate behavior for teenagers. Punjabi girls, in particular, must cope with conflicting standards regarding suitable behavior and these differences can impede educational progress.

Valleysider students provide sharp contrast to the Punjabis. They face no social or cultural barriers of similar magnitude to those encountered by the Punjabi students, either immigrant or native born. Their parents have more education, better jobs, and higher income—all factors commonly correlated with academic success. Yet the Valleysiders' academic achievements, on the whole, are generally no better than those of their American-educated Punjabi peers. Although Valleysider performance, as measured by standardized test scores, compares favorably with national norms, it is nonetheless well below their obvious potential. As a group they invest less effort in their education, have more discipline problems in school, and are more frequently absent than Punjabi classmates. Valleysider educational aspirations are also lower.

Punjabi students seek to sidestep anticipated social disadvantages in the job market by securing training and credentials beyond those of their white peers. Formal education, from their perspective and that of their parents, is the single most important key to future job opportunities in America. They learn from their parents to apply themselves to their studies, to avoid trouble with their classmates, and to heed their teachers' advice. Punjabi parents provide strong support for education, although they themselves have little contact with school officials and rarely become involved in school affairs.

Punjabi youngsters succeed in school to the degree that they do in spite of sharing group characteristics that many researchers have correlated with school failure—parents with low-income, low-status jobs, little formal education, little or no proficiency in English, and a cultural tradition regarded as "backward" and un-American by many in the larger society. Not all Punjabi adults fit the standard description, but enough do that their success strategies merit attention.

Theoretical Perspective on Minority Schooling

In this book I want to draw together two distinct theoretical perspectives used to explain the school performance of minority students. The first, which may be called the cultural discontinuity theory, assumes that educational problems arise, in large part at least, because of a mismatch between the culture and language of the school and that of the students. Research drawing on this framework has shown how schools fail to build on the knowledge and skills minority children bring with them from home. Thus, minority youngsters not only feel less comfortable with the teaching-learning environment at school but are at a competitive disadvantage with those who reach school already skilled in the ways of the dominant culture.

Anthropologists have long been interested in the relationship between a student's home culture and language and his or her performance in school (Hewitt 1905). A growing body of research supports the thesis that learning difficulties in school may result from differences between language styles, patterns of interaction, and values at home and in the school (Byers and Byers 1972; Dumont 1972; Erickson 1984; Erickson and Mohatt 1982; Gay and Cole 1967; Gibson 1982; Heath 1982; Ogbu 1982; Philips 1972, 1982; Scollon and Scollon 1981). Many of these studies have focused on how "negative transfer" between home and school learning environments impedes school progress (Cazden 1982:211).[4]

In Valleyside, too, areas of sharp contrast, even conflict, arise between the values and behaviors learned by Punjabi children at home and those taught at school. These differences in some instances, as for example in matters pertaining to independent versus group decision making or relations between the sexes, are so severe as to interfere directly with school performance. At the same time there are many areas of congruence in which the attitudes and values learned within the Punjabi family and community—for example, beliefs about discipline, authority, work, and individual achievement—reinforce the expectations of the school environment and help to promote academic

[29]

success. The present case provides opportunity to explore how some aspects of the home culture of Valleyside Punjabis contribute positively, others negatively, to the teaching-learning process.

The second perspective, which may be called the structural inequalities theory, emphasizes the status of a particular minority or social class group within the socioeconomic structure of the host society and the group's relationship with the dominant majority. It assumes that low achievement in school is an outgrowth of the system of social stratification and that schools function to maintain the status quo (Bourdieu 1974; Bowles and Gintis 1976; Willis 1977). Some students, most frequently those of higher socioeconomic status, are prepared for professional and technical jobs, while other students, generally minorities and whites of low socioeconomic background, are prepared for blue-collar and lower-level white-collar positions. Studies that draw on this framework have shown how the educational system, through curriculum and methods of counseling, testing, and tracking students, creates barriers that result in very unequal opportunities for poor and minority students (Erickson and Shultz 1982; Leacock 1968; Mehan 1978; Mehan et al. 1986; McDermott 1977; Ogbu 1974; Rist 1970; Rosenfeld 1971; Sieber 1978). This book provides further evidence of these sorts of barriers.

Both theories, that which focuses on cultural differences and that which focuses on the social structure of a society and its schools, help account for the below-average academic performance of disproportionate numbers of poor and minority youngsters. Neither explains, however, why some groups of recently arrived immigrants, such as Cubans, Salvadorans, Koreans, and West Indians, along with Valleyside Punjabis, are, by some measures, more academically successful than majority-group students. Nor do these theories explain why immigrant minorities are, as groups, often more successful in transcending cultural and structural barriers than other, more established minority groups, such as American blacks, Puerto Ricans, and American Indians.

Writing about the development of bilingual proficiency in language-minority students, James Cummins (1981:34–36) questions the validity of the "linguistic mismatch" explanation of school failure. Certainly children who enter school limited in English face a barrier that does not exist for native English speakers. As Courtney Cazden has pointed out, however, "All human beings, even young children, are capable of coping with differential demands, and of switching their response styles—e.g., from one language to another—with finely tuned appropriateness" (1982:211). The issue is why some language-minority children seem to have a much easier time than others in learning a second language and in adjusting themselves to the other demands of the classroom situation.

Increasingly, studies in the field of minority education point to the interaction among cultural and structural (or contextual) variables and suggest the need not only for a synthesis of existing theoretical perspectives but increased attention to a minority group's particular situation within the host society.⁵ Newer studies focus on the dynamics of minority-majority group relations, looking not only at how members of the majority group view the minority but also at the minority group's perceptions of the majority and of the opportunities available to its members.

John Ogbu, for example, has written extensively about the impact of the job ceiling in this country on the academic performance of American blacks and other "castelike" minorities. He suggests that if minority students believe they will be unfairly rewarded for their academic accomplishments, they may have trouble accepting school rules and may reduce the effort they invest in their schooling. The result is poor academic performance (Ogbu 1974, 1978, 1982). School failure, from this perspective, may be seen at least in part as an adaptive strategy related to a realistic appraisal of unequal opportunities in the job market. Not all groups view schooling as an avenue to occupational mobility (De Vos 1975; Giroux 1983; Willis 1977).

In more recent discussions of the impact of family and community forces on student achievement, Ogbu suggests that minority students who do poorly in school appear to equate school learning with the loss of their separate identity; they therefore resist following the school's rules of behavior for academic success (1984). Pursuing a similar line of analysis with regard to second-language learning, Cummins (1981) offers "bicultural ambivalence" as explanation for why certain minority groups, such as the Finns in Sweden, Mexican Americans in the United States, and Franco-Ontarians in Canada, perform poorly in the dominant language of the country.

Other researchers have noted that minority beliefs about the majority culture and the role of public schools can interfere with student achievement. Referring to indigenous minorities, such as Hawaiians and Navajos, Cathie Jordan asks: "Is the process of becoming educated necessarily the process of becoming assimilated? If so, a very terrible

[31]

choice is involved" (1986:1–2). Similarly, Betty Jo Kramer (1983) observes that Ute Indian students learn from their parents to view school as the "enemy" because it fosters assimilation into the majority culture and contributes to a rejection of tribal society and traditions. "The fundamental issue," says Judith Kleinfeld, a specialist on the education of native Alaskan children, "is that some cultural groups in some circumstances decide that they do not want to acquire the attributes of the majority culture" (1983:286; see also Lambert 1975:61; Matute-Bianchi 1986:254; Taft 1983:11; Troike 1984:48).

There is increasing evidence to suggest that minority performance in school is influenced not only by home-school cultural discontinuities and structural inequalities but by students' beliefs about the majority language and culture and about schools as agents of cultural assimilation (Lambert 1975:61; Taft 1983:11; Troike 1984:48). Closely related are perceptions of and responses to prejudice and discrimination. If minority students do no wish to become skilled in the ways of the majority group or if they believe schools and teachers are treating them unfairly, they may have difficulty accepting school rules, these rules having been established by the dominant group. In such cases, academic performance may suffer (Cummins 1981, 1984; Erickson 1984; Kleinfeld 1983; Kramer 1983; McDermott 1974; McDermott and Gospodinoff 1981; Ogbu 1985; Ogbu and Matute-Bianchi 1986).

Most studies of minority school performance in the United States continue, understandably, to focus on those groups of students whose school performance lags farthest behind national norms. Far less attention has been given to the school-adaptation patterns of those minority groups or subgroups that meet with a comparatively high degree of academic success once initial language barriers are transcended. Ogbu's comparative research on the variability in patterns of school performance among different types of minority groups is a notable exception (Ogbu 1978, 1983; Ogbu and Matute-Bianchi 1986). His work, together with my previous research in the U.S. Virgin Islands (Gibson 1976, 1982, 1983c), suggests distinctly different perceptions of status and patterns of adaptation among immigrant minorities and indigenous or involuntary minorities.

I use the term *minority* to refer to groups that are racially, culturally, or linguistically distinctive from the majority group and that occupy a subordinate position in terms of their power either to sustain the dominant value system or to allocate rewards (Schermerhorn 1970:12–14).[6] By *immigrant minorities* I mean groups that have voluntarily left their own country, have settled legally in a new country, and enjoy the possibility of remaining there permanently. The situations of guest workers, undocumented workers, and refugees differ significantly from those of voluntary immigrants, and the degree to which their adaptation patterns are similar merits further comparative analysis. School performance data for Cuban, Central American, and Vietnamese refugees settled in the United States indicate, however, a high degree of academic success. The children of West Indian guest workers in the U.S. Virgin Islands also do comparatively well in school. Unlike the children of guest workers in the countries of Western Europe, who have been reported to do poorly in school, these West Indian students face no substantial language or cultural barriers (Gibson 1983c).

Involuntary minorities are those groups that have been incorporated into a society by colonization, conquest, annexation, or slavery (Ogbu 1985:863). Ogbu refers to these groups variously as "subordinate," "castelike," "nonimmigrant," and "involuntary" minorities. Cummins has recently called these "dominated" groups (1986). I prefer the terms "involuntary" and "nonimmigrant," although I also use the term "indigenous minority" when referring to native peoples such as Hawaiians or American Indians. *Nonimmigrant minority* thus, in my usage, refers not simply to those who were born in the United States but to those who have been incorporated into this country involuntarily.

In the American context blacks, Puerto Ricans, and American Indians are examples of involuntary or nonimmigrant minorities, while Punjabis, Koreans, and Jamaicans are examples of immigrant minorities. An immigrant minority group, according to my usage, refers not only to the first generation—those who are actual immigrants—but also to a group whose ancestors settled by choice in America and which continues to maintain a separate minority-group identity.

For some groups, such as Mexican Americans, there are no clear group boundaries between voluntary immigrants, undocumented workers, and those whose ancestors became a part of this society involuntarily by way of military defeat in the 1840s. A number of recent studies focus on how the differing histories and situations of each subgroup affect their perceptions of and adaptations to schooling (see, for example, Matute-Bianchi 1986; Romo 1984). Filipino Americans are another group whose members, by my terminology, have been incorporated into U.S. society both voluntarily and involuntarily, although I am unaware of any studies on Filipino Americans using this framework.

[33]

My own earlier work, and Ogbu's, provided the stimulus and the theoretical rationale for this study. Although the Valleyside school district had provided me with statistical data showing a serious disparity between the academic achievement of Punjabis, as a group, and the other students attending Valleyside High, both white and Mexican American, I hypothesized that Punjabi students would become competitive academically once they had overcome the basic challenge of learning English (Gibson 1980:10). I assumed from the start that second-generation Punjabi students would exhibit patterns of school performance distinctly different from those of the newer arrivals. I assumed, too, that at least some of the barriers to school success could be characterized as temporary and, thus, that the problems of school failure would prove less persistent for the Punjabis than for involuntary minorities such as blacks and Puerto Ricans or the Mexican Americans who make up the other large minority group at Valleyside High.

The differing perceptions and adaptations between the two types of minority groups appear to be related less to the cultural attributes of the individual groups or the current structure of American society than to the particular historical context of contact with the majority group, the minority's ongoing experience of subordination, and its perceptions of the opportunities available. Here the sociological literature on immigrant minority enclaves proves instructive.

The central concern of this body of work is not educational performance but why immigrant minorities are typically overrepresented in self-employment and why small business entrepreneurship has existed and persisted among selected groups. In seeking to explain this pattern of economic entrepreneurship among immigrant minorities sociologists have looked, with more or less attention, at cultural variables—the cultural characteristics and experiences the immigrants bring with them to the new society; contextual variables—the general characteristics of the receiving society (also referred to as structural variables); and situational variables—the special nature of the immigrant situation (see Turner and Bonacich 1980:145; Bonacich and Modell 1980:24–33). Recent studies note that in order to understand the socioeconomic attainments of immigrant groups—and I would add their educational attainments as well—we need "to go beyond the 'culture versus structure' debate" and look instead at the dynamic interplay between the two as immigrant groups respond to "historical situations and changing economic structures" both in the host society and in their country of origin (Nee and Wong 1985:282–302; see also Boissevain and Grotenbreg 1986; Brooks and Singh 1979; Hirschman and Wong 1981; Kim and Hurh 1985; Lieberson 1980).

The literature on immigrant economic enclaves is directly relevant to my analysis here because factors that have been found to contribute to immigrant socioeconomic achievement seem also to contribute to immigrant academic achievement. Just as educational anthropologists point increasingly to the historical context of minority-majority relations and to the minority group's perspective on its situation as critical to minority school performance, so too do sociologists point to similar factors to explain the socioeconomic adaptations of minority groups.

With respect to immigrant minorities, Ivan Light distinguishes three factors, all well documented in the literature, which, independent of cultural factors, appear to produce entrepreneurship: first, the immigrants' relative satisfaction with their new country; second, the ethnic and class resources available to immigrants through social networks with coethnics; and third, what is commonly called a sojourner orientation (1984:199; see also Bonacich 1973; Turner and Bonacich 1980).

Most immigrants have come to the United States because it offers better opportunities than were available in their country of origin. They are likely, therefore, to view social and economic hardships encountered in this country from a perspective distinctly different from that of the native-born American population. Until fully adapted to the standard of living in their new homeland, they are more willing to work hard at low-paying jobs and to endure the prejudice and discrimination of the dominant group than members of involuntary minority groups. In the present case, as we shall see, the Punjabis' relative satisfaction with their situation in this country has direct bearing on their response both to the nature of economic and educational opportunities available and to the prejudice and discrimination they encounter.

The immigrants' shared experience of being a minority in the new country draws them together and creates a sense of communal solidarity, which proves to be a particular source of strength in the new setting and furthers the development of ethnic entrepreneurship. In other words, a sense of solidarity emerges out of the new situation among people who did not necessarily share a sense of unity prior to emigration. Light terms this collective response a "reactive solidarity." Immigrants draw upon the collective resources of coethnics, including their knowledge, skills, money, community institutions, and a set of values that promote socioeconomic success in the new setting (see also

[35]

Light 1985). In the Valleyside example, the processes of chain migration have directly contributed to the formation and growth of a strong ethnic enclave that not only helps the Punjabis get ahead economically but also helps promote their positive response to schooling.

The third factor, a sojourning orientation, arises from the migrants' plan "to amass as much money as possible as quickly as possible" and then return home (Light 1984:200). Few of the recent wave of Punjabi migrants—those who have arrived since 1965—come with the intention of returning to India to live. The symbolic option remains, however, and has important bearing on how Punjabis respond to both opportunity and adversity in the new country. They feel that they can return if they absolutely must. Most important perhaps, in the present case, this possibility may help immigrants view school learning as the acquisition of an additional set of skills to be drawn upon when appropriate, rather than as a replacement for their traditional culture.

This book looks not only at how cultural and structural, or contextual, variables shape Punjabi adaptation patterns but also at the influence of situational variables on these patterns. It draws upon both the sociological work on immigrant economic enterprise and the anthropological work on minority school performance. Like the more recent studies in both fields, this book moves away from the culture-versus-structure debate and attempts instead to look at how the different classes of variables—cultural, contextual, and situational—interact to shape Punjabi adaptation patterns. Such a framework, used comparatively to study a number of different minority groups, promises to increase our understanding of why some groups meet with a great deal more success in school than others.

[3]

Asian Indian Immigration
to the United States

> All of our brothers and sisters want us to call them over here. In our area in India in every household there is a person who is living in another country. In some households the whole family is living in a foreign country—England, Canada, or here in the United States.
>
> Punjabi farmer, 10 May 1981
> Valleyside, California

> Many people are in England. I have two brothers there, and my parents. But my children want to go to the United States, or to Canada.
>
> Punjabi farmer, 3 April 1984
> Jullundur District, Punjab

Valleyside, California, located about two hours by car from San Francisco, is home to one of the fastest growing Punjabi Sikh communities in America. Although the state of Punjab accounts for only 2 percent of India's total population, approximately 15 percent of all immigrant visas issued each year by the U.S. Embassy in India go to Punjabis. Some two-thirds of these go to Sikh farmers and their families, many of whom give Valleyside as their destination.[1] So many do so, in fact, that this small and obscure town, largely unheard of in the United States, is a familiar name to American consular officials in India. The total Valleyside Punjabi community numbered upward of six thousand at the time of fieldwork (1980–1982).[2]

The 1965 amendments to the Immigration and Naturalization Act, which took effect in 1968, set in motion a process of chain migration, the full impact of which is still being realized. The 1965 legislation established an allocation system for immigrant visas which places highest priority on the reunification of family members. In recent years, approximately two-thirds of all immigrant visas have gone to relatives of American citizens and permanent residents (see Table 1). In Valleyside, the proportion of Punjabis sponsored by relatives is even higher. Almost every new arrival has family already settled in the area.

The size of America's Asian Indian population throughout the twentieth century has been closely tied to this country's immigration and naturalization policies. Political and economic conditions in India and the opportunities open to Indian immigrants in other parts of the world have, of course, influenced migration patterns. American immigration law, however, has been the predominant factor affecting Indian settlement in this country.

Settlement in the United States, 1900–1965

Fewer than seven hundred Indians entered the United States during the nineteenth century. Between 1900 and 1920, however, nearly seven thousand Indians arrived (U.S. Bureau of the Census 1975:107–8). Most were illiterate farmers and agricultural laborers from Punjab Province on British India's northwest frontier. They came as sojourners, expecting to return home to their families once they had accumulated sufficient savings to purchase farm land back in Punjab.

During the second half of the nineteenth century, following the British annexation of Punjab in 1849, many Sikhs were recruited by the British for service in the British Indian army. Some served overseas in other parts of the empire, and in 1887 a detachment of Sikh soldiers passed through Canada, as they returned to India from Queen Victoria's Golden Jubilee (Singh 1953:120). Sikh soldiers carried word back to Punjab of economic opportunities in North America. Service in the British army also provided Sikhs with some knowledge of English and confidence in their abilities to meet the demands of life in foreign countries. In the early 1900s, furthermore, British steamship companies recruited laborers from Punjab with promises of riches to be made in North America. By 1907 some five thousand Indian migrants, most of them Punjabi Sikhs, had reached the west coast of Canada (Chadney 1976:31) and, within a few years, an equal number had arrived in California (U.S. Bureau of the Census 1975:107–8).[3]

A number of factors related to political and economic developments in Punjab contributed to this early wave of emigration. Most of the migrants came from the Doaba region of Punjab, an area bounded by the Beas and Sutlej rivers (see Map 2).[4] Migration has long been one answer to Doaba's population pressures, particularly for small land-owners of the Jat caste.[5] Within the Jat Sikh social system, land tradi-tionally is divided equally among all sons. As members of a cultivator caste, all Jat men have access to agricultural land unless ancestral property has passed from family ownership, but rarely is a man's inheritance sufficient to support a wife and children. Wealth must be accumulated anew by each succeeding generation. Within a single family it is not at all uncommon to find some brothers who have become wealthy and others who are far less fortunate; yet all maintain close relations with one another. The egalitarian principles of Sikhism work against the formation of social classes.[6]

Beginning in the late 1800s, young Jat Sikh men, whose share in their family's landholdings was small, looked to other opportunities beyond Doaba to maintain or enhance their status. Enlistment in the British Indian army and migration were two common alternatives (Kessinger 1974; Singh 1966b). Many moved to the newly opened canal colonies in the western regions of Punjab Province, a section that fell to Pakistan in 1947. Others migrated abroad to various countries within the British empire.

The majority of those coming to the United States took up farm work in the Central and Imperial valleys of California, where, in spite of their small numbers, they were viewed as the newest Asian threat. Some 300,000 Chinese had migrated to this country during the latter half of the nineteenth century, and the number of Japanese immigrants was on the rise, with over 140,000 arriving between 1900 and 1910 (U.S. Bureau of the Census 1975).[7] Measures designed to bar further immigration from China and Japan and to reduce the political and economic rights of the Chinese and Japanese already settled in this country were rapidly extended to Asian Indians.[8] Most troublesome were the laws prohibiting Asian immigrants from owning land and from becoming naturalized American citizens.

The Punjabis had left behind an oppressive situation in India expect-ing to find a much greater degree of freedom in America. Unhappy with British rule, they readily identified with America for her own revolution and her Bill of Rights safeguarding individual and religious freedoms. Punjabis were much distressed, however, by the realities of anti-Asian sentiment and the legal barriers to their advancement.[9]

[39]

India in those days was commonly known as Hindustan, and few Americans knew anything of India's religious diversity; they called all Indian immigrants Hindus. Many Sikhs, unable to explain their background adequately in English, simply went along with the designation, which quickly took on derogatory connotations.

Punjabis had arrived in this country with considerable skills as farmers and were accustomed to toiling long hours under the hot Indian sun. Most found work as laborers and foremen in California farm communities, stretching from the northernmost parts of the Sacramento Valley down through the Imperial Valley to the Mexican border. Within a few years, some were able to save sufficient sums to lease and even purchase their own land. Many white American farmers, however, who were themselves pressed by difficult economic times and influenced by the pervasive anti-Asian sentiments of the day, resented Indian competition and lent their support to measures restricting Indians' ability to purchase their own farms (Leonard 1985).

Some of the most racist legislation in the history of the United States was directed at Asian immigrants, Indians included. California's Alien Land Law, designed to prevent the rise of the Japanese in farming, prohibited all those ineligible for citizenship from owning or leasing agricultural land. Although Chinese and Japanese immigrants were specifically barred from naturalization, based on court decisions in 1894 and 1895, the status of Asian Indians remained a disputed issue. Some sixty-seven Indian men acquired American citizenship by arguing successfully that they were Caucasians, thus of the same racial stock as Europeans and eligible, therefore, to become naturalized citizens (Jacoby 1958:1).

The U.S. Naturalization Law of 1790 had limited naturalization to "free white persons," and in 1870 the law had been amended to include "persons of African descent." It said nothing, however, about "persons of Asian descent." Although a 1922 Supreme Court decision had equated the words *white* and *Caucasian*, those opposed to citizenship for Asian Indians argued that Indians were Orientals. In 1923, in a landmark decision, the U.S. Supreme Court ruled that Indians, though Caucasian, were not "white" in the sense intended by those who had written the 1790 law. Over the next several years, on the basis of the decision in the case of *U.S.* v. *Bhagat Singh Thind*, a Sikh immigrant, the United States government revoked the citizenship of forty-two Indians. Twenty-three years were to pass before Indians could once again apply for citizenship (Jacoby 1958).

[40]

Following the *Thind* decision, Indians were legally prohibited from owning or leasing farmland in California because the Alien Land Laws of 1913 and 1920 now unquestionably applied to them as well. The Supreme Court decision, furthermore, made clear that the 1917 Immigration Law, which had barred from immigration those ineligible for citizenship, applied also to Indians. This law was specifically designed to restrict entry into the United States of unskilled Asian laborers. By barring all those over age sixteen who were also illiterate, the law affected many would-be immigrants from southeastern Europe, as well as those from Asia (Vialet 1980:15).

Immigration from India, which had slowed to a trickle following the outbreak of World War I and the passage of the 1917 Immigration Act, came to an official halt after 1923. Over the next twenty-three years the only new arrivals were a few hundred students and some three thousand "illegals" who found their way across the Mexican border or jumped ship in Atlantic seaports (Jacoby 1956:8). The overall population of Indians actually declined sharply during this period. Many Indians returned home voluntarily. Others died or were deported.[10]

Of the Punjabis who remained in California, the large majority, even those who had held professional and technical posts in India, were unable to find economic opportunities apart from farm work. When one Valleyside old-timer, a man who had come to this country in 1923 to pursue graduate studies, described these early days, he told of grueling summers cultivating beans and peas in Stockton, picking grapes in Fresno, and then moving on to Yuba City to pick the peaches. In spite of his education, this man could find no work except as a migrant laborer in the Central Valley. Most educated Indians shared his situation.

In 1940, 85 percent of all Asian Indians residing in the United States held blue-collar jobs, less than 4 percent professional positions. The California Punjabi community of this period was overwhelmingly male, rural, agriculturally oriented, uneducated, and aging. More than half were over forty, and a third were over fifty. The majority had less than four years of schooling and one-third had no formal schooling at all (La Brack 1982a:61). Only a handful of Indian women had immigrated to America. Unable to be reunited with their families or to arrange marriages with Indian brides, a number of men married non-Indians, many of them women from Mexico. Others, especially in northern California, remained single, either unmarried or faithful to their wives in India.[11]

The Immigration Act of 1946 brought some relief by legalizing Indian immigration and by permitting Indians the right to become naturalized citizens. The new law made it possible, at least in principle, for married men to reunite with their wives and children still in India and for bachelors to choose brides in accordance with traditional Indian marriage patterns. Life for California Punjabis remained much the same, however. The rate of immigration from Eastern countries was strictly controlled by a national origins quota system. Only one hundred immigrant visas per year were allotted to Indians. Hostility against "Hindus" persisted, based on fear of cheap labor and resentment of a way of life considered at odds with the "American" way.

During this same period the long-awaited goal of an independent India was achieved. The jubilation at the victory, for which many overseas Punjabis had long struggled, was dampened by India's division into two separate nations. The accompanying partition of Punjab caused over eight million persons to relocate, including two million Sikhs, or approximately half the entire Sikh population (Akbar 1985). The larger and agriculturally richer western portion of Punjab became part of Pakistan, and refugees moving east, the Sikhs and Hindus, were allotted smaller and less productive pieces of land than they had farmed previously. At the time of partition Sikhs were only 13 percent of undivided Punjab, but the most prosperous segment of the rural population (Singh 1966b:267).

Following independence, large numbers of Indians, particularly Punjabi Sikhs, emigrated to England, men first, wives and children following somewhat later.[12] As Britain's post–World War II economic boom gave way to recession, however, and the number of South Asian immigrants continued to mount, the anti-Asian sentiments of British whites grew to distressing levels. Sharply curtailed economic opportunities, coupled with a general climate of racism and increasingly restrictive British immigration and naturalization laws, caused Indians to shift their sights once more to North America.[13]

The Present Period, 1965–1985

The 1965 Immigration and Naturalization Act repealed the national origins quota system and removed other racist features of earlier laws, thus ending more than eighty years of exclusionary policy toward Asia. The 1965 legislation, together with more recent amendments, has set an annual worldwide ceiling on immigration of 270,000, exclusive of refugees and "immediate relatives" of U.S. citizens, and a per-country limit of 20,000 (Vialet 1980:25). The spouses, minor children, and parents of U.S. citizens are subject to no numerical limitations; they may freely enter the country as permanent residents. Numerically limited visas, 80 percent of which are reserved for relatives of citizens and permanent residents, are distributed according to a seven-category preference system that places highest priority on "family reunification."

The new regulations have resulted in a dramatic increase in Asian immigration to the United States. From only 6.8 percent in 1965, the Asian percentage of all immigrants had climbed to 44.3 percent by 1981 (see Table 2). During the same period the number of new arrivals from India increased from only 467 in 1965 to 21,522 in 1981 (U.S. Bureau of the Census 1975; U.S. Department of Justice 1981). During the 1950s, only 5,268 immigrants from India were admitted to the United States. Another fifty thousand arrived during the 1960s, most of them after passage of the 1965 Immigration Act (U.S. Bureau of the Census 1975, 1984b). During the 1970s, new immigrants from India totaled 176,800 (U.S. Bureau of the Census 1984a). In that decade, India was the seventh largest source of immigrants to the United States (see Table 3); moreover, about one-third of all Indian immigrants came from countries other than India, including Guyana, Jamaica, and other Caribbean countries (Bachu 1983:5). Indians are one of the fastest growing immigrant communities in America. In 1980 they were the fourth largest group of Asians residing in the United States, exceeded only by the Chinese, Filipinos, and Japanese (see Table 4). By 1985, the total Asian Indian population had grown from a low of 2,405 in 1940 (Hess 1982:31) to over 500,000 and may actually have been nearing 600,000.[14]

In sharp contrast to the early arrivals from rural Punjab, nearly 80 percent of all adult male immigrants arriving from India today are professional and technical workers or managers and administrators.[15] The median age of the new arrivals is 30.8; 70 percent are under the age of 35 and 20 percent under 20. Half are females. As a group, these recent arrivals are extremely well educated. Of those twenty-five years old and over, 87.2 percent are high school graduates, 63.1 percent have finished four years of college, and 46.1 percent have some graduate training; only 2.8 percent have had less than five years of schooling (U.S. Bureau of the Census 1984b). With a median family income in

[43]

1980 of $23,935, recent Indian immigrants are an affluent group (U.S. Bureau of the Census 1984b).[16] Many have previously visited or studied in this country. Almost all speak English fluently and are familiar with Western values and beliefs, factors that facilitate their adaptation to life in America.[17] They come from all over India, and they have settled throughout the United States, most in urban areas and over half along the eastern seaboard.[18]

The Valleyside Punjabis are noteworthy because they represent a case of unskilled and largely uneducated immigrants who must accept low-wage occupations generally identified with the peripheral economy. As the emerging literature on ethnic economic enclaves makes clear, however, some low-skilled immigrants, far from being trapped in dead-end occupations, have demonstrated a high degree of socioeconomic mobility (Bonacich and Modell 1980; Kim and Hurh 1985; Light 1972; Model 1985; Nee and Sanders 1985; Wilson and Portes 1980). The Valleyside Punjabi case provides further evidence of how a strong ethnic enclave can help promote rapid economic self-sufficiency. It indicates, too, how the current U.S. immigration law, with its emphasis on family reunification, serves to promote the formation of immigrant enclaves.

The overwhelming majority of new arrivals from India are sponsored by relatives already settled in this country. Table 5 shows the distribution of immigrants admitted to the United States during 1981 by class of visa issued. The most important visa categories for Indians in general, and for those who continue to emigrate from rural Punjab in particular, are the second and fifth preferences. The second preference, which allocates visas to the spouses of permanent residents, makes it possible for Punjabis settled in the United States to arrange marriages back in India, and there currently is a backlog of Indians seeking visas under this preference.[19] For U.S. citizens there is no delay in arranging a visa for a bride or groom who is a citizen of another country.

The largest number of immigrants from India each year comes under the fifth preference, a category that permits U.S. citizens to sponsor their adult brothers and sisters, as well as those siblings' spouses and minor children. Persons wishing to enter under this category currently face a wait of several years for visas.[20] It is the fifth preference that has contributed most directly to chain migration and the sharp increase in the number of Indians now living in this country. Eager to reunite their extended family, many Indian immigrants move forward as rapidly as possible to become naturalized citizens.

Author and daughter visiting a Sikh family in Punjab. This couple's six children and eleven grandchildren all live in California. The younger woman, a relative, now lives in Canada.

Valleyside as a Sikh Settlement

Because of the availability of agricultural work, the Sacramento Valley has long been an important center of Punjabi settlement. Punjabis leased large tracts of land during the 1910s, and a few even managed to purchase their own farms. During the 1920s and 1930s Punjabi landholdings were diminished because of the Alien Land Law and bad economic times. By 1947, Punjabi Sikh farmers owned just under a thousand acres of fertile, well-irrigated land in Yuba and Sutter counties, most of it planted with peach trees (Miller 1950). Although

[45]

the total Punjabi population in the bi-county area was probably less than four hundred and largely male, when the Immigration Act of 1946 was signed into law (La Brack 1980:204), these early settlers served as a magnet to Punjabis elsewhere in California and to relatives back in Punjab.[21] Indian men were finally able to reunite families that had been separated for two decades or more.

Table 6 shows the rapid growth that has occurred in the Valleyside area since 1965. Recent arrivals are notably similar to the earliest Doabi migrants except that they come now as settlers, not sojourners, and they come as families. Most immigrate directly from rural Punjab, where their families had small to medium-sized landholdings (ten to thirty acres). Few speak English or have any experience of urban life in India. Most have no salable skills apart from farming. They come because relatives already settled in Valleyside have urged them to immigrate and have promised to help them adapt to the demands of life in this country. They come, too, because they believe America offers opportunities for them and for their children far greater than those available in India.

New families arrive each year. The current situation of political unrest in Punjab and the feeling, shared by many Jat Sikhs, that Sikhs are being unfairly treated by the government of India, have only enhanced the desire to emigrate.[22] Punjab's green revolution has improved the standard of living for landowners, but it is the large farmers who have benefited the most. Farmers with smaller holdings, even middle-sized farms, although they live more comfortably than they did a decade or two ago, may not have enough land to divide among their sons. In one Doabi village I visited in the spring of 1984 I found young people particularly interested in leaving the village. A number wished to migrate abroad. "Not to Britain," they said. "To America, or Canada."

[4]

From Punjab to Valleyside

> Like they say, "America is the leader of all countries. America's leader is California and California's leader is Valleyside."
>
> Punjabi Sikh farmer

Most immigrants come to America in search of better opportunities for themselves and their families. The strategies they employ to take advantage of the opportunities available to them are shaped, I have suggested, by the interaction between the cultural traditions and experiences the immigrants bring with them, characteristics of the host society that either promote or impede socioeconomic opportunities (what I call contextual variables), and the immigrants' particular situation in the new country. The contextual variables in the United States sharply restricted the numbers of Asian Indian immigrants throughout the first part of this century and severely limited their economic opportunities. Moreover, American policy made it impossible for these immigrants to maintain traditional cultural patterns of family life.

Since 1965, however, the context has changed. Most Indian immigrants have arrived as families and with the intention of settling permanently in this country. Gone is the sojourner orientation of earlier immigrants, which stemmed not only from prior intentions to return home but also from the discriminatory attitudes and actions of the dominant group, which made life in America difficult to endure (see Bonacich 1973). Punjabis can now marry according to rules of caste endogamy and clan exogamy, and they have moved rapidly into farm ownership.

Despite their rural background, that the Punjabi settlers have turned to farming in America seems to be more a consequence of the local California context than of their vocational preferences and skills. Settlement patterns in other parts of the world suggest that the California Punjabis would have pursued new trades had there been opportunities apart from farming. In East Africa, Jat Sikhs were recruited by the British to build the railroads (Bhachu 1985a). In British Vancouver, Punjabi Jat migrants found their first jobs in rail construction and later moved into the lumber industry (Buchignani and Indra 1985; Chadney 1980; Joy 1982; Mayer 1959). In Britain, where farm ownership was never an option, Jats found their first jobs in foundries and factories (Helweg 1979). Although their agricultural skills may have helped California Punjabis get ahead economically, Punjabis took up farming in America less from cultural tradition than from sheer necessity. Common to each setting, however, from Africa to Britain, Canada, and California, was the Punjabis' reliance on kin and countrymen. In each of these overseas settlements, family and communal solidarity have helped to advance Punjabi economic interests and to maintain their Indian identity and traditions.

The economic adaptation strategies of Valleyside Punjabis at the time of fieldwork will provide a fuller understanding of Punjabi success strategies and the forces that shape them and will also set the stage for the discussion of schooling which follows in later chapters. There is a strong relationship between the adults' views on life in America and their strategies for exploiting the economic and educational opportunities available to them and their children. I am concerned, thus, not only with an objective description of the Punjabis' socioeconomic situation in Valleyside but also with their subjective evaluation of their situation.

This chapter and the next quote at length from several of the Punjabi parent interviews in order to give the reader a feel for these Sikh agriculturalists, their colorful language and folk sayings, as well as their perspectives on life in this country. The quoted passages give a range of responses, not merely the typical. They represent the essence of the full set of interviews and provide a context for the analysis of school performance.[1] Some passages are exact quotations from single interviews. Others are constructed from several interviews, in order to provide as full a response to specific topics as possible. All names are pseudonyms.

The average parent interview lasted two to three hours and covered a range of topics. Most of the interviews were conducted in Punjabi, tape recorded, and later translated in full into English. Passages here quoted are taken from the English translation. It is important to bear in mind that the interviews were carried out by a team of researchers,

Punjabi and non-Punjabi, male and female, community insiders and outsiders.[2]

Most Valleyside Punjabis come from villages of five hundred to two thousand inhabitants in the Jullundur and Hoshiarpur districts of Punjab. Only two of the parents in the core sample, both men, had been in the United States prior to 1946; one of them was born here, and the other, an elderly man, had come to America in the early twenties. Six other men had arrived during the 1950s and early 1960s, after the 1946 law reopened the door to legal immigration. The rest had all immigrated after 1965, two or three each year, most coming with their spouses and children, a few sending for their families after several years. Only three men had found their first jobs in this county in nonagricultural work, regardless of their educational level or previous work experience.

In certain respects the Punjabis of Valleyside are an extremely homogeneous community, the overwhelming majority sharing not only caste and religious affiliation, but their Doabi village background. Common values and attitudes were reflected throughout the set of interviews. They are, by and large, a far more homogeneous group than the Valleysiders we interviewed.

Diversity of background was also apparent. One in ten of the families sampled was Hindu or Muslim, not Sikh.[3] All were Punjabis, however, and their perspectives on most topics were similar. The Sikhs were divided between the more orthodox *amritdharis* (baptized members of the Khalsa who have pledged to keep unshorn hair as one of the marks of their faith) and the *sahajdharis* (literally, "those-who-take-time"). *Sahajdharis* may choose to keep these outward symbols of their faith, but they have made no formal commitment to do so. Within one family some members may be baptized, others not, and the distinction suggests no necessary difference in adaptation to America. To most Valleysiders, however, the short-haired and clean-shaven *sahajdharis* appear more westernized.

A split had occurred within the Valleyside Sikh community well before this research commenced, ostensibly because of differences regarding the maintenance of the Five Ks and other traditional Sikh values and customs. As newcomers had increased in numbers, they had assumed control over *gurdwara* affairs, insisting that traditional ways be observed. A second *gurdwara* (Sikh temple) was soon built, in part at least, to accommodate differences between the more traditional and the more "modern," or westernized, segments of the Sikh commu-

[49]

nity. But Sikhs do not formally belong to one *gurdwara* or another, and the mass of Sikhs felt free to attend ceremonies at either location. The building of the second *gurdwara* was in large measure the product of community factionalism, each party wishing control over its own temple and, thus, a leadership role in local affairs.

Before immigrating most Punjabi families had spent their entire lives in India or in parts of Punjab which now fall within Pakistan, but a significant minority had previously lived in Britain, Fiji, and East Africa.[4] The overwhelming majority of those coming directly from India were from villages, but some had lived in urban areas and had held white-collar jobs. A number of Punjabis with professional degrees from Indian universities had also settled in the area, although none was represented in the core sample.

"America Is Like a Paradise"

Whether old-timer or newcomer, rich or poor, high school graduate or illiterate, the Sikh parents we interviewed held a great many views and values in common. Almost all found Valleyside a good place to live and to raise a family. They appreciated the rural atmosphere, rich farmland, and good weather, similar in most respects to that in Punjab. When asked about their financial situation, most said they were better off in America than in India. This was the opinion of agricultural laborers and factory workers, as well as farm owners.

Punjabis especially welcomed the opportunities for finding work and, with work, the ability both to save and to purchase goods. In America, one man explained,

> if you want to become something, you can. If you want to start a business, there are opportunities. You can have money from the banks. You can buy everything. What you need is money. In India, even if you do have money, you can't get something. It is not available. . . . There, you are shown pictures of things. Here, you can actually get it for yourself. Even if you work as a laborer, there are opportunities. In India you cannot do this. Working as a laborer you cannot even eat your *roti* [unleavened whole wheat bread, the staple of the Punjabi diet].

In 1984 an agricultural laborer in Punjab earned fifteen rupees a day. Although the exchange rate was ten rupees to the dollar, one rupee could purchase about what one dollar would buy in the United States.

Thus, even at minimum wage, a U.S. farm worker at the time of fieldwork was better off than his equivalent in India.

A small farmer in Punjab, although able to feed his family, operates at a subsistence level. Those with middle-sized farms—perhaps fifteen or twenty acres—may be quite comfortable by village standards but still have little opportunity to increase their wealth. Good agricultural land in Punjab, if available at all, has become extremely expensive. An acre of land may cost four thousand dollars, and only large landowners or those with relatives abroad can hope to raise such a sum. The government of India, moreover, has been squeezing the Punjabi farmers by holding down the price it will pay for their grain. As a result of the green revolution the larger landholders have greatly improved their status, but the average farmer with only ten to twenty acres, who is typical of those who emigrate to America, cannot afford to mechanize and, thus, cannot compete with the bigger landowners. Nearly half of all farmers in Punjab (44 percent) must attempt to make do with ten acres or less.[5] Farmers may be better off in real terms than a decade or two ago (Leaf 1984), but comparatively they are slipping behind, with little prospect of improving their or their children's situation (Sharma 1981). Those who have emigrated to Valleyside may not be satisfied with their wages, but in a relative sense they see themselves as better off because there is the possibility to advance.

Valleyside Punjabis also comment on the high quality and availability of all sorts of food, the ready-made clothes, the washing machines and televisions, the air-conditioned housing, good roads, and automobiles—all things the average American has come to take for granted but which, in most cases, these Punjabis had never before enjoyed. For women, the job of managing the household is far easier than in Punjab. No longer, for example, must they cook squatting over an open fire of sugarcane stalks or dried cow dung, use cinders to clean pots and pans, grind wheat for flour, milk the cow, or collect manure for fertilizer. While all villages in Punjab now have electricity, few families there have refrigerators. Almost none has a flush toilet. Housekeeping is far easier in Valleyside than in an Indian village.

These Punjabi immigrants appreciate, too, the openness and fairness of American institutions and the laws that safeguard individual rights. In India the system is more personalistic, more tied to family connections, influence, and wealth. The children of a small farmer in India, even if they become educated, have few prospects. In spite of Punjab's expanding economy, many young people with high school and even

A typical kitchen scene in rural Punjab.

college credentials are unable to find work. Well-to-do Indians have little desire to emigrate and the very poor cannot arrange the cost of transportation. For those in the middle, America is like a promised land.

When farmers in Punjab hear stories of how their countrymen have prospered in Valleyside and elsewhere in California, they, too, begin to think of emigrating. When they see immigrants, back in Punjab for a vacation, lavish gifts on relatives, make expensive improvements to their village landholdings, and donate sizable sums of money to the local *gurdwara*, they, too, come to believe that in America money simply "grows on trees." Valleyside Punjabis also note, however, that few can appreciate how hard it is to "pick this money down."

[52]

Life is far from easy for the Punjabi immigrant, whether orchard farmer or laborer. Laborers have to work harder than they ever imagined. Farmers, too, work hard in their own fields, unlike in India, where most of the heavy physical labor is done by lower-caste migrant workers. In addition, they have the constant worry that they may be unable to renegotiate their cannery contracts or meet the payment schedules on their mortgages and production loans. Back in Punjab most Jat farmers own their land outright, at least ancestral lands, and while there is little hope of substantially improving one's situation, there is also little fear of losing what one has.[6] In Valleyside, however, because of their indebtedness, few farmers can hope to hold on to their land if they experience, as they well may, a total crop loss.

Still, in spite of their worries and hardships, few Punjabis regret coming to America. Unlike the early immigrants, who expected to return home, these families come with the intention of remaining permanently. They consider themselves the fortunate ones and they speak constantly of "calling over" other family members.

The decision of whether or not to apply for American citizenship is frequently tied to family considerations. One man explained: "You should become a citizen so that you can bring your brothers and sisters over, so that they can lead a good life. . . . The whites think individually, saying 'How will I benefit if I do this?' We think of all our relatives, either to bring them over, or their son or daughter."[7] He was referring, here, to arranging for a niece or nephew, or some other young relative back in Punjab to marry in the United States. Punjabis take very seriously their obligations to help family members improve their situation; they try to find suitable mates for nieces and nephews or to become citizens themselves so they can arrange immigrant visas for their closest kin. In so doing, they themselves gain honor and power within their family circle.

Having relatives already settled in Valleyside was central to the new arrivals' decision to leave India. "We came from home, and came into a home," one observed. Several men noted that they might not have come at all had they not had extended family already living in the area, and they certainly would not have come with their wives and children. Some family networks were extensive, and within our sample it was quite common for one parent, either the father or mother, to have all of his or her siblings now resident in California, usually in the immediate vicinity of Valleyside.

[53]

"We Help Our Relatives"

Family and kinship networks play an essential role in Punjabi settlement patterns and are a pivotal force in these immigrants' ability to adapt as successfully and as swiftly as they do to their new surroundings and new circumstances. When newcomers arrive fresh from Punjab, they are almost totally dependent on the relatives who "called them over." They work as rapidly as possible, however, to become self-sufficient. One couple described their first weeks.

> Mr. Dosangh: My brother is here, two sisters. We lived with my brother for about a month and then we started working. He was the one who found us work.
>
> Mrs. Dosangh: [Our relatives] also paid for our tickets [from India]. They fed us. They took us everywhere we needed to go in their own car. Whenever there was work available [in the fields] they took us with them. After this we bought a car. From then on we were able to take care of ourselves.
>
> Mr. Dosangh: There is a lot of cooperation between our families. Our people are able to make a stand very quickly. But no one helps you totally. They help with a little money so you can start eating your *roti*. After that we had to do everything ourselves. Slowly we were able to stand on our feet.

Many others related similar experiences, telling of how relatives had helped them find a place to live, arranged for some work, and guided them through the initial period of getting established in their new homeland. Even with the help of relatives, the first years are extremely difficult.

"We Are Running About like Chamars"

The move to Valleyside requires major adjustments for all family members. Many of those we interviewed were unprepared for how hard they would have to struggle to make ends meet. Those working as agricultural laborers noted that in India they were their own bosses. In Punjab today, moreover, even many lower-caste Punjabis shun field labor, seeking instead what they consider to be better opportunities in towns and cities. Farming has become more mechanized, reducing the need for year-round workers, and at harvesttime, farmers hire migrant laborers from the nearby states of Bihar and Uttar Pradesh, where economic conditions are far worse than in Punjab. For Jat farmers to have to take positions as laborers is difficult both psychologically and physically.

Recent arrivals often work for less than minimum wage—$3.35 at the time of fieldwork—because peach farmers in Valleyside generally pay seasonal labor by the piece, a practice that favors the faster and more experienced workers. Rates also vary between farmers. One man, who had been a village teacher in India, said of the system: "The rich farmer will pay $1.50 a tree for pruning and a small farmer will pay in pennies. You may be earning less than the minimum. . . . The new people don't care. Still it looks good. The reason is that they don't have any money, so $10 a day is better than nothing, staying home." Some Valleyside farmers, this man explained, keep the workers oppressed all the time, not only the new immigrants but also those who have been in Valleyside a number of years, yet lack the connections or education to find better employment.

Picking peaches is unpleasant work. The sun is hot, the fields dusty, and an irritating layer of peach fuzz soon penetrates the picker's clothing. A farm laborer who had lived briefly in England prior to coming to the United States described his first days:

> Just when we got here we started picking peaches. My eldest son, who is twenty, and I spent all day picking, and how many bins did we fill? Two! It was seven dollars a bin. We said, "We cannot do this," and we just went back home. We had a very difficult time. . . . We even decided to go back to England because we just couldn't manage. Our relatives, my sister who sponsored me, said, "At least stay one year. Then, if you want to go back, go back."
>
> If a person comes straight from India, he has been doing farm work, but still the work here is hard. Climbing ladders, we have never done before and this is difficult. . . . Here, we are running around like Chamars working for our people [other Punjabis] in their fields. In India, even if you might go hungry, you wouldn't work for someone else, not even your brother. The farmers in Punjab only work for themselves. You hire Chamars to do the work for you. When a person comes he feels disheartened. But then you get used to it. [8]

This theme came up again and again—the discomfort Jat Sikhs experienced when they had to take work as farm laborers, the hardness of the work, and the social adjustments it required. In India, not only was the position of farm laborer associated with the lower castes, but it was a dead-end job. Small farmers, however, though they had little hope of ever becoming wealthy, enjoyed high status as Jat landlords.

In America both the context and the Punjabis situation have been altered. All Valleyside Sikhs can cite examples of fellow countrymen who have managed to move from the ranks of laborer to that of farm owner, some within only a few years. Sikhs, furthermore, appreciate American attitudes toward work and toward pulling oneself up by the bootstraps. Such values fit closely with their own sense of egalitarianism.

In India, because of the caste system, Jats, no matter what their economic condition, would not only refuse to work on someone else's farm but would also shun other trades and types of employment considered inappropriate to their status. Nevertheless, Punjabis readily adapt to their new circumstances. One immigrant commented: "Whether an orchard belongs to your relatives or your brother or Chamars, no matter whose, there is no difference. You have to work. Here, even the family of the farm owner, the children and everyone, works hard doing the same work as we do. The method here is better. If they worked like this in India, then no one would die of hunger." Jat Sikhs respect hard work, including hard physical labor.

"Here, Women Work Outside the Home"

In Punjab, as recently as the early 1970s, less than 2 percent of the women were in the labor force, compared with 13.2 percent for India as a whole.[9] Punjab remains culturally conservative, especially in the rural areas, and landowners continue to "consider it below their dignity to allow their women to work outside the home," even if their farms are small (Singh 1979:3). This value carried over to America, and until the 1970s, only the well-educated, urban, westernized Punjabi women worked outside their homes. The large majority, however, were illiterate or semiliterate and had neither occupational skills nor previous work experience. They remained at home because their husbands would have considered it shameful for them to be seen doing physical labor in the fields or canneries.

The first women to break with village tradition, even to work in their own orchards, became the object of much teasing, but by the late 1970s almost every woman in our core sample was engaged in some sort of agricultural labor during the summer months. Farmers' wives either helped on their own farms or found work each season in the local canneries. These jobs were less physically demanding than field labor, and both hourly wages and job benefits were far better.

Again, the Punjabis have made a pragmatic response to the new context. Not only have they observed "respectable" Valleysider women working outside their homes, they have also seen that a woman's earnings can contribute substantially to the family income. This was not the case in Punjab. One man, an old-timer, described the change:

> Now that they see others working, they say, "Why shouldn't I earn money too?" But it took us time to adjust to this. Now there is no problem. When someone arrives from India, they no longer tease or joke. There are more women working now. One reason is that they can claim unemployment. The rest of the winter they are saying, "Sister, what new *salwaar-kameez* have you sewn? How much money are you claiming [getting from unemployment]? I am claiming this much."[10]

Seasonal laborers who are unable to find steady work, like the uneducated Punjabi women, are eligible for unemployment compensation during the months when they are laid off. Although some would prefer year-round work, seasonal labor has its advantages for women who wish to be at home during the school year tending to their families' needs, including the sewing of new outfits, most frequently the traditional Punjabi *salwaar-kameez*, for themselves and their daughters.

Valleyside Punjabis have proved themselves extremely adaptable in areas that further their economic interests, even in matters touching most directly on family honor.[11] Now women work outside the home and men accept jobs as laborers on another's farm, although in Punjab such behavior continues to bring serious loss of respect to a Jat landlord and his family. A new situation has produced a fresh response and a redefinition of the criteria for judging a family's prestige.

Today, few Punjabi women whose husbands are farmers or farm laborers feel that they can afford to stay home. Their work is both strenuous and monotonous and, like many women in America, they find it difficult to juggle the demands of housekeeper, mother, and wage earner. These are, nonetheless, tough, strong women, and they and their families need the additional income or, in the case of farm-owning families, the additional family labor.

[57]

A full-time farm worker may earn no more than five hundred to six hundred dollars a month in the off season; yet in 1981 it cost even the most frugal Punjabi family a thousand dollars a month to meet its basic living requirements. An experienced worker, one who drives a tractor or supervises a crew, will earn more, but still he is paid only for the days he works. In the winter, when it rains, he stays home. He can work for years as an agricultural laborer and still earn little more than minimum wage, with none of the standard benefits, such as sick leave, medical insurance, or retirement. Most agricultural workers count on the summer earnings of their wives and often their children, sons in particular, to tide them through the year. In the height of the picking season, families will put in twelve- or fourteen-hour days. With husband, wife, and children all working, a family of four or five can earn $200 to $250 a day.

"Gradually a Person Is Able to Stand on His Feet"

With their skills in surviving at a subsistence level and their willingness to work long and hard, most of those we interviewed had managed within a few years not only to make ends meet but to save substantial sums of money, despite low wages. In many instances, these people had arrived from India with only their clothes and eight dollars apiece, the amount of cash that they were legally permitted to take from India.

Life in India has taught Punjabis frugality, an attribute that serves them well in America. The average Valleyside Punjabi family spends far less on food than the average Valleysider family, and the same is true of clothing and entertainment. Families with older children may pool their earnings. Savings will be used to repay the costs of their move from India—airfare alone runs around nine hundred dollars per family member—or as a down payment on a house. A daughter's earnings are usually used for her own expenses or saved for her dowry, rather than spent for general household expenses (Bhachu 1985a), but it is not uncommon for adult sons to live at home for a time, even after they marry, thus permitting several wage earners to share household expenses. Less typical, but still a distinct pattern in Valleyside, are households with two adult brothers, their wives, and children all living together and sharing expenses.

One indicator of economic mobility among Punjabi families in Valleyside is eligibility for free or reduced-price lunches at the high school. Whereas 66.7 percent of those who had been in the United States for less than four years were on the eligibility list for low-price or free lunches, among those who had lived in the United States eight years or more, only 18 percent were on the list. In 1980 the typical farm-laborer family earned about fifteen thousand dollars a year, with the father working full-time and the mother and older children working seasonally.

Home ownership is another indicator of economic mobility. Recent figures show that in California only one in five farm-worker families owns a home (*Sacramento Bee* 31 March 1985). Yet, within five years of reaching this country, most Punjabi Sikh families in Valleyside have become home owners.[12] More specifically, within my sample of thirty-eight Sikh families, thirty-one owned their homes. Of the seven who were renting, only two had lived in the United States more than four years. Eleven of the home owners also owned orchard land, sixteen were farm laborers, and four held non-farm-related jobs.

Punjabi farmers live in modest houses situated on their ranches. Laborers, however, generally have little choice but to live in town in the newer tract housing. Such properties were selling for forty to forty-five thousand dollars in 1976 and by 1980 had increased in price to sixty-five thousand dollars or more. In one case, to avoid the steep cost of single-family dwellings, an extended family had pooled resources to purchase a multiunit apartment building. The venture, from the Punjabi perspective, had the added advantage of enabling a set of married siblings to live in close proximity.

Fruit picking is the job of last resort for most Americans, but for many Punjabi immigrants who lack technical skills or higher education, it is a new beginning, the first rung on the ladder to a better life, if not necessarily for themselves, then for their children.

"Whenever We Can, We Work for Ourselves"

Of necessity, most Valleyside Punjabis accept work as farm laborers, but their goal is to become their own boss, as a farm owner if possible or by taking up a trade, say as a mechanic, or beginning a small business. In India these Jat agriculturalists raised wheat, rice, sugarcane and beans, but they rapidly learn the requirements for orchard farming, either on the job as laborers in the orchards or by talking to others about successful farming techniques. Punjabis are willing to take risks and they are also willing to start small, buying just a few acres in partnership with others, in the hope that they will eventually be able to increase their holdings.

To finance their first purchases, Punjabis may lease their holdings in India, go into partnership with village mates and relatives, or arrange for loans from members of the extended family who are already established farmers.[13] If Punjabi immigrants had to rely on banks and other credit agencies to obtain their first loans, most would never be able to buy land in Valleyside or to begin some other venture.

One Sikh man contrasted the Punjabi system with the "American way":

> I could raise thousands of dollars by asking my relatives and buy a business. After I set up the business, I could pay them back. Here, you go to the bank. They ask you, "Where are you working? How much are you earning?" You say, "Nowhere." Then they say, "We can't give you the loan and you can't go into business." We Punjabis go into business very quickly with the help of the relatives—the corporate family system.

Another man described how in 1970 with thirty thousand dollars borrowed from his uncle, an old-timer who had arrived in California in 1922, he was able to buy a thirty-acre ranch, including a farmhouse. The land cost eleven hundred dollars an acre. Within a few years, using this ranch as collateral, he was able to secure a conventional bank loan and purchase additional acreage.[14]

Most of the Punjabis who have bought any substantial farm acreage in Valleyside are those who migrated to this country during the late 1960s, or earlier. The more recent arrivals—and it is this group that forms the majority of Valleyside Punjabis—were simply priced out of the market by the rapid rise in land prices and the unprecedented interest rates of the latter half of the 1970s. Within the core sample of Sikh families, three out of four of those who had arrived in the United States by 1970 were farm owners by 1980 (see Table 7).[15] Not one of those arriving after 1970, however, had become an orchard farmer. The newer arrivals simply have had no option but to remain agricultural laborers or, in the case of those with sufficient education and some knowledge of English, to shift over to factory work when they can find it. Younger, better-educated immigrants—those with at least a high school diploma—may also seek some further training in order to qualify for a trade.

A Valleyside Sikh farmer harvesting prunes.

By 1980, Punjabi farmers owned somewhat more than half of all the peach acreage in the Sacramento Valley, plus additional acres of prunes, almonds, and walnuts.[16] Between 1974 and 1980 Punjabis more than doubled their agricultural acreage in the tri-county area surrounding Valleyside (La Brack 1982b:56). Several Punjabi Sikh farmers have become quite wealthy. In the early 1980s, the largest Punjabi landholder owned approximately six thousand acres in the vicinity of Valleyside, with additional properties elsewhere in the state and in Canada. Most have only small farms, however (see Table 8). In 1980 more than half of all Punjabi peach growers (55.3 percent) owned forty acres or less and nearly one-third (31.4 percent) owned twenty acres or less.

With their confidence as farmers, their skill in surviving at a modest

[61]

level, and the financial backing of relatives and village mates already settled in this country, many Valleyside Punjabis have done well for themselves and their families. Few, however, are financially secure, and few of the coming generation look to farming as a desirable occupation. Farming may be their traditional occupation, but in Valleyside, Jat Sikhs take up farming out of necessity, not out of choice. No other jobs are available to those lacking facility with English. Even factory work is difficult to find and requires commuting long distances or moving to an urban area. The cost of living is far cheaper in Valleyside than in the San Francisco Bay area, or even in Sacramento. In Valleyside, too, the immigrant has the support of relatives and the larger Punjabi community, and it is possible for Punjabi women and older children to find summer employment. Such jobs are far scarcer in urban areas.

The Decline of Peach Farming, 1980–1985

Between 1980 and 1985, the total number of peach farmers in Valleyside, Punjabi and non-Punjabi, declined by 30 percent.[17] Some farmers sold their orchards in the early 1980s when land prices were high. Others have shifted their crops—kiwi fruit, for example, is now being grown in the area—in hopes of achieving a better return. Many, however, have simply been forced out of business. In Valleyside most farmers lost some or all of their peach harvest in both 1982 and 1983 because of heavy rains. Moreover, like their counterparts throughout the nation, Valleyside farmers have been burdened by loans taken out when mortgages were costing over 15 percent and production loans ran even higher. Unable to meet their monthly payments, some have been forced to sell, taking whatever they can get for their land. Some had no choice but to default on their loans. Prime orchard land, which in 1980 sold for seven to eight thousand dollars an acre, was in 1986 being offered for twenty-nine hundred an acre, and still there were no buyers.

Not only is the demand for canned peaches down substantially from a generation ago (almost all the peaches grown in Valleyside are for canning), but California processors have been particularly hard hit by competition from the European Economic Community, which since 1978 has provided direct subsidies to its fruit processors. As a result, canned California peaches are being displaced by the European product, which sells for as much as 20 percent less in American super-markets.[18] The export market has been even harder hit, with the shipment of California peaches abroad dropping from 1.9 million cases in 1981 to only 560,000 cases by 1984.[19] Unable to market their fruit, many canneries have simply closed their doors. Others have had to substantially reduce the amount of fruit they will contract with growers to buy. Farmers who are unable to obtain contracts with processors have no outlet for their crop and must leave their trees unpicked.

Table 9 shows the decline since 1975 both in the number of cling peach farmers in the Sacramento Valley and in the number of acres planted in peaches. Paralleling the statewide decline, the overall number of farmers in the Valleyside area decreased by one-third in the first half of the 1980s, and the number of bearing acres declined comparably. During this period Valleyside Punjabi farmers managed to hold on as well, if not better, than other farmers. They still own about half the peach acreage in the area. Even some old-timers, however, because they purchased new acreage when interest rates were high, have lost at least a part of their land.

Many Valleyside Punjabis are having to look for jobs apart from farming. Because of limited opportunities in Valleyside itself, some families or individual members of families have moved to San Jose, to take up work as computer assemblers. Others are moving to Sacramento. Meanwhile, many in the younger generation are pursuing higher education so they can enter white-collar and professional fields.

Immigrant Adaptation Patterns

The economic success of Punjabi orchard farmers stems both from preexisting agricultural skills and from their ability to draw support from Punjabis already settled in the area. Although the butt of many jokes by more sophisticated, urban northern Indians who view these "peasant farmers" as backward, "all brawn and no brains" (Rama-krishna 1979:27), Jat landlords consider themselves inferior to none. They take great pride in their religious and cultural heritage and enjoy a high sense of self-esteem. They share a belief, forged from their history, in their ability to overcome adversity. They are confident of their skills as farmers, and they are willing to take risks for the sake of profit. In the Valleyside setting, moreover, they are able to find work immediately upon arrival in the one trade they know well. The crops

[63]

are different, but with their confidence and experience as farmers, they make the transition swiftly. Thus, it is possible for newcomers, with little or no formal education, no English, and no employment experience in India apart from farming, to become economically productive within weeks or even days of their arrival in this country.

The 1965 immigration and naturalization law has proved to be a major contributing factor in the growth and development of the Valleyside Punjabi enclave. Kinship networks among some families are now extensive. One clan, all relatives and in-laws of the wealthiest Punjabi farmer in the county, now numbers several hundred. New arrivals provide a steady stream of cheap labor for Valleyside orchards. At the same time, established residents help the newcomers make the transition from life in rural India to life in a highly developed Western society. Each group, old-timers and new arrivals, benefits from the presence of the other.

Recent immigrants have little need to turn to public or private agencies for housing, job placement, job training, counseling, or any other type of assistance. Their needs are met within the enclave itself. Newcomers, moreover, have an immediate sense of belonging to a community. Valleyside is not unique in this respect. Punjabi migrants have established strong settlements in Britain, Canada, Fiji, East Africa, and many other parts of the world.

Nor is this sense of communal solidarity and use of ethnic resources peculiar to the Punjabi Sikhs. Such a pattern exists in other immigrant groups (Light 1984). Kenneth Wilson and Alejandro Portes (1980) note the importance among the Cubans in Miami of a numerical concentration of immigrants, sufficient capital within the immigrant group to set up business, and renewal of the enclave through sustained immigration. Also applicable to the Valleyside Sikh case are many of the characteristics associated with the so-called middleman minorities, including many Indian communities in Africa, Australia, and Britain.[20]

In Britain the early Punjabi settlers tended to work in groups, relying on coethnics for help not only in securing employment but also in dealing with white bosses. In such a fashion Punjabi factory workers were able to participate in the larger economy without making many of the adjustments that would have been required had they set off on their own to find employment (Desai 1963). In Valleyside, too, Punjabi immigrants rely on friends and relatives to find them work, in factories as well as on farms, and, in the case of those who speak little English, to deal not only with their employers but also with other institutions, such as schools and hospitals.

Valleyside Punjabis also turn to established members of the community to serve as intermediaries with banks when they apply for loans to purchase a home or buy some orchard land. Although detailed investigation of how farms are financed in Valleyside was beyond the scope of this book, Punjabis seem generally to piece together the necessary funds for buying their first orchards through a combination of personal savings, loans from relatives, and loans from banks.[21] As a Punjabi farmer becomes established, reliance on financial backing from relatives decreases and the use of bank loans increases.[22] Several farmers in the course of their interviews specifically commented on the importance of maintaining good relationships with the local banks and were quick to point out that Valleyside bankers would give Punjabis loans when they "refuse the whites."

While the more established Punjabi farmers may no longer need to turn to relatives for loans, they continue to rely on family labor, particularly at harvesttime. Because labor is the major production cost in peach farming, Punjabis, by involving the entire family, can substantially reduce overall costs (La Brack 1982b), increasing their profits in good years and minimizing their losses in bad. The ethnic enclave also serves as a major resource to small farmers, including those who are unable to read, write, or speak English, by helping them to keep abreast of the latest developments in orchard farming.[23] Some Punjabi orchard farmers have managed, by drawing on the resources of more acculturated members of the community, to become quite successful economically without learning English or becoming proficient in the dominant culture.

Only a small minority of Valleyside Punjabis have become economically successful in American terms, but their perspectives on success are shaped by their prior experiences in India and by their knowledge of the opportunities available to Punjabi settlers in other parts of the world. Those we interviewed saw themselves as having improved their opportunities and those of their relatives by coming to America. They also believed that through a combination of hard work, perseverance, and the support of family members they could improve their situation. Such a belief was bolstered by the example of the many Punjabis in Valleyside and elsewhere in America who have become quite prosperous.

[65]

Although the interaction of cultural, contextual, and situational variables has brought different responses from other immigrant minority groups, the Valleyside Sikh case shares many characteristics with ethnic enclaves described in the literature on immigrant entrepreneurship. Psychological satisfaction with their new surroundings is particularly characteristic of those who have experienced hardships in their homeland far greater than those faced in the United States or who share the belief that greater opportunities are available to them in the United States than back home. Group members' subjective assessment of the opportunity structure, together with their relative satisfaction with their situation, has a direct impact on their economic adaptations, including their willingness to accept menial employment. These factors also have direct bearing on their perceptions of and responses to prejudice and discrimination.

[5]

Ethnic Relations

> The whites may think of us as inferior because we are in their
> country, but otherwise it is okay. When you go to another country
> you go there knowing something like this [prejudice] is possible.
>
> Punjabi farm laborer,
> Valleyside

Ethnic relations are here viewed through the eyes of both the Punjabi minority and the white majority. Much of the data is drawn from the interviews with the mothers and fathers of high school seniors and its primary perspective, therefore, is that of these parents.[1] The purpose is to describe the social context within which schooling takes place in Valleyside and to suggest that the ability of a group to achieve in school, or society, is affected not only by the degree of prejudice and discrimination it encounters but also by the minority group's perception of ethnic and racial conflict and by the nature of its response to such conflict. Theories of intergroup conflict and intragroup cohesion have largely focused on "real conflict," as opposed to "perceived conflict"; yet perceptions play an important role in shaping a minority group's response to prejudice and discrimination (cf. Buchignani and Indra 1980:149; Troyna 1978).

A minority group's response may be shaped by the direct experience of prejudice, by the particular situation of the group within American society, and in the case of an immigrant group, by its prior situation and experiences in another country. Immigrant minorities have often proved themselves willing to endure prejudice and discrimination so long as they are not totally barred from economic advancement. Even adverse conditions may look good to immigrants because from a comparative perspective they see themselves as better off in the new country than in the country of origin. A sense of relative satisfaction with their new situation persists until the immigrants are fully adapted to the standard of living in the new country (Light 1984:199).

South Asian emigrants have faced prejudice and oppression in many parts of the world (Tinker 1977). The combination of their economic success and their resistance to assimilation has contributed to host society hostility. Writing about Asian Indians in Britain, Rashmi Desai (1963:83) notes that immigrants, because they work together in groups, have less need to adapt themselves to the ways of the larger society. Their voluntary separation fosters the maintenance of traditional Indian ways, and it also contributes to tensions between themselves and the dominant group. In a dynamic process, the hostility of the majority group serves to strengthen ethnic boundaries and communal solidarity, which, in turn, reinforce the negative attitudes of the host society (Anwar 1979; Ballard and Ballard 1979). Such is also the case in Valleyside.[2]

Views of Valleysiders

For lack of any other satisfactory term, I call the white majority group Valleysiders. I could refer to them as white Valleysiders to distinguish them from Punjabi Valleysiders and Mexican American Valleysiders. Or I could call them simply Americans or whites, in keeping with their own view of themselves and in keeping with the Punjabis' terminology. "Valleysiders," however, has the advantage of simplicity.[3]

Today's Valleysiders may be divided into three major groups according to their date of arrival in the area. First, there are the old-timers, those whose families have been in the area for several generations. Among them are a handful whose ancestors were among the earliest settlers in California. The second major group migrated to California from Oklahoma or Arkansas during the 1930s and 1940s. One in three of the Valleysider students sampled had a parent or grandparent who came to California during this period, most to escape poverty. The final group comprises the newcomers, many of whom came as the result of a job transfer from another location in California.

Although a diverse lot, far more diverse in background and views than the Punjabis, the Valleysiders share a sense that Valleyside is a good place to live and to raise children. Like the Punjabis they cite the favorable climate, the location between ocean and mountains, and the quiet, small-town atmosphere.

[68]

Valleyside, the county seat since 1856, grew slowly in its early years, reaching 3,600 residents by 1908. In 1940 the town still had a population of only 4,968 and the county 18,680, but over the next twenty years the population doubled, and by 1980 the county population had surpassed 50,000. About 20,000 people lived in the town proper.

In years past most Valleysiders were farmers, but times have changed. Not only has the overall population grown, creating more job alternatives, but many small farmers have sold out, either to the larger Valleysider landowners or to Punjabis. Although agriculture remains the county's largest employer, few Valleysiders today farm for a living. In recent years, they explain, it has become increasingly difficult to make a profit from the small, family-run farm.

Today Valleysiders hold a wide variety of jobs. In our core sample, about a third of the fathers ran their own businesses, some of them farm related—renting equipment, selling fertilizer, setting up irrigation pipe. The rest were equally divided between the public and the private sectors. One in ten commuted to work, returning either daily or weekly. Several were retired from the military services. Almost all the mothers were also employed for at least part of the year. Although they held relatively low-paying positions—bookkeeper, secretary, clerk, school cafeteria worker—their salaries were an important part of the family income. Median family income for these Valleysiders was thirty thousand dollars, excluding children's earning. More than a third reported incomes of thirty-five thousand dollars or more. Almost a quarter, however, had incomes of less than fifteen thousand dollars; in six of nine cases, these were female-headed households.

Most Valleysider parents were satisfied with their employment and had no plans to change. At the same time, they noted a general lack of opportunity for advancement and lower wages than in nearby cities. Young people, parents observed, could always find summer employment in the area because of agriculture, but for full-time, permanent employment, opportunities were limited.

Quite a few Valleysiders, especially those whose families had moved to the area a generation or more ago, had many relatives throughout the county. Others had no kin nearby. Regardless, family was important to Valleysiders. Some noted, though, that they found it increasingly difficult to maintain a strong and united family. It was hard, they pointed out, to do things together on a regular basis. Even family meals could be difficult to arrange, since each member of the family had a separate schedule.

Valleysiders spoke proudly of this country's greatness. Most especially they valued their freedom and the economic opportunities available in America. They supported free enterprise and believed that initiative pays off. They appreciated the right not to conform. "Perhaps we do conform," one woman observed, "so as not to be viewed as weird. But it is our right to do what we want, so long as we are not infringing on others and not causing problems." The combination of freedom and opportunity was the reason, Valleysiders noted, that people from all over the world, including "East Indians," wish to immigrate to the United States.[4]

Valleysiders are very much aware of the increasing number of East Indians, or Punjabis, in their midst, and almost all have strong opinions about them, though few have much direct contact with them. Their places of work are separate, as are their places of worship. Although most Punjabis have non-Punjabi neighbors, the reverse does not hold. Since Punjabis represent only 10 to 12 percent of the county population and most old-timers live outside of town on their own ranches, the large majority of Valleysiders have no near neighbors who are Punjabis.

Yet all Valleysiders see Punjabis in shops and banks or simply driving about town. Punjabis are distinctive, both in dress and physical appearance, and thus are easily noticed. In the course of fieldwork, many Valleysiders expressed interest in learning more about the Punjabis, but it is clear from their comments that most lack even the most basic factual information about Punjabis in India or in Valleyside.

When asked how Punjabis fit into the community, one Valleysider couple responded as follows:

> Mrs. Ross: I don't think they are part of the Valleyside community. I have never seen Americans, people like us, have social contact, or religious contact, or anything else. The only time I have come in contact with them is at work [at a local cannery] and you don't socialize.
> Mr. Ross: I see this in the summertime. They sit in their groups and I guess we sit in ours to a certain extent.
> Mrs. Ross: I feel like we're indifferent. We don't greet each other, say "Hi" when we pass them on the street or anything. We can't talk to them because we can't speak their language. There is one [Punjabi] gal who is going through our schools and she [speaks some English]. The floorleader goes and gets her and she becomes the interpreter.

Other Valleysiders reported the same pattern. One woman noted, "When it comes right down to it, I don't think I have ever talked to one." Association between the two groups is minimal.

[70]

Those few Valleysiders who have Punjabi friends, through work or socially, comment positively about the relationship. "I know one girl at work," a Valleysider woman remarked. "She's fantastic. You couldn't ask for a better person." Such remarks were rare, however. Where social contact does exist it is usually with those Punjabis who are the most acculturated to mainstream American life, often those whose families have been in America for two or three generations or who have professional positions. All Valleysiders, regardless of how minimal their actual relationships with Punjabis, have something to say about this growing immigrant population in their midst. Their views are based largely on casual observation, hearsay, or the opinions of their children.

One Valleysider woman, herself a Dust Bowl refugee who had migrated to California in 1940 in search of better economic opportunities, compared her background to that of Punjabi immigrants. Mrs. Nelson's remarks reflect both understanding and hostility, and she welcomed the chance to comment:

> I was thinking the other day that when we came we probably met the same kind of thing that East Indians do because at that time there was a horde of Oklahoma people coming in and the California people really resented it. . . .
>
> There were no jobs in Oklahoma. We came without a job, but my husband found farm work. The day after we arrived my husband went to work milking a cow. Eventually we got our own ranch. We had peaches and walnuts. I remember we felt very discriminated against. In fact, the first job we had, the wife told the husband: "Don't bring any Okies here." I had never considered myself an Okie. Maybe that's the way we are with these people. I was thinking about this the other day and remembering back about how we felt that people treated us.

Mrs. Nelson went on to comment about how she saw the Punjabis fitting into the larger Valleyside community.

> I don't talk with them very much. I see them and that's about it. . . . I do notice once in a while how erratic they drive and I have been hearing about how they act in the grocery stores. I was looking for it when I went in, but I have never had anyone [a Punjabi] shove me aside. I think I was just hearing this. It is so easy when we hear people complaining about them. And then when one of them does this to us, it is easy for us to get mad. But when one of our own does it to us, we don't get as mad.

[71]

And about a year ago there was a big scare about East Indians having malaria. There were quite a few cases. I think all of us worried about it.[5] I did, and then when the [Sikh] temple was built down here I worried about that. I envisioned all kinds of traffic and that our dogs wouldn't be safe. I was listening to all of this and because we have to drive right by the temple on this back road when we go to church, I was thinking we'll never be able to get through the traffic. I really built it up in my mind. I let myself think about all these things—about the traffic, about how I was going to get shoved in the grocery line—and I really haven't found it happening.

Like Mrs. Nelson, many Valleysiders worried about the impact Punjabis were having on their community. Although their day-to-day lives were actually affected very little by the influx of the Punjabis, Valleysider attitudes have grown noticeably more negative as the Punjabis increase in number.[6] The negative image of Punjabis cuts across all groups of Valleysiders without regard to professional position, family income, education, or years in the area. Punjabis are the subject of numerous stories, often told in jest but laden with a sense of derogation. "People don't think they're being hostile," commented one Valleysider woman, "but they really are."

Punjabis are also the subject of many stereotypes, often contradictory. Those most frequently cited by Valleysiders in the course of formal interviews and in casual conversation include:

They've bought up all our land. They're all rich, even though they don't show it.

Most collect some sort of welfare.

In stores they tear through things, rip open packages, block the aisles, are very loud, and let their children run wild.

Basically they're very submissive, shy, with fear in their eyes, frightened.

They show no respect for others, don't try to fit in, are demanding and arrogant.

They're good businessmen, always pay in cash.

They have low moral standards, shoplift, cheat you every chance they get.

They're terrible drivers, a hazard on the roads.

[72]

They don't believe in bathing, smell bad, are not very clean, have lice in their hair.

Many of these characterizations have little or no basis in fact. Although new arrivals tend to be defensive, cautious, and slow drivers, the Valleyside police department could provide no evidence to support the "bad driver" image. It seems to be largely prejudicial myth. Statistics for traffic violations are not summarized by ethnic identity, but the strong impression of one officer familiar with department records was that Punjabis are actually underrepresented in the number of traffic citations and arrests, as well as for other types of misdemeanors and crimes. Managers of local stores frequented by Punjabis also flatly refuted the accusations of shoplifting and unruly behavior. Assumptions about body odor and Punjabis on welfare are equally unfounded.

Like many Valleysiders, Mrs. Nelson worried about the rapid escalation in the size of the Punjabi enclave and its growing impact on the majority community.

I expect more hostility, don't you? I fear that, I really do. . . . I really do feel like maybe we should stop so many from coming because I feel that at some time we may be in the minority. We have limited other nationalities. And yet I don't know how we would do that. We have said, "Give us your poor, your hungry," and I think this is why we've got them. It does hurt us. I hear my husband every once in a while complaining. I know he thinks here he is out working and supporting them on welfare. I don't know how many of them are on welfare.

This complaint about Punjabis on welfare, although not so prevalent as comments about body odor, emerged as a clear theme in the Valleysider parent interviews. Yet county statistics for 1980 indicated that proportionately far fewer Punjabis than Valleysiders participated in programs administered by the Department of Welfare. For example, even though Punjabis constituted some 10 to 12 percent of the county population, they represented only 3 percent of the Medi-Cal recipients and less than 1 percent of those receiving either Aid to Families with Dependent Children benefits or food stamps.

Valleysiders also complained that "their" tax dollars were being spent to support the teaching of Punjabi in the schools. The implementation of a federally supported Punjabi-English bilingual education program in one local elementary school in the late 1970s had stirred intense debate in the community at large. Some Valleysiders claimed that bilingual education and other special programs for Punjabi chil-

[73]

dren were disrupting their own children's education (Gibson 1985: 127). Many Valleysiders also shared the view that children taught in Punjabi would not learn English. Mrs. Nelson noted: "At the school for a while they wanted to set up [bilingual] programs for these children. Instead of making them learn the English language, they wanted a teacher to teach them in their own language. I didn't quite approve of this." It mattered little to Mrs. Nelson and others we interviewed that a major objective of the bilingual education program was the development of English skills. Most were simply opposed to the idea of teaching Punjabi in the schools.

The language issue was symptomatic of Valleysiders' deeper concerns that Punjabis were not assimilating rapidly enough into the mainstream and that they were getting ahead economically, by whatever means. These two issues, economic competition and cultural distinctiveness, were the most bothersome issues to Valleysiders, and the interviewer discussed them with Mrs. Nelson.

> Mrs. Nelson: I don't know how long they have to be here before we'll claim them as our people. I think we will always think of them as foreigners and intruders. How long does it take?
>
> Interviewer: Do you think of the Japanese as intruders?
>
> Mrs. Nelson: No I really don't and I never did. Maybe we didn't see the influx. They came during Gold Rush times, didn't they? We brought them over to do things for us. I think we are seeing the East Indians in a different light. We are not seeing them helping us. We are seeing them taking from us. We are seeing them buy our land. It took these other minorities a much longer time to get a hold.
>
> Interviewer: How are they able to do it so much more rapidly?
>
> Mrs. Nelson: I think because of the way they stick together. They help one another.
>
> Interviewer: You were saying, "How long will it take for them to be accepted?" I think one of the things about the East Indians is that they want very much to maintain their cultural identity, while maybe some other groups have wanted to assimilate more quickly, and when they do, they cease to be as visible.
>
> Mrs. Nelson: I think that this is what most people want. Maybe we feel threatened by seeing these people not becoming Americanized. I don't think the people already here are going to make any effort to socialize unless they do westernize themselves.

Like Mrs. Nelson, many Valleysiders seemed both to respect the Punjabis' pioneer spirit and to resent their economic success.

Some Valleysiders were most hostile than Mrs. Nelson in their attitudes toward Punjabis, some more knowledgeable. A few were indifferent. Most, however, seemed disturbed that Punjabis appeared to be moving ahead economically while seeking to maintain themselves as a separate community. Immigrants, they believed, should conform to American ways.

Another Valleysider tried to pinpoint her annoyances by contrasting Punjabi ways with those of the majority community:

Their consumables are food. They don't buy that much clothing the way we do. Like, well, we say, "I'm going to a party next weekend so I have to go get a new pair of shoes, get my hair done, my nails done, etc." They don't go to McDonald's. They don't go to Mr. Steak. And they don't go to the movies. I think the very main objection to them is they don't spend their money. They're making lots of money, but they're not spending it. I'm sure they put it in the bank, but then they send a lot back to India. They don't buy new cars. They don't do all the traveling back and forth to Lake Tahoe. They are just not consuming people.

Well, people object to that. They think, "Here I have to send this damned kid to dancing school and I have to take this kid skiing and why are their kids so happy with wearing old clothes?" You know they've got money because they've got three peach orchards. And here I am having to put on this big show and I really don't have the money to do it.

Few Valleysiders seemed to realize that it was, by and large, only the old-timer Punjabis—those who had arrived during the 1960s or earlier—that owned their own farms, and most of these had only small holdings. Nor did they seem to appreciate that most Punjabis, newcomers in particular, were struggling to make ends meet on an income less than half the average Valleysider's.

Those Valleysiders who knew anything about Punjabis recognized that they worked hard, saved what they could, and cooperated in joint business ventures. Said one, a real estate agent, "They are very industrious, hard to beat as far as ranching goes. . . . The whole family gets out there, and when it's irrigation time, you can't catch them at home. They're all out there putting up ditches, irrigating, or pruning. . . . You give them forty acres and [by the next year] they get enough credit and enough cash to go out and look for some more." Many Valleysiders recognized, too, that Punjabis lived frugally, worked hard, and took jobs that "no white guy" would do: "It's terrible wages for picking, pruning, and cultivating in the heat of the sun. Their goal is to get land.

[75]

They are willing to do whatever is necessary. The whole family gets out there. All the relatives pitch in. They cut down their standard of living to make their payments. They will combine families. They will combine incomes. They're not afraid to go into partnership with a whole bunch of people." One Valleysider, referring to their economic success, asked, "Who are we to criticize them? Anyone can do it." More, however, were clearly uncomfortable with this culturally distinctive and economically thriving enclave in their midst.

Even those Valleysiders who were quite well informed about the Punjabis wondered how they managed to buy houses and orchard land within just a few years of their arrival in this country. Unable to explain these economic achievements through their own cultural framework, some Valleysiders had invented a myth of the cheap bank loan, which ran as follows:

> If you got 3 percent interest money, wouldn't you buy all this land and make these investments? The American government has this lend-lease money that they send to India—millions and millions of dollars. India turns around and sends that money back to Canadian banks. These East Indians go to this Canadian bank, withdraw that money for 3 percent interest to buy up all this farmland. It is the money sent over there to develop those poor nations through our federal government.

Various versions of this story were current. All shared these elements: money originally "ours" had been made available at discounted rates to Indians through special banks.[7]

The myth of the cheap bank loan symbolized the majority group's resentment of the Punjabis. It rationalized the majority's prejudices. Unable to accept the economic achievements of a group of largely uneducated immigrants from rural India, some Valleysiders preferred to believe that Punjabis had purchased the county's best orchard land through unfair economic competition.

Some Valleysiders even declared the Punjabi system to be un-American because "they put three families to a house" and are willing to "skimp and slave." Valleysiders also worried about their ability to compete on the open market with Punjabis who were willing to work for low wages. One man explained: "They work for basically nothing and it's unfair competition. The Hindu landowner has a crew working for him. They're driving out the guy who has to pay for legitimate labor and wages. If we don't watch out, they are going to control our farmland." This man failed to note that non-Punjabi farmers in the area also

[76]

benefited from the cheap labor. Nor did he mention that Punjabi agricultural workers were often exploited by area farmers, and not only their own countrymen. Similarly, while Valleysiders expressed concern that the county's prime agricultural land was falling into Punjabi hands, few noted that it was the Valleysider farmers who were selling out.

Although most Valleysiders had negative views of the Punjabis as a group, some of which were only mildly negative and largely unconscious, others were more sharply and at times openly negative. Regardless of their views, most Valleysiders were generally courteous and helpful to Punjabis when they did interact with them. Those few who had some close personal association with Punjabis liked them as individuals. Although some who had business dealings with the Punjabis found them too eager to drive a bargain, most Valleysiders respected them for their initiative and hard work. As the Punjabis themselves were quick to point out, only a small minority of Valleysiders were openly hostile.

Views of Punjabis

Our interviews revealed that almost every Punjabi family had experienced prejudice, but it was the newcomers that suffered most. The old-timers, generally farm owners, were better established in Valleyside and were respected, albeit sometimes begrudgingly, for their agricultural skills and substantial influence in the county's largest industry. Most knew at least some English, and those who hired Mexican migrant labor often some Spanish as well, and they were able to go about their day-to-day business without concerning themselves with Valleysider prejudices. Newer arrivals were less acculturated and seemed not only to attract more attention, but also to be more preyed upon by that minority of Valleysiders, often teenage males, who were openly hostile to the Punjabis. Punjabi farmers, moreover, were less visible because they lived out of town on their own ranches where houses are set far apart. Newcomers, on the other hand, lived in town and daily came into more direct contact with neighbors. Those who rented, furthermore, tended to live in poorer neighborhoods, where, by their assessment, teenage youths were often rowdy and poorly disciplined by their parents. In spite of these differences, newcomers and old-timers differed little in their perspectives on ethnic relations.

[77]

In the interviews we probed not only incidents of hostility which the Punjabi parents or members of their family had experienced but also whatever friendships or positive social relationships they had enjoyed with members of the majority group. We were interested both in the parents' descriptions of social relations and in their response to these relations.

In almost every case, the Punjabi parents we interviewed chose to minimize the negative aspects of their relations with Valleysiders, regardless of whether the interviewer was Punjabi or non-Punjabi, community insider or stranger to Valleyside. Informal conversations and participant observation revealed similar response patterns. Punjabis generally described acts of hostility as isolated incidents, rather than as a significant part of their day-to-day experiences. They noted, too, that it was Valleysider teenagers, not adults, who were to blame for the problems that did occur. The following passages, drawn from parent interviews, are characteristic of the Punjabis' perceptions of prejudice:[8]

   Mr. Singh (an old-timer): The white children do cause mischief, kids fifteen to twenty years old.
   Mrs. Singh (old-timer): They shout "Hindu, Hindu," swear at us, put up their fingers. Anywhere you go there is always someone who walks past you and says, "Hindu go home, go back to India." We say never mind. Let them do it.
   Mr. Singh: The kids do call us Hindus, but they don't know what a Hindu is. To them it is swearing. They don't know that the Sikhs are a separate religion.
   Mr. Atwal (arrived late 1970s): All white people are not alike. Some treat us well. Others look at us with an evil eye. They feel as if we have dropped from space. Like, for example, where we first lived on Robbins Road our neighbors broke the windows of our cars, flattened the tires, spit on us, used abusive language.
   Mr. Takhar (arrived early 1970s): Some of the whites are very prejudiced. Some boys sprayed red paint on our windshield. We had to take the paint off with razor blades. They also drove their cars across our lawn. We had to put pipes in our yard to keep them from doing this. They did this on purpose. One [white] neighbor who teaches at the high school said it was a disgrace to the community. He said he would go to their parents, but we moved. Where we live now is okay.

Others, including Punjabi young people, reported efforts by Valleysiders to right the wrongs of unruly neighbors. One American-born

Punjabi girl, a high school senior, commented on her aunt's white neighbors: "Where my aunt lives, my father's sister, the neighborhood is kind of rowdy and they have gotten their windows broken. But they have other neighbors who are nice. One man went around the neighborhood and got donations to get the windows fixed. He said it didn't look nice in the neighborhood. The windows were always broken and had tape covering them." As in this case, descriptions of prejudiced attitudes and actions were almost always balanced with examples of friendliness. Punjabis share a strong sense that not all Valleysiders are alike. "Some are good, some bad, just like Punjabis." Few Punjabis, even those whose families have been the most victimized, harbor negative attitudes toward Valleysiders, or white Americans, as a group. Quite the reverse. Punjabis respect members of the majority group but decry the actions of certain individuals.

Most Punjabi parents observed that majority-group ill will did not have much direct impact on their ability to go about their day-to-day lives. The only contact most Punjabi farmers and farm workers had with Valleysiders was in the stores and banks or with their neighbors. Punjabis worked separately and ate at home. Few went to bars or even the movies. There was not much prejudice in the stores, they said, because businessmen wanted all the business they could get and could not afford to alienate Punjabi customers. The same with banks. Bankers, they believed, were concerned with Punjabis' ability to repay their loans and not with the color of their skin.

Most Punjabis also reported positive relations with at least some Valleysider neighbors. They described typical acts of cooperation and friendliness such as watching out for one another's children, keeping an eye on each other's houses, or borrowing jumper cables to start a dead battery. Punjabi farmers reported sharing vegetables, fruit, and even farm machinery with their neighbors.

One man, an agricultural laborer and a relative newcomer to Valleyside, recounted how a total stranger, "a white man," drove him fifteen miles into town when his car broke down. "They [white Americans] are really good. They treat you even better than our own people." Others made similar comments. Punjabis wish to have positive relations with members of the majority community and deeply appreciate Valleysider efforts to help. Likewise, they too wish to be considered good neighbors and a solid part of the larger Valleyside community.

Seva, or service to others, is a major aspect of Punjabi Sikh culture, and for overseas migrants *seva* includes providing help not only to

[79]

Valleyside Sikh temple and fruit orchards (© 1985 Peter Menzel).

family members and other fellow Sikhs but to members of the larger community where one has settled (Helweg 1979:13). An example of such assistance was the opening of one Valleyside *gurdwara* to victims of a recent flood in neighboring Yuba County and the contribution of several thousand dollars to the Red Cross for emergency relief. Free lodging and meals, moreover, are always available to all who wish them at any *gurdwara*, and the soccer field at the largest Valleyside *gurdwara* is also available to local soccer clubs for their games.

Most of the Punjabi parents whom we interviewed advocated a strategy of ignoring the hostilities. The troublemakers, most Punjabis believed, were white youths of lower-class background, often unemployed and with nothing else to do but "tease." Such difficulties, they explained, arise in every country. It was, according to one old-timer, "the 'new' whites, those from Oklahoma, from the poor states, that arouse these things." Other Punjabis echoed this theme, explaining that "people from good families don't do this" or that "only the loafers, some of those living in rented houses—the labor class—create problems." Most believed that "the whites who are working don't have time to do this type of thing." Several noted specifically, moreover, that it was not white farmers who treated them poorly. "This is a farming area," they said, and "farmers need each other."

Only rarely did Punjabis appear downcast over the majority group's negative attitudes or angry about Valleysider hostility. Rather, it was their deliberate strategy to avoid a situation of response and counter-response. One man, a longtime resident of Valleyside and a community leader explained:

> Now if we started swearing at them, what is the point? If some white children pass by in a car and shout, "Hey Hindu," and give us the finger, it would make things worse if we go after them in our car. If they abuse [us] and we abuse them, then we will have bad feelings amongst us. If I start swearing at them, do you think they will treat me well? If we don't allow anyone to cough, no one else is going to let us cough either. If we keep patient and truthful, it will remain this way.

Some Punjabis responded to teenagers' pranks by reporting the offenders' actions to their parents. In more serious cases Punjabis called the police. Neither approach, it seemed, was much of a deterrent. Those with some knowledge of English also tried to deal with errant youth directly, instructing them about Sikh history and culture or setting the record straight about their "taking" jobs from Valleysiders. One man, a Punjabi farmer, related a conversation he had had with two Valleysider boys intent, he supposed, on stirring up trouble for a Punjabi shop owner.

> One time Lal Singh had two white boys come into his store. I went in, too, to ask if they were causing a problem. Lal said, "No. What they were saying was that since our people have come here, we have taken over all their jobs, and now what can they do?"
>
> I said to the boys, "Yes, you are right. Would you like a job?" One said, "Yes." I said, "To everyone else I give $3.50 an hour. I'll give you $4.00. Come with me and start irrigating the fields." He goes, "Shit, that job?" So I said, "You son of a bitch, do we work in offices! This is the job that I have taken from you, so take it. . . . If you are complaining about Pun-

jabis taking other jobs, at the moment, we don't have other jobs. There are Hindu [*sic*] doctors, but you have a lot of doctors, too. And there aren't enough doctors anyway." The boys said, "Yes." I said, "Do we have a mayor here? Is there a Punjabi supervisor?" They said, "No." I said, "Well, how many Punjabi teachers are there?" They said, "About three." I said, "Which jobs have we taken over? Can you tell me? We have taken over the farm work."

I'll tell you another thing. I said, "You son of a gun, we are developing this country. We have been here for so many years and all we have bought is land. We have never sent back money home.[9] We are using this country's money in this country. Your country is benefiting. What's more, this country does not belong to you either. You came here just before us and we came a little after. If you want a job, then come with me. We irrigate the fields, prune the trees, drive the tractors. There is a lot of dirt flying and whenever you want to do this, come along. We have not taken over any of the other jobs. These are the jobs we have taken and you can have these back."

Other Punjabis reported a similar strategy of explaining to Valleysiders just what their economic status actually was.

Many of those we interviewed attributed the animosity largely to jealousy. It was a widely shared Punjabi belief that they were doing well and that the majority group resented their success. Several parents commented on Valleysider attitudes:

They figure that in twenty years they did not get anywhere, no money saved.

Wherever we go, we work hard and try to stand on our feet as quickly as possible. These people, they earn and they spend.

They think, "These people have only been here for two years and already they have bought their own house. We cannot do anything like that."

When we first come we work as laborers, but in a short time instead of our working for them, they start working for us. You tell me who is going to like us when they have to work for us. They think that we have taken over something which actually belongs to them.

Even newcomers, working for minimum wages in jobs shunned by Valleysiders, seemed to accept that the animosity was a natural outgrowth of Valleysider jealousy. In spite of all the difficulties recent arrivals faced in making ends meet, they shared the general Punjabi belief that they were doing well for themselves, and better than many poor whites and Mexican Americans.

The Punjabi response to prejudice is shaped not only by the attitudes and actions of the majority group and by their particular economic niche in Valleyside but also by their past experiences in other countries. Punjabi Sikhs have settled all over the world and their view of life in America reflects their international and comparative perspectives. Punjabis say that the prejudice they experience both here in the United States and in other countries stems in part from the fact that they "look different," "live separate," and pursue a different "style of living." They assume, moreover, that in all countries the indigenous lower classes, down and out and unable to get ahead, lash out at those who do well, especially immigrants. "When you go to another country," one Punjabi newcomer explained, "you go there knowing that [prejudice] is possible."

The situation in Valleyside, although difficult, is, in the Punjabi view, far better than in England or Canada. Several parents commented:

It is nothing here compared to Canada. There is a lot of hatred there. Our people are successful and they hate us. In England it is even worse. They don't want the Asians. Our people have a lot of property in England— businesses, shops, cinemas, small factories.

In England, the whites are very prejudiced. If you go to a pub in the evening you have to go together in a group of five or six, not alone. If you are by yourself, they beat you up.

Also the English are prejudiced because they ruled over us and now they feel that they are superior and we are inferior.

They are all color minded. They think they are the greatest. But the world has changed. It is only a little island.

Parents also explained that unemployment is high in England and that relatives settled there now want to emigrate to the United States. To many Punjabis both here and abroad, America is the "leader of all countries." In spite of the difficulties, Valleyside Punjabis count themselves among the fortunate.

Only a few of the Punjabi adults we interviewed had firsthand experience in competing with white Americans for jobs. Their perceptions about job discrimination were, therefore, formed largely through the experiences of friends and relatives who were better educated and who had looked for work apart from farming. Although some of our informants clearly felt that Punjabis were hired last, after whites and even after other minorities, and that their only option was to take jobs no one else wanted, most nevertheless had a positive attitude about the American employment system. A certain amount of discrimination was to be expected, Punjabis believed, because "in all countries they wish to hire their own people."

Most also believed that employment opportunities in the United States were far better than in Britain or back in Punjab. Several parents contrasted the American employment system with that of India. In India, they explained, to get a job one had either to be rich and well connected or from a lower caste. Since the small Jat Sikh farmer is neither, he has difficulty finding work apart from farming, regardless of his qualifications.

Under India's affirmative action laws the Chamars and other disadvantaged castes are given preference in hiring and in gaining admission to universities. For example, 22 percent of all central government civil service jobs go to the Chamars and other "backward" groups. Additional places are reserved by the central government for the intermediate castes, who traditionally have had low social status (Scully 1985). Each state also sets quotas for civil service jobs. Many members of the higher castes, including many Jats, feel the quota system produces unwarranted reverse discrimination. They advocate an employment and university admissions' system based on objective criteria such as test scores, not caste background, especially since some castes that continue to be designated as "backward" are today no longer economically disadvantaged.[10]

By comparison, most Punjabi immigrants find the American system extremely fair and open. Here, they say, a person is hired based on educational credentials and experience, not according to caste or class background. They noted, moreover, that U.S. laws provide greater protection to the individual than Indian laws. They assumed that their children, armed with an American education, would be able to find desirable jobs. In general, they believe in the American system and its ability to safeguard their rights.[11]

[84]

Punjabis consciously seek to project a good image of themselves as a group. They attempt, therefore, to avoid confrontation with members of the majority community, even when they feel themselves wronged. The following story, told by a Punjabi farmer, expresses such an attitude:

> I know one man who went to work in a factory. He said that they told him to take off his turban if he wanted the job, that he would have to wear a helmet. Otherwise the insurance would not cover him. He said, "They are trying to take off my turban. Our religion is in danger." Why go into all this? Either wear the helmet, or go and seek work elsewhere. Why create difficulties? In case the man dies with injuries, they would have to pay. We don't think about these things. We just try to arouse something. If Punjabis continue to arouse things like this, it will create prejudice. Next time a Punjabi goes looking for a job, they will say, "There are no jobs because Punjabis don't listen to what we say."

Others noted that if they were passed over for a job, they simply looked elsewhere.

Punjabi parents' response to the prejudice, and discrimination where it existed, was not simply a passive reaction but rather a deliberate and calculated strategy. Jat Sikhs do not shy away from confrontation when they feel their honor or interests are threatened, but in the Valleyside context they find accommodation serves their interests better than confrontation.[12] Although their willingness to subordinate their ways to the requirements of the dominant culture stems, in large measure, from a realistic appraisal of their limited ability to alter the status quo and a concern that fighting back quite likely would only lead to increased tension between groups, Sikhs also have a genuine wish to get along with members of the majority group.[13]

Some Punjabis, especially those better educated and more westernized, disagreed with this approach, believing that Punjabis must take a collective stand. One Punjabi professional, raised in urban India and a graduate of an American university, described these Doabi village folk as "dense." He believed that they should get together and insist upon their rights. Short of this, he said, the situation in Valleyside would never change. Most, however, believed that Punjabis faced less discrimination in the United States than in many other parts of the world. So long as they perceived themselves to be progressing economically, they found little reason to alter their strategies.

Impact of Prejudice

As unpleasant as they have found it to be the object of prejudice, most farmers and farm workers observed that majority-group hostility had little direct impact on their daily lives. The climate of prejudice detracted, however, from the quality of life enjoyed by all Valleyside Punjabis, whether old-timer or recent arrival, laborer, farmer, or professional. Said one woman, the wife of a farm worker and herself a seasonal laborer, "You do feel it. If someone treats you badly, obviously you are going to be upset about it. The reason why we don't do anything is because it is their country."

Like other immigrants, Punjabis see themselves, at least for a time, as guests and outsiders. To avoid trouble many keep themselves separated. Some even assume that Punjabis bring trouble upon themselves if they "go to bars" and "wander around" in town. "If after work you just come and sit at home and only go to the stores if you want groceries, then what kind of problems will you have?" asked one man, a farm laborer who had lived six years in Valleyside. Younger and better-educated Punjabis disagreed, noting that they had every right to use public facilities without fearing that they might be subjected to verbal or physical abuse. At the time of fieldwork, however, the dominant view was that a strategy of separation and low visibility was best.

Punjabi adults are shielded from the most injurious effects of prejudice not only by their strategy of separation but by their positive sense of self-esteem, even cultural superiority,[14] their egalitarian ideals, strongly rooted in the Sikh religion, and their strong sense of community. In Valleyside they have pulled together not only as a response to prejudice and the constant pressures for cultural conformity but also to advance their economic interests. Their communal and family solidarity resembles that of other immigrant groups and is, in part, a response to their subordinate position in this society (Light 1984; see also De Vos 1975).[15] But Sikhs also have a long history in India of pulling together to overcome hardship and protect their identity and economic interests.

As a group, moreover, the Punjabis have become a major economic force in Valleyside. They own approximately 50 percent of the county's farmland, and they recognize that their presence has become increasingly important to the local economy. One Punjabi, the owner of a hundred acres of prime orchard land, explained: "The Punjabis work for the whites and the whites work for the Punjabis as well. It is not just that we depend on them. They depend on us too. . . . They bring their machines and harvest our crops. Their mechanics work for us. . . . Even the banks benefit. We have good connections with the banks. We buy their fertilizers. Diesel gas. I think the prospects are good." He was referring to the prospects for social relations. Not all agreed. Some old-timers observed that prejudice had increased with the rapid influx of new immigrants and that the situation would continue to worsen as Punjabis increasingly competed for jobs currently held by white Americans.

Yet if discrimination mounted, Punjabis stated explicitly that they could always return to India. "All of us who have come to America," said one farmer, "we have some property in India too. Even if they tell us to leave the country, we will have a good place to go back to." Punjabis maintain strong ties to their villages in Punjab. Although few actually expect to return permanently—and their investment in this country is clear indication of the wish to remain here—many have experienced catastrophic moves in the past. Many families were uprooted at the time of India's partition in 1947.[16] And they all know families who were forced to flee East Africa in the 1960s, often losing all their investments. If discrimination mounted here, as it had in other countries, they had a homeland to which they could conceivably return.[17]

In sum, a combination of cultural, contextual, and situational variables enables most Punjabi adults to maintain a positive attitude toward America and white Americans in spite of the prejudice. They encourage their young to adopt the good traits of the majority group and to take advantage of the educational and economic opportunities that residence in this country affords. At the same time, they worry that their children might take up with the wrong sorts of whites and fear that the constant pressures to Americanize will cause their children to feel caught between cultural systems. And they are deeply concerned about the impact of racial hostilities on their children's academic progress.

[87]

[6]

Academic Performance
at Valleyside High

> My duty is to educate them. If they study, they will be successful,
> otherwise not.
>
> Punjabi parent, Valleyside

The most common measures of school achievement at the secondary
level are standardized test scores, grades, and graduation. Perhaps
more important, but less frequently analyzed, are the actual courses
taken in high school. Track placement is another measure and a particularly significant one for examining the school performance of minority students and students of low socioeconomic status. College attendance, although not necessarily related to academic success in high
school, is a further indicator of overall educational achievement. Finally, for language-minority students, the degree of proficiency in
English is critical to educational success. We shall consider each of
these measures in our analysis of school performance.

School district records showed that in just eight years, between 1972
and 1980, students of Asian origin had grown from less than 3 percent
to almost 13 percent of the total student population, grades kindergarten through twelve. More than 90 percent of these students were of
South Asian origin.[1] At the time of fieldwork 231 Punjabi students
attended Valleyside High. Only 12 percent of these students were
American-born (Table 10). Only 30 percent had begun their schooling
in America, and another 5 percent had arrived by the end of second
grade (Table 11). Half had lived in the United States for five years or
less. Both length of residence and age on arrival in the United States
will be considered in analyzing school performance, as will location of
previous education for those whose schooling began in a foreign country.

In sharp contrast to the Punjabis, all Valleysider students were American-born and two-thirds had received all their schooling in Valleyside. About three-quarters of the twenty-one hundred students attending Valleyside High were Valleysiders. Students of Mexican origin made up another 10 percent of the high school enrollment. Although one in three of these students was foreign-born, only one in five had started school in Mexico, the others having migrated to this country during their preschool years. Punjabi performance profiles will be compared with those for Valleysiders and Mexican Americans.

Valleyside High School

Valleyside High, a large, four-year high school with a wide-ranging curriculum, serves nearly three-quarters of the county population and at the time of fieldwork was the only comprehensive high school in the area. The buildings, playing fields, and parking lots cover several city blocks. Classrooms, administrative offices, and a multipurpose room used mostly as a cafeteria surround a central quad, where students congregate between classes. By tradition, a certain section of the quad is reserved for seniors.

In an experienced faculty of 124 full-time teachers, over half have taught for at least ten years. All but two have a master's degree or equivalent course work. At the time of fieldwork, two-thirds were male, including all seven administrators.[2] Only eight were nonwhite, including two Punjabis.

Academic achievement at Valleyside High compares favorably to that at other comprehensive high schools across the nation. Valleyside seniors, for example, have consistently scored from twenty-five to fifty points above state and national averages on the math Scholastic Aptitude Test; verbal SAT scores have surpassed the state and national averages in five of seven years recently, but by a smaller margin.[3] Scores on standardized tests taken by students in junior and senior high show a range and distribution similar to those at school districts of comparable size and composition. Valleyside High also compares favorably with state averages and its state comparison group for the percentage of high school students taking advanced classes in math and science. Significantly fewer Valleyside High students, however, take four years of English than in the state as a whole (49.6 percent in Valleyside, 73.0 percent statewide in 1983–1984).[4]

Punjabi Performance Patterns

Analysis of school performance data for all 231 Punjabi students revealed two widely disparate achievement patterns. Students raised in this country do comparatively well in school. Newer arrivals do far less well. The two most important—and closely related—factors influencing the academic performance of Punjabi students are their *age on entry in English-medium schools* and their *proficiency in English*.[5] A third factor, which influences both course selection and general response to schooling among students at the high school level, is the student's sex. Punjabi girls and boys have different performance profiles. These three factors provide a framework for the present analysis. Other factors commonly associated with minority students' performance in school, such as parents' education, occupations, income, English fluency, and their familiarity with the prevailing culture and the American system of education, seemed to be of less importance in the present case.

High School Graduation

To graduate from Valleyside High students at the time of fieldwork needed a total of 220 credits, including 20 credits of English (equal to four semesters), 10 credits each of science and mathematics, 30 credits of social studies, 5 credits of driver's education, and 20 credits of physical education.[6] All other credits were electives. In order to graduate students also had to receive "passing" scores on standardized tests, reflecting minimum levels of competency in reading, writing, and mathematics.

High school graduation in Valleyside, as elsewhere in America, is an especially important measure of school success. For some, it is the chief means of distinguishing successful students from nonsuccessful. By this criterion only two-thirds of the young people attending Valleyside High at the time of fieldwork were successful. About one-third of the students dropped out, and this attrition rate was similar to that for the state as a whole.[7]

A distinctly higher percentage of Punjabi students finishes high school than either majority-group Valleysiders or Mexican Americans. This is true regardless of how long the Punjabis have lived in this country, their previous educational background, or their proficiency in

English. Of the Punjabi students who enter Valleyside High as ninth graders, an estimated 88 percent finish four years later, compared to 75 percent of the Valleysiders and 60 percent of the Mexican Americans.[8]

Of the forty-five Punjabi students classified as seniors in October 1980, forty received their diplomas in 1981. Only six of these students were American-born and only twelve had begun their schooling in this country. Eight had lived in the United States for less than three years.

Three of the five who failed to graduate were recent arrivals. Two were girls who had failed the competency test. Both planned to spend an additional year at Valleyside High so they might receive their diplomas in 1982. The third, a boy, had to drop out midway through senior year when his father became so seriously ill that he was unable to support his family. This young man, an able student with aspirations to a career in engineering, planned as soon as practicable to take evening classes at the community college. Another boy, who had arrived in the United States during eighth grade, was a slow learner and a borderline special education student.[9] He, too, was unable to pass the competency tests. The fifth student was a girl who had lived in Valleyside since fifth grade. She dropped out for health reasons.

Punjabi students were far more likely than either Valleysiders or Mexican Americans to elect early graduation, if eligible. Although Punjabis accounted for less than 9 percent of the class of 1981, they totaled 39 percent of those who graduated midway through their senior year. Many Punjabis saw little point in remaining in high school once they had completed all their requirements. Few were involved in the social life of the senior class, and once all graduation requirements were completed, they wanted to move on promptly to a higher level of education. Of the Punjabi seniors finishing at midyear, two-thirds began classes at Valleyside Community College that same month.

Grades

The Punjabi seniors, as a group, received better grades in high school than non-Punjabi classmates. While the cumulative grade point average for all seniors was 2.47 on a 4-point scale, the mean for Punjabis was 2.59. The boys received higher grades on average than the girls (2.72 versus 2.50). A similar pattern emerged from analysis of grades received by Punjabi students in grades nine to eleven. Fluent-English-proficient (FEP) students tended to receive higher grades than those

[91]

classified as limited-English-proficient (LEP). The cumulative grade point average for all Punjabi FEP students, grades nine to twelve, was 2.67. Again, boys received the higher marks.[10]

No clear correlation was found between parental income or education and Punjabi students' grades in school. Within the core sample of forty-five seniors, children of farm laborers were as likely, possibly more likely, to receive top marks as children of farm owners. This finding merits testing with a larger sample.[11]

It is clear from the Valleyside study that Punjabi students earned better grades in school than their majority-group classmates, even though their parents had far less formal education, spoke little English, and had a median family income of just half that of the Valleysider group. The comparatively good grades of students who had only recently arrived from India were related to the higher grades that teachers tended to give in ESL (English as a Second Language) classes than in the regular academic classes.[12] This, however, is no explanation for the even higher grades received by Punjabi students who took no ESL classes.

Other Measures of School Success

Another finding that emerged clearly from the study is that neither graduation nor grades are sufficient measures of school achievement, in spite of the importance generally accorded them. Many students, majority and minority alike, finished four years of high school without taking even a single high school level math or science class. Some language-minority students also graduated without taking even one high school level English class.

District policy permitted limited-English-proficient students to meet the graduation requirement of twenty credits of English through their ESL classes. They were also able to meet science and math requirements through ESL classes in these subjects, even though the instructional level and content of the ESL classes was, at best, equivalent only to that of the upper elementary grades. This policy enabled LEP students to graduate at the end of four years of high school along with their age-mates. District policy has since been changed, however; now all students, minority and majority alike, must complete the same English requirements in order to graduate. When necessary, students are permitted to attend high school for more than the customary four years in order to meet these requirements.

English Proficiency and Age on Arrival

For all too many Punjabi students school success was more apparent than real. Many students—generally those with limited English skills—graduated from high school with far less than a high school education. Nearly one-third of the Punjabi seniors received their diplomas without taking any English, science, or math classes beyond the ESL or remedial level. All were distinctly limited in English. Most were recent arrivals, but several had been attending schools in the Valleyside system for as much as seven years.

The study revealed a close relationship between English proficiency and the grade at which Punjabi students entered English-medium schools. Almost 90 percent of those who emigrated from India after fourth grade continued to be weak in English through high school. Those who entered in the earlier grades, although often not as proficient in English as native speakers, had sufficient English skills to pursue college-preparatory classes in high school. The difference between the earlier and later arrivals was striking.

The Valleyside school district classified every student whose family spoke a language other than English at home as either FEP, LEP, or NES (non-English-speaking). The classification was based on fairly cursory tests of students' ability to read and write English, as well as to speak it. While perhaps not an adequate measure of academic English proficiency (California State Department of Education 1983; Cummins 1981), the classification system did reveal clear group patterns. The system was also consistent with our own informal assessment of students' English skills. Those classified as FEP had, as a group, stronger English skills than the LEP students, and the latter stronger skills than the NES group. Within the core sample, most of the LEP students preferred to be interviewed in Punjabi. Some were unable either to be interviewed in English or, unaided, to complete a written questionnaire in English. The FEP students, on the other hand, were very comfortable in conversational English and had no difficulty completing the questionnaire without help.

Table 12 shows the relationship between grade of entry into U.S. schools and the English proficiency of Punjabi high school students. Over three-quarters of the students who entered American schools by second grade were classified FEP by the time they reached high school, as were two-thirds of those arriving in third and fourth grades. But only 12.5 percent of those entering the system in fifth or sixth grade were classified as FEP in high school. Students who had previously lived in either England or Fiji, countries with substantial Sikh settlements, were omitted from the analysis, but most of these students had attended English-medium schools prior to their arrival in Valleyside and their school performance patterns were similar to those of the American-educated group.

We found English proficiency to be more closely related to students' age on immigration, or more specifically their grade of entry into the U.S. school system, than to their length of residence in the United States. The critical point appeared to be fourth grade. Those who arrived by then were likely to be academically competitive in high school. Those who arrived later lagged far behind their age-mates in English skills even after attending American schools for five to seven years.[13] Juniors and seniors, for example, who had entered the system in fifth and sixth grades had been in the United States as long as freshmen and sophomores who had entered the system in third and fourth grades. Nevertheless, the younger arrivals were far more likely to be classified as fluent in English. Of the younger arrivals, 63.2 percent were classified FEP, the remainder LEP. Of the older arrivals, only 25 percent were considered FEP, the rest LEP. An almost identical pattern was found to exist between grade placement on arrival and English proficiency for the Mexican American students attending Valleyside High (Gibson 1983a:120–21).[14] Reasons for the difficulties experienced by the older arrivals in mastering English and their implications for educational policy are discussed in later chapters.

Track Placement of Early Arrivals

Many departments of the high school tracked all students, that is, they geared their general course offerings to several different levels of ability and achievement. The English department, for example, grouped courses in two ways. First, courses increased in difficulty, progressing from English 1 (generally taken in ninth grade) to English 4 (a college-preparatory course taken in twelfth grade). Additionally, students were placed in one of three instructional tracks—remedial, average and accelerated—according to standardized test scores and past classroom performance. On entering high school, those students who were unable to write at what Valleyside teachers described as a sixth-grade level were required to take remedial English or, if LEP/NES, one or more classes of ESL English. Students were also placed in math, science, social studies, and foreign language classes according to their ability level and past performance.

Our focus here is the track placement in high school of Punjabi students who began their schooling in this country or entered the system by second grade. The academic progress of the older arrivals, in particular those arriving in fifth grade or later, is examined in Chapter 8 as part of the discussion of barriers to educational opportunity.

In several important ways all Punjabi students are clearly at a competitive disadvantage when they enter school. Not only do most Punjabi students, including those born in Valleyside, enter school knowing little or no English, their parents are largely unable to help them with their school work because their own skills in English are limited, as are, in many cases, their educational backgrounds. Moreover, during the early and middle 1970s, when the high school students we studied were attending elementary school, the Valleyside school district offered no ESL or bilingual education to limited- and non-English-speaking students. Few of the elementary schools had even a single teacher who spoke Punjabi.[15] The students, thus, received virtually none of the special assistance that is now generally available to language-minority children when they enter school. The Punjabi students also had to cope with widespread ignorance about their cultural background and endure what may be characterized as pervasive and active prejudice toward them.

The tracking system at Valleyside High was in a state of flux at the time of fieldwork, with placement criteria and groupings shifting from year to year. The general trend was toward more levels, remedial through accelerated, and toward increased reliance on standardized test scores. Teachers' recommendations, past classroom performance, and the students' and parents' wishes were also considered.

The track placement of students on entering ninth grade proves critical to their later ability to progress into the more advanced academic classes. It is rare for a student who begins in the slower track ever to take a third or fourth year of high school level science, math, or English. Students who do take these more demanding academic classes, which are generally required for university admission, almost always begin high school in the "fast track."

At Valleyside High far more fast track students than slow track students were college bound. Students who needed remedial work at the start of high school usually shifted to vocational or general education classes after meeting basic requirements in math, science, and

[95]

English. Some took a course or two beyond the minimum, but rarely did they take these subjects in all four years of high school.

Students scoring below the 35th percentile on the California Test of Basic Skills, taken in eighth grade, were placed in remedial math, general science, and a slow section of social studies when they entered ninth grade. Students scoring high on this test were eligible as freshmen for an accelerated math class and for foreign language instruction. All other students were placed in what may be called the "average" track.

Punjabi students in the class of 1984 were *less* likely than the Valleysider students to need remedial instruction in math but also somewhat less likely to be placed in the accelerated math group (see Table 13). Since the standardized tests in math included word problems and were timed tests, some Punjabi students, in spite of strong math skills and a strong interest in math, undoubtedly scored lower than native-born English speakers because they were less proficient in English. The Mexican American students were more likely than either group to require remedial assistance and less likely to qualify for the accelerated math class.

Science placements revealed no difference between the Punjabi and Valleysider groups. Again, the Mexican American students were more likely to require remedial work than the other groups. Students whose scores on the California Test of Basic Skills showed them to be weak in "math concepts and applications" were generally placed in a one-semester remedial, or "general science," course, which satisfied graduation requirements in science. Most other students took a two-semester course called Introduction to Physical Sciences, which was a prerequisite to more advanced science classes offered at the high school. Some students took no science as ninth graders, waiting until later grades to satisfy their science requirements. These students subsequently took either IPS, general science, or some other science class meeting graduation requirements.

All ninth graders took one semester of cultural geography and one semester of physical geography. As was the case in science, more than 70 percent of the Valleysider students were placed in the faster track, but only 64 percent of the Punjabis and 45 percent of the Mexican American students were similarly placed. Placement was tied to students' scores in reading comprehension.

Students were placed in remedial English if they had not passed the minimum competency test in writing and were not identified as limited-English-proficient. The LEP and NES students were placed in one of three levels of ESL English. The passing score on the writing competency test was quite low. Only 11 percent of the Valleysider students had failed to pass the test before entering high school, compared to 25 percent of the Punjabis and 24 percent of the Mexican Americans. Placement in the accelerated English class was based on a combination of test scores, class performance in eighth grade, and teacher recommendations. Considerably more Valleysider students than Punjabis or Mexican Americans were placed in the accelerated English class.

In sum, the Punjabi students raised in the United States were about as likely as majority-group students to be placed in the advanced courses when placement was based on math test scores. When English comprehension was the major placement criterion, the Punjabis fared less well, but even here only one-quarter of the Punjabis were placed in either remedial English or ESL English. In all subject areas the Punjabi students were more likely than the Mexican American students to be placed in the faster tracks.

The sample of Punjabi students in the class of 1984 was small, only twenty-eight students, but the patterns that emerged were similar to those found for the classes of 1981–1983. Analysis of the courses taken by these older students over four years of high school provides further evidence of Punjabi school achievement.

Advanced Academic Courses

Less than 20 percent of the students attending Valleyside High in 1980–1981 took four years of high school English. Only two-thirds of the students took even one high school level class in either math or science. We were interested to learn how the performance patterns of the American-educated Punjabi students compared to this overall pattern. The analysis will concentrate on the percentage of students taking progressively more advanced classes each year in math, science, and English.[16]

In math, students who took Algebra 1 as ninth graders were able to progress by twelfth grade either to Advanced Algebra and Trigonometry or to Math Analysis. In science, top students typically took Introduction to Physical Sciences in ninth grade, followed by Biology 1, Chemistry, and either Biology 2 or Physics. The top English students, after completing English 1 and 2, proceeded into a two-year, college-preparatory course sequence (English 3 and 4). English 3 was also offered as an average track class for those who did not qualify for or wish to take the more accelerated course.

As shown in Table 14, the American-educated Punjabi students did well academically, remarkably well considering the substantial barriers to their success in school. Throughout their four years of high school they took, on average, somewhat more math and science than their Valleysider counterparts and almost as many English classes. Different patterns emerged, however, for Punjabi males and Punjabi females. Nearly half the boys took three years of both math and science and more than one-third took a fourth year. Yet only 13.6 percent of the girls took a third year of science or math and fewer still a fourth year. In English, as many girls as boys took a third year, but substantially more boys took a fourth year. Reasons for these differences are discussed in the next chapter.

There was no similar disparity between the sexes within the Valleysider group. Approximately the same percentage of Valleysider males and females took three years of English, math, and science. A few more males than females took a fourth year.[17] Overall, however, only two-thirds of the Valleysiders took Algebra 1, only half took Geometry, one-fourth Algebra 2, and one-tenth Trigonometry or Math Analysis. In science only half took Biology 1, one-third Chemistry, and 15 percent either Biology 2 or Physics. More Valleysider students took a third year of high school level English than Punjabis, 69 percent to 55 percent, respectively. Only one in four of the Valleysiders took a fourth year of English.

Standardized Test Scores

Every school district in California establishes a minimum level of competency in reading, writing, and mathematics that students must attain in order to graduate from high school. For this purpose the Valleyside school district used a nationally normed testing program. Passing scores, which were felt to reflect community norms in Valleyside, had been set considerably higher in math than in reading or writing. To pass the math portion of the test required a score equal to the 55th percentile for a national sample of eighth and ninth graders. In reading and writing the passing scores were set at the 23d and 20th percentiles, respectively.

Test results for Valleysider students compared favorably with a national sample, as shown in Table 15. Over 80 percent passed the reading and writing and over 40 percent passed the math the first time they took the tests, which for most students was during junior high or on entering high school.[18] Students who failed in one or more areas were retested following a period of remedial instruction. More than 90 percent of the Valleysiders had passed both reading and writing after their second attempt, and three-quarters had passed the math.[19]

The minority students, both Punjabis and Mexican Americans, had considerably more difficulty than the majority-group students passing the competency tests. Of the American-educated students—those who had entered U.S. schools by second grade—only 27 percent of the Punjabis and 15 percent of the Mexican Americans passed the math test when they first took it. Some of these students were undoubtedly handicapped by the heavy use of word problems in the test. Students had less difficulty demonstrating minimum competency in reading and writing because of the lower passing scores in these two areas. Still, more than a third of the language-minority students failed both the writing and reading tests the first time they took them. Following remedial instruction, however, about 90 percent of both groups were able to pass the reading test and nearly 80 percent the writing test. Only half the students passed the math test on the second attempt.

The competency tests were administered to all students, regardless of their proficiency in English. As might be expected, students weak in English had great difficulty with the tests (see Table 16). The tests were themselves a measure of English language proficiency. That some students designated as non-English-speakers actually passed the tests indicates either that they were improperly classified or that they received assistance in taking the tests. Since students had to attain passing scores in order to graduate, some took the tests again and again, once or twice a year, until they passed, all the while taking remedial or ESL classes.

Standardized test scores were the one measure of academic success that showed the American-educated Punjabis lagging behind their Valleysider classmates in any substantial fashion. The differences are most apparent in comparing the distribution of competency test scores, as indicated in Table 17. About twice as many Punjabis as Valleysiders scored below the 25th percentile and less than half as many scored above the 75th percentile in reading, writing, and math. A similar pattern emerged for the American-educated Mexican Americans,

[99]

whose competency test results overall were somewhat less strong than the Punjabis and far below those of the Valleysiders.

College Attendance

Fully three-fourths of the Punjabi students in the class of 1981 enrolled in college the year following their graduation from high school (80 percent of the girls and 74 percent of the boys). Of these, all the girls and most of the boys attended Valleyside College, the local community college on the outskirts of Valleyside. Three boys went away to college, two entering a four-year college program directly. Both were excellent students planning careers in electronic engineering.

More than half of those who enrolled at Valleyside College went on to complete a two-year course of study and received an A.A. or A.S. degree (50 percent of the girls and 64 percent of the boys). Based on students' high school and community college records, together with information available through informal follow-up interviews with a few key informants, some 40 to 50 percent of the Punjabi boys in the core sample appeared likely to complete at least four years of college. Far fewer of the Punjabi girls—no more than 15 to 20 percent—were likely to earn a B.A. or B.S. degree.

Punjabi students not only aspire to a college education, but most actually continue their schooling beyond the secondary level. Their record of school persistence and achievement is all the more impressive given their family backgrounds. More Punjabi students enroll in college than Valleysider students and, in the case of the boys, it appears that far more actually complete a four-year degree. Approximately two-thirds of all Valleyside High graduates attend college, but only about 12 percent receive a four-year degree.

Valleysider Performance Patterns

Most Valleysider parents commended the educational program at the high school. Even those whose children had done poorly praised the high school faculty and curriculum. Parents noted that the system worked well for those who arrived in ninth grade with the requisite basic skills and who knew what they wanted and needed from high school. Many Valleysider parents explained, however, that their children either were bored by their classes, were too shy to ask for assistance, or lacked motivation. Some pointed out, in addition, that their children were simply unable to handle the academic demands of high school because they were poorly prepared in math and English.

Teachers and administrators noted similar problems. They explained the root cause as a lack of parental support for education. More specifically, they cited too little discipline and supervision at home and a general failure by parents to be meaningfully involved in their children's education. They also believed that many other problems related to these.

Most Valleysider seniors themselves were pleased with their high school experience. They reported that they had taken the courses of their choice and that they were satisfied with the grades they had received. Many admitted that they had deliberately chosen "easy" classes once basic requirements had been met. Only those who planned to go directly into a four-year college felt the need to take increasingly advanced academic courses every year. These courses were viewed as "college prep," and other students simply saw little reason to take them. They also knew that should they later decide to attend college, they could make up missing courses at some community college, where, in California, the only requirement for admission is graduation from high school or a minimum age of eighteen.

One Valleysider student explained that he had not taken any math course beyond first-year algebra because he did not feel the more advanced courses would prove useful in the future. The "peak" of his education, he reported, had come in tenth grade, when he had taken algebra 1, biology, and English 2. After that his interests and energies had turned away from school to an after-school job, playing in a rock band, and activities with friends. Following high school he hoped to support himself through a lawn maintenance business.

Many other Valleysider students, especially the boys, expressed similar attitudes. One college-bound senior, well liked by peers and teachers, noted that getting an education meant more than just going to school. He reported: "I go fishing and skiing a lot. I get my work done, and to miss school and do these other things is educational to me too. . . . Obviously there are people that never cut school, and what if something did happen and you are stranded some place out in the wild somewhere? You wouldn't know how to survive. So it is a different type of education. I don't miss [school] because I'm lazy. I miss it and do something worthwhile." This student missed ten days of school his

[101]

senior year, four less than the typical senior in our Valleysider sample. He also worked close to forty hours each week in the family business, played two varsity sports, and participated in a variety of social activities both in and out of school. He was in fact very far from lazy. His busy schedule permitted him little time to study and his senior year he deliberately took the minimum course load. Only one of his four classes, senior English, required homework, and this he was taking because the college of his choice required it. Senior year, he explained, was "kick back time."

Valleysider Success Theory

Valleysider parents, and teachers too, saw high school as preparing young people to go out on their own. Parents wanted their children to master the "basics," which for most meant passing all required courses, and to graduate from high school. They were extremely disappointed if one of their children failed to graduate. Most placed equal emphasis on vocational and academic classes. Many were particularly pleased with the vocational classes that provided work experience and job-related skills. They wanted their children to be ready to earn a living after high school. It would be nice, some said, if their children were to finish college, but most did not expect their children to do so, nor, they reported, had they stressed higher education as either a goal or a necessity.

Other qualifications beyond formal education were at least equally important to their children's ultimate success as adults, Valleysiders believed. Initiative, drive, a willingness to knuckle down and do the job were basic. Opportunity—by which they meant being in the right spot at the right time in order to have a chance to get ahead—was also essential. Connections, too, were felt to be extremely important. A college education was simply one more ingredient and not necessarily the most important one. While some parents saw college as a means to advancement, others observed that even a college degree was no guarantee of a job. It depends on what you want, one parent commented, noting also that hard-labor jobs paid well. Another observed pointedly that mechanics made more money than schoolteachers.

The median level of education for the Valleysider fathers in our sample was thirteen years (excluding kindergarten) and for the mothers twelve. While 15 percent of the fathers and 26 percent of the mothers had never finished high school, more than half the fathers (56 percent) and almost half the mothers (44 percent) had pursued some postsecondary education. Few, however, had completed four years of college (23 percent of the fathers and 12 percent of the mothers), and many of those with some college education had attended the local community college as adults, often years after finishing high school.

Most Valleysider students said they would be pleased to have their father's job and income. Over half the girls reported that they would be happy with their mother's job and even more with her income. Valleysider students, by and large, believed their parents had done well in their jobs, even without a college degree or, in a number of cases, without a high school diploma. One student explained his father's views: "He feels that if you get straight A's and work really hard, that doesn't mean you are going to be successful. But he says, 'Just give it your best. You prove yourself when you work hard and don't let anyone down.'" Almost every Valleysider youth, by the time he or she was finishing high school, had worked in several jobs. These students felt confident of the skills they could apply to new positions. Most frequently they noted their ability to get along with others.

The ability to get along in society was stressed also by teachers and parents, many of whom placed social criteria for success ahead of academic ones. In defining a successful high school experience teachers avoided ascribing success to intelligence or academic achievement. Academic achievement, some said, was based largely on innate ability and, moreover, was not necessarily a predictor of adult success. Again, it was a view they held in common with Valleysider parents. More important, some faculty members explained, were social skills and a sense of self-worth. For them, the nonsucceeder was not the one with poor academic skills. It was the student who could not "fit in," who did not "feel part of it," and who did not value many of the things that other students enjoyed at school.

Taking part in extracurricular activities was considered particularly important. The school stressed it. Parents encouraged it. Students enjoyed it. Almost every Valleysider boy in the senior sample had participated in at least one school sport. In almost equal numbers the girls had been involved in some school activity, a sport, perhaps, or more generally one of the many clubs. Top students continued their participation throughout high school, often involving themselves in multiple activities each year. Students in the bottom half of the class were more inclined during their junior and senior years to spend their time in nonschool activities and working in part-time, after-school jobs.

Valleysider parents supported both part-time work for their children and a "good social life." Parents were pleased when their children had many friends and were busy with outside activities. When their children were out with friends, parents wanted to know where they were going, with whom, and when they planned to return. Some were very strict about these expectations, others more casual. Some set curfews, generally more lenient on weekends than week nights. A few limited the number of nights during the week a child could be out. Quite a few felt they were stricter than other parents. Most believed that at least some other parents were too permissive. In general, however, parents wanted their children to enjoy themselves during these years before they had to take up full adult responsibilities.

Two-thirds of the Valleysider students in our sample held jobs during their senior year. All but one of the remaining third had worked previously. Both parents and students concurred on the importance of jobs for teenagers. For many, the value quite simply was the pay check. Most of these young people earned between fifty and a hundred dollars per week, some of which they saved—girls more than boys—but much of which they spent. Jobs provided teenagers with money to go out with friends, attend movies, keep up with the latest clothing styles, and even to purchase and maintain a car. From the parents' perspective, jobs also taught young people responsibility and the realities of the working world.

Self-reliance was the goal. This theme came up again and again, in the responses of parents, teachers, and students. Parents pointed out that their children would soon be eighteen and legally adults. Parents assumed, furthermore, that after high school, or two years of college, their children would leave home to live on their own. To prepare them for this day, Valleysiders encouraged their offspring from the time they were small to make decisions independently and to take responsibility for their actions. As their children approached age eighteen, most Valleysiders saw their parental role as largely reduced to that of loving and concerned adviser. Even when they disagreed with their children's plans, they usually did not stand in their way. "That's apron-string tying," one mother said, and "I don't believe in that." Another parent, a father, said much the same thing about his son: "Right now I would encourage him to stay where he could have some guidance, because I think even at eighteen he has some things to learn. But I wouldn't hold him back. I would explain to him that he has to make his own decision because he has to live by it." This man was pleased his son still came to him to discuss his problems but admitted that the boy quite often did not follow his advice.

[104]

On the whole, Valleysiders believed they could not protect their teenage children from temptation or difficulty. Rather, they sought to teach them to make wise decisions and, when necessary, to learn from their mistakes. Thus, by late high school they placed few controls on their children and expected them to make their own choices in matters of friendship, education, jobs, use of time, place of residence, and marriage.

"On their own" is a phrase used frequently by Valleysider parents in conversations about child rearing. No theme was more prominent in the interviews, with students as well as parents. Valleysiders often brought the subject up almost gratuitously it seemed, in response to questions that had no direct bearing on it.

Throughout the interviews Valleysider parents emphasized the importance of raising girls, as well as boys, to be independent and self-sufficient. Girls, no less than boys, were encouraged to make decisions for themselves and to take full responsibility for their actions. Many parents stressed that women in today's society must be able to support themselves and, if necessary, their families. It would be up to their daughter, they said, to decide if she would maintain a career while raising children. They wanted her to be prepared, however, to make it on her own and to feel confident in her ability to do so.

Mexican American Performance Patterns

Full analysis of the Mexican American performance patterns lies beyond the scope of this book. We did not have the opportunity to carry out comparative interviews with Mexican American students or parents. Nor was it possible to assume that the sample of students attending Valleyside High was representative of the total group of high school age Mexican Americans residing in Valleyside. While Mexican Americans constituted 13.6 percent of the student population, grades kindergarten through twelve, in 1980, they made up only 10.2 percent of those attending Valleyside High. Some students dropped out of school before reaching ninth grade. Others were placed as ninth graders in one of the two continuation high schools in the district and, thus, never attended Valleyside High.[20] Local educators estimated that the overall dropout rate for Mexican American youths, including those who never reached high school, ran between 45 and 50 percent, a figure similar to both state and national estimates for Mexican Americans.[21]

Comparing the students who did reach high school, it is clear that the Mexican American students, *as a group*, were academically less successful than Punjabi students, *as a group*. The discussion that follows refers only to group patterns. Some of the Mexican American students attending Valleyside High were able and diligent students whose overall school performance placed them at the top of their classes. As shown in Table 13, however, substantially more Mexican American students were placed in remedial classes on entering high school than were Punjabi students. Although both groups had about the same rate of success in demonstrating minimum competency in reading, writing, and math, the Mexican Americans were less likely than the Punjabis to score above the 50th percentile on the math and writing tests.

The Mexican American students also received significantly lower grades than the Punjabis. While the grade point average for all ninth graders in the fall of 1980 was 2.10, the median GPA for Mexican Americans was 1.80, and for Punjabis 2.40. Only those students who had entered U.S. schools by second grade were included in this comparison. Many of the Mexican American students were failing one or more classes and half the girls had a GPA of 1.20 or lower. The boys received better grades—their median GPA was 2.06—but there were only half as many boys attending ninth grade as girls, suggesting that some of the less academically inclined male students had dropped out of school after junior high or had transferred to continuation high school.

Attendance records revealed a similar gender difference among the ninth graders. Nearly half the American-educated Mexican American girls (thirteen of twenty-seven) were absent eleven or more days during their first semester at Valleyside High, while only one Mexican American boy missed over ten days and one-third (four of twelve) never missed a day, a pattern similar to that of the Punjabi group.

More of the Mexican American ninth graders were classified as LEP or NES than Punjabis (31.1 percent and 17.9 percent, respectively, of those who had entered U.S. schools by second grade), and language proficiency was clearly a factor in the generally poor performance of these students. A disparity remained, however, even when we controlled for language proficiency. The fluent-English-proficient Punjabis received an average 2.40 GPA, compared to a 2.00 GPA for the fluent-English-proficient Mexican Americans. Some of the Mexican Americans had incomplete school records, suggesting that they had moved between districts or returned to Mexico for a time and may not have attended school continuously since entering U.S. schools. No similar breaks appeared in the Punjabi records.

Absenteeism was cited time and again by teachers, counselors, administrators, and migrant education staff as a major factor contributing to the difficulties Mexican American students experienced in school. It came up repeatedly in our conversations with school personnel, who frequently made comparisons, often unsolicited, between the Punjabi and Mexican American students. Some Mexican American children were absent for weeks at a time, we were told, particularly those in the early grades, when their parents moved to Washington to pick apples in the fall or returned to Mexico in the winter to visit relatives.[22] Even when they were in Valleyside, it was reported, Mexican American youngsters attended irregularly.

Elementary principals also observed that the Mexican American children seemed to have less sense of purpose and direction in school than the Punjabis and that they learned English more slowly. Several principals noted that the Mexican American parents favored bilingual education rather than ESL and that they looked to the schools for assistance in helping children develop and maintain their Spanish skills, while the Punjabi parents favored all-English instruction and would request that students not be aided in Punjabi even if they were having difficulty understanding English.

One principal commented that the Mexican American parents tended to be more defensive than the Punjabi parents when called to school about a discipline problem. They were more likely to assume that the root cause of the difficulty was not their child's misbehavior but discrimination. One ESL teacher observed that even after parent conferences, inappropriate classroom behavior would persist. Another noted that the Mexican American peer group was not supportive of schooling and that this was a difficult force to counteract.

These seemingly invidious comments by Valleyside educators were expressions more of frustration and concern than of ill will. Teachers and administrators were clearly disturbed that many Mexican American students attended irregularly and performed poorly. A high school counselor, himself Mexican American, made home visits to discuss students' difficulties with their parents and to encourage more regular attendance. A Mexican American teacher commented that many of the students seemed uninterested in their studies. He also observed that recent arrivals from Mexico often appeared more eager to apply them-

[107]

selves to their school work than American-born youngsters. He noted, too, that these immigrant students sometimes stopped working as hard in school once they became absorbed into local peer groups.

The role of the Mexican American peer group in influencing school-adaptation patterns has received all too little serious research attention. It is clear, however, that some Mexican American youths resist following the school's rules of behavior for success (Matute-Bianchi 1986; Ogbu and Matute-Bianchi 1986). It seems, too, that while Mexican American parents want their children to do well in school, they may not insist on the behaviors that lead to school success.

[7]

Community Forces and Schooling

> When we do farming, if we don't take full care of it, if we just drive
> our pickups around the fields instead of working, we fail. . . . It is
> the same with the children in school.
>
> Punjabi farmer, Valleyside

> Dress to please the people, but eat to please yourself.
>
> Punjabi saying, often repeated
> by Valleyside Sikhs

Punjabi Success Theory and Education

Valleyside Punjabis, no matter their educational background or financial status, infuse their discussion of education with a sense of its importance. Everyday folk sayings, repeated vigorously and with great feeling, permeate their conversations: "Education is the third eye." "If you don't have knowledge, you cannot do anything." "If you are blind yourself, how can you lead others?" They are the same sayings one finds inscribed on the walls of primary schools throughout Punjab.

Beyond such sayings, Punjabis stress the necessity of formal education for obtaining "good" jobs and a "good" income. The basic purpose of education is pragmatic, as they see it. Almost all the parents we interviewed saw a strong positive correlation between the amount of education one has and the type of employment one can expect to obtain. The more educated person, they say, gets the better job and the better income. They tilt education itself always in the direction of the practical and the material. We found little interest in the social sciences or the humanities.

Parents also noted other advantages of education. One explained that an educated man is able to go wherever he wants and without education a person is dependent on others. Those who have been to school, parents said, can "stand on their own feet," be self-reliant. They can serve as role models for the younger generation. Education strengthens the entire family; the educated person can help less-educated family members. The educational achievements of young Punjabis, moreover, bring credit to their parents and, significantly, enhance marriage arrangements for the entire family.

The importance of maintaining and improving family status serves, among Valleyside Punjabis, as a strong incentive to success in school. One man explained: "If you go the right way and have a good character, you will have a good name. People will say good things about your home, and the Punjabi community will get respect from other people. If you do bad deeds, you will give a bad name to your community, your home, your mother and father." Children are told that school is like a job and that to do well one must work hard. They are reminded, too, that their parents have come to America for them, so that they may have a better life. The parents' lives will have been wasted, some warn, if their children are not successful in school.

Punjabis are much concerned with maintaining and improving their family's good name, and parents worry that their children's behavior may somehow detract from their honor. The concept of *izzat*, or honor, is important for Valleyside Punjabis, and children learn early that their actions affect not only their own reputations but those of the entire family. To do well in school is one way a child may bring credit to his or her parents.

Punjabis place high value on the kind of education that leads to a specific profession or provides job-related skills. They believe a child should learn a skill while in school so that he or she is prepared for a job. The successful student, in their view, is the "child who is able to support himself after education." The parents praised Valleyside High for its vocational program. Indian high schools have no such emphasis. Even colleges in India, they noted, offer only academics.

Most Punjabi boys sign up for some shop classes. Of those in our senior sample, more than half took both welding and auto mechanics. One-third took electronics. Three-fourths took small-engine repair. In equal numbers, they enrolled in classes that promised to provide hands-on work experience.

The most able male students aspire to careers in engineering or computer science. Accounting and agricultural business were goals of several other students in our sample. Students not bound for college hope to pursue such trades as mechanics and welding. While some farmers' sons do choose to carry on the family business, none of those we interviewed wanted to farm for a living. Farm work remained a ready option, however, for those fresh from India, as well as those who showed little promise in any other area.

For many Punjabis the expense of a college education is a major concern, not only because of the actual cost but also because of the lost income. Such costs are generally seen in terms of the whole family. A young man just out of high school could earn eight to ten thousand dollars a year doing farm work, more perhaps at some other job, and if he lived at home, most of his earnings could be saved. In four years the family would have thirty to forty thousand dollars, which could be used to buy some land or begin a family business.

Several parents worried that college might change their sons. A college graduate might consider it beneath his dignity to "dirty his hands" in jobs requiring physical labor. Rarely, however, did parents stand in the way of a son's educational aspirations if he showed both academic promise and motivation. Most, in fact, took great comfort in their sons' educational accomplishments. Practically speaking, a successful son could bring honor to his parents and promise them security in their old age as well.

With daughters it is different. Most Valleyside Punjabis want their daughters to have sufficient education to obtain a "clean" and secure job. Positions in banks, schools, businesses, secretarial work, typing—these are the sorts of jobs Punjabi parents desire for their daughters. Any kind of office work with regular hours and a steady income is considered a good job. If girls can prepare for such positions while still in high school, so much the better. If an additional two years at the local community college are required, most parents are willing to consider the possibility. One must remember, however, that for many of these rural Doabis even allowing their unmarried daughters to work outside the home has been a major adjustment.

The girls in the senior sample generally earned one-third or more of all their high school credits from business and other vocational classes. Typing and bookkeeping were particularly popular, as was "school-office skills," but they also enrolled in a wide variety of off-campus work-experience classes. The girls said they aspired to a four-year college degree, but few seemed actually to expect to pursue one. By their junior and senior years, after all basic requirements had been completed, most girls turned away from classes in math, science, and

English. Labeled "college prep," these classes seemed inappropriate. Many of the girls seemed unsure, even in their final semester of high school, whether their parents would in fact permit them to attend classes at the local community college.

Their parents were concerned that something might happen in college that would injure their daughter's and the family's reputation. They realized, too, that in college their daughters would be much more on their own than had been the case in high school. No longer could parents count on someone phoning them if their child cut her classes, misbehaved, or performed poorly.

In rural Punjab there continues to be a feeling that too much education can "spoil" a girl, make her too independent in her ideas, quite likely "snobbish" and outspoken. This is the traditional view among uneducated Punjabis and, as one Valleyside Punjabi explained, there are a lot of uneducated Punjabis in Valleyside. Valleyside Punjabis were worried, too, that if a daughter went away to college she might fall in love and wish to arrange her own marriage or become so Americanized that she would no longer fit into the Punjabi community. A highly educated woman, moreover, could find it difficult to take up her proper role within her future husband's family. She might say, as one parent explained, "I've just finished college; how can I make the *roti?*" It is customary for a Punjabi woman when first married to carry a heavy share of the cooking and other daily chores in her in-laws' house, including cooking for the male members of the household and their friends. In this context to "make the *roti*" takes on a very broad cultural meaning.

A less-educated woman, Punjabi parents asserted, would be less likely to question her role and more comfortable with the joint decision-making processes that are the norm within Punjabi households. Accordingly, many Valleyside Punjabis said that if their daughters wanted to pursue higher education, beyond the community college level, they should do so after they were married. The decision then could be made jointly by the girl, her husband, and her in-laws. This is the usual village view, but young women raised and educated in Valleyside were helping to reshape parents' more traditional attitudes.

Education in Rural Punjab

Indians have an ancient literary tradition and great respect for books and learning. They have also been exposed to British-style Western

Class in session at a village elementary school in Punjab.

schooling for more than a century (Metha 1926:9). Within rural Punjab, however, book learning has not been considered a necessity, and books are rare. The views of rural Punjabis have shifted somewhat as a consequence of the green revolution and the opening of primary schools in nearly every village, but attendance continues to be lax in many areas.

Schools in rural Punjab provide sharp contrast to those in Valleyside. Many are overcrowded and inadequate facilities. Even new schools may lack desks, chairs, and instructional materials considered indispensable by American standards. The teacher-student ratio is high, particularly at the primary level (grades one to five). Primary school teachers are not college graduates and are poorly prepared and poorly paid. Few curriculum materials exist and those that do are of poor quality. Children and teachers make do, however, with such resources as are available. Children, typically, sit on woven mats instead of chairs, and out-of-doors, weather permitting. Instead of paper and pencil, both of which are consumable, they learn to write with home-made pens on wooden slates coated with a thin layer of replaceable clay.[1]

Indian students are expected to show complete deference to teachers and others in authority. Little encouragement or reward is given to independent thinking or critical analysis. Discipline can be extremely harsh and some children drop out of school because they are afraid of being physically punished by their teachers. Only the most educated parents are in a position to help their children with their studies. Most parents assume, simply, that those who wish to learn will learn.

Education in Punjab is free only through middle school (grades six to eight). Although the fees for secondary school (grades nine to ten) are nominal, any fee serves as a deterrent to those of modest means. To send a child through ten years of school, when he or she could be at home helping to support the family, was and still is an economic hardship for many families in rural Punjab. Only prosperous families can afford to send their children to college.

In recent years the state of Punjab has made the expansion of education a top priority, and pupil enrollment, especially in the primary grades, has increased sharply. By 1978, Punjab led all Indian states in the percentage of primary age males who were enrolled in school and was second highest for female enrollment (NCERT 1980). Even so, many children, particularly girls, attend school for only a few years. Punjabis continue to be especially reluctant to send their daughters away to school, even to a neighboring village or nearby town.

Table 18 shows the sharp attrition rate as students in rural Punjab progress through school. In 1978 more than twice as many children were enrolled in grade one as in grade five and the decline continued throughout the higher grades. Approximately ten times the number of students entered primary school as completed secondary school. The dropout rate was steep for boys, steeper yet for girls. By the end of middle school girls made up only one-third of the enrollment.[2]

Only recently has it become customary, even among Jats, for all sons to complete secondary school—ten years in India—and within our sample somewhat less than half the fathers had gone that far. A quarter of the men had attended school for five years or less. More than a third of the women had no formal education. Only 10 percent had attended

Punjabi girl doing her times tables on a slate in an Indian village school.

middle school or beyond. Few Jat village women work outside the home, nor are there job opportunities for them.[3] Unless they plan to live and work in urban areas or to emigrate from India, formal education continues to be of little practical value.

The situation in America is completely different. Punjabi women, even those with little or no education, can become wage earners by working in fruit orchards and canneries. Their daughters, equipped with an American education, can do far better. Almost all Valleyside Punjabis want their daughters to finish high school and to work outside the home; it is a dramatic shift in values from those prevalent in rural Punjab.

Attitudes about American Public Education

Valleyside Punjabis support the concept of free public education, readily available to all takers. The parents interviewed had few qualms about sending their children to school with students of other social classes, religions, and ethnic backgrounds. "We all belong to the same God," one woman explained. "Even in India," she said, "there is no separation." In fact, of course, there is much separation in India between persons of different castes and classes. This woman's comments represent the Sikh ideal of a casteless, egalitarian society. It is true, too, that in Doabi villages all children attend the same primary school, rich and poor, high caste and low caste together. Like most other Valleyside Punjabis, this woman believed that all children were entitled to the same instruction.

The parents also believed that their children, if they were to live and work in America, must be exposed to different cultures and different ways of thinking. They wanted their young to speak English well and to become competitive in the larger society. By attending American schools and by learning the ways of the majority group, their children could achieve these goals.

At the same time, many of the parents were strongly opposed to coeducational schooling at the secondary level. Adolescent males and females, they believed, should attend separate schools, as is customary in India. Punjabis may allow young children to play together with members of the opposite sex, but about teenagers mixing freely they have serious reservations.

Valleyside Punjabis permitted their children to attend Valleyside

A Valleyside elementary school in session.

High in large measure because they had no other choice. This was the American way and they felt they must adjust themselves to it. There was no private high school in the area, nor could most have afforded such an alternative. Neither did they wish to establish separate Punjabi-run schools. They wanted their children to attend American schools with other American children. They were, nonetheless, distinctly uncomfortable with the social environment at Valleyside High.[4]

Growing Up in Valleyside

Like Valleysiders, Punjabi parents want their children to be able to support themselves when they grow up. Unlike Valleysiders, Punjabis

[117]

place no emphasis on preparing young people to leave home and to live on their own. Self-reliance, Punjabi style, means taking one's place and pulling one's weight within the family group. Punjabis call it "standing on your feet," a phrase frequently used by those we interviewed.

All Punjabi parents expect the younger generation to defer to elders for direction and approval. Adolescence, from the Punjabi perspective, is a time when young people need especially strong parental supervision and guidance. Teenagers, parents explain, naturally "question everything," including their parents' values, but they lack the maturity to make wise decisions for themselves.

For Punjabis, decision making is usually a joint process. Even a grown man will consult his parents and siblings before making major decisions, for example, the choice of a mate for one's child or a business transaction involving the purchase of land. This practice, Punjabis explain, both maintains family unity and reduces the risk of making the wrong decision. Punjabi parents were much disturbed by what they perceived to be the American emphasis on encouraging young people to make decisions on their own, even to question adult advice. Said one parent: "When someone becomes like this, we feel that he no longer belongs to our community. He does not listen to anyone, does everything as he pleases—the way the Americans do. To us that is not right. We do not like this." Another observed that "the actual Americans listen to you," but that one of our own who "becomes 'American' is the one who does not listen." Many others said that those who insisted on going their own way were "cut off" and that they disliked such people. The impact of "American" values on their children deeply worried these parents. In India, they explained, if a parent says, "Don't, they don't," but in Valleyside Punjabi children would respond, "It's none of your business" or "I'm going to make my own decisions."

Valleyside Punjabis are particularly concerned that young people might want to select their own marriage partners without regard to parental wishes. Punjabi parents told us that they considered it their duty to arrange the best possible matches for their children. Marriage is seen as the union of two families, not just two individuals, and parents believe that they have more experience, more contacts, and better judgment about what makes such unions successful. "Love marriages," in their view, rarely work. Once the attraction ends, there is nothing left. To bolster their position, they cite the prevalence of divorce in America. Punjabis are deeply disturbed by the frequency of divorce in this country and believe that it stems, at least in part, from the emphasis on placing individual interests ahead of family interests.

[118]

Americans, in the Punjabi view, give far too little supervision and guidance to their children, particularly in their teenage years. One Punjabi, a longtime resident of Valleyside and an American citizen, explained: "They are not making the right life for the kids. NO, NO. The poor kids. They have no sense, what to do, where to go, or who to meet. We were talking a minute ago about that, that it is a bad stage— you know, sixteen, seventeen, eighteen. . . . I don't want to ruin their life. NO. So I tell them, 'Do this, it is better. Do that, no good.' They listen, too." Most of those we interviewed believed they could make better decisions than their children and that it was their duty to do so. The children would learn by example, and after they had studied and were married, they would be able to shoulder responsibility for their own decisions.

Not all agreed fully with this approach. One man remarked that Punjabi adults were typically "very arrogant," always discounting their children's advice. He insisted that children should be consulted and their viewpoints considered. If children demonstrate that they can make good decisions, another commented, then they should be given "full freedom." Both parents, however, were referring to sons.

Punjabi parents encouraged no such freedom for their daughters. Most believed that they should make almost all decisions affecting their daughters. Punjabi girls themselves described how boys had far more opportunity to make everyday decisions in such matters as clothes, hair style, and activities with friends. Boys, for example, were free to join friends after school for a game of soccer or hockey or to go out in the evening to the movies. Girls, by contrast, were expected to return home directly from school. Only rarely was it possible for them to get together with girl friends outside of school. Most of their social activities revolved around the immediate family or cousins and other relatives living in Valleyside. Of course, most had many cousins, so they seldom lacked companions.

In an Indian village everyone is known and news of misbehavior travels rapidly. Moreover, because Sikhs customarily marry someone from another village, teenage boys and girls growing up together are not viewed as potential mates and parents need not be especially worried about village boys pursing their daughters. Local sanctions are very strong.[5]

Valleyside is different. Punjabi adults who themselves have had little contact with the larger society expressed uncertainty about what dangers might befall their children and tend, therefore, to be very protective of them. The parents hear stories of drunken driving, drugs, wild

[119]

teenage parties, and unwed mothers. They see Valleysider girls in skimpy clothing and boys and girls embracing in public. Many are convinced, moreover, that Valleysiders push their children out on their own against their will and best interests. Such behavior would be unimaginable in village India and is best avoided in America.

Punjabis worry in particular about their daughters' reputations. "All our respect is in their hands," the parents told us. A girl's indiscretions could jeopardize marriage arrangements not only for herself but for her siblings as well. A family's good name is of paramount importance in arranging a marriage, and parents expressed a heavy responsibility to keep their daughters', and thus the family's, name untarnished.

If a teenage girl "steps out of the house, goes out to play, or is seen sitting with other girls," one parent explained, it brings a loss of respect. Another, the father of an eighteen-year-old girl born and raised in Valleyside, objected to his daughter's having a driver's license. Even a trip to the county library was cause for concern, since his daughter might meet up with friends and start "fooling around."

Not all parents were as traditional as these. Most agreed, however, that girls should not be given too much time on their own. Even unchaperoned time with girl friends could foster independent thinking. It was best, most parents said, for adolescent girls to be safely at home, when not at school or work.

One Punjabi father spoke at length about the differences between Punjabi and Valleysider ways:

> We have different customs and attitudes. Especially relating to our girls, we think differently and they think differently. For example, when I came from India my brother-in-law took me to his next door neighbor's [a Valleysider]. My brother-in-law started asking about his seventeen-year-old boy and eighteen-year-old girl. I will never forget what he said: "The boy has stopped going to school and I am going to tell him to get out and get lost, if he doesn't go back to school, [instead of] always staying at home. For the girl, I have to take her to the doctor." My brother-in-law asked him, "Why?" He said, "She's finished high school, and [yet] she is not going out with any boy!"

This man went on to contrast the two sets of values: "Here is a man who thinks that there is something wrong with his daughter because she is not going out with boys, that there is something wrong psychologically. We don't even want our daughters to go out of the house, and they don't want their daughters to sit at home. . . . I even want my daughters to marry someone whom I choose. It is my responsibility. These people think the girl should do it herself."

Commenting on the attitudes of the older generation, one young Punjabi man, raised from the age of seven in this country and at ease with both Punjabi and Valleysider ways, observed that the Punjabis "need more knowledge [of the majority culture] to base their opinions on. They base it on our culture. . . . It is taboo in ours, so it should be taboo in theirs. [Punjabis] are very possessive about their kids. Since they have raised them up and everything, [the parents believe that] they should have something in return from their kids. They tend to feel that the Americans should do the same. It is very different." Punjabis, he noted, believed their children wanted to stay at home and, furthermore, that they should remain nearby for the mutual benefit of young and old, but Valleysiders, he explained, "don't care either way," telling their children that it was their future and they must decide what was best for them.

Cultural Variation

In emphasizing differences between Punjabi and Valleysider views on child rearing, I do not mean to overlook either the similarities between the two groups or the variations within each. Both sets of parents want much the same thing for their offspring—that they be happy and successful. They hope their children will become economically secure, adopt good moral standards, become responsible citizens, marry well, and have a good home life. Both groups also teach young people to pull their own weight by the time they reach their late teens or early twenties. Parents will continue to assist as necessary, but they expect their children, at this point, to shoulder adult responsibilities.

Both groups place high value on family, while respecting independence and individualism. Punjabis, once married, have few qualms about setting off on their own to begin new lives in places more distant than many Valleysiders ever travel. In their new surroundings, moreover, they have shown remarkable adaptability. Punjabis carry with them their strong traditions, sense of history, and respect for family and community. These become building blocks in each new location, and they pass them on to their children, as their parents' parents have done before them. Our ways, they say, "are best for us." Valleysiders are, in many respects, rather similar.

[121]

Variations in values and life-styles also emerged within each group. A number of Valleysider parents spoke out against children's "doing their own thing" and commented that there is too much emphasis in American society today on readying children to be on their own. One Valleysider father noted that he still went to his parents "for counseling" and he expected his grown children to do the same. Never, he said, would he tell his children because they had reached age eighteen that they were on their own. Several Valleysider parents also worried about the messages their children were picking up at school about "their rights" and the feeling that they could do as they pleased. "No man is an island," one Valleysider father commented, and his happiness, he noted, came not from doing things just for himself but for family or others.

Some Punjabis, on the other hand, emphasized the necessity for risk-taking among youth. "We train them to take responsibility," one Punjabi man noted with respect to his children. "Responsibility means to take risks and risks mean responsibility. If you take responsibility, you will succeed in life. Otherwise, no." In addition, some Punjabis were far less strict about the maintenance of traditional values. A few, generally those of urban background and with a college education, have encouraged their children to participate fully in the activities of Valleysider friends. They told us that their children's lives would be easier in the future if they were allowed to adopt a way of life similar to that of the majority group.

The contrasts between Punjabis and Valleysiders are, nonetheless, substantial. Despite the shared respect for the individual and the group, the balance is different, the view of family is different, and roles considered appropriate according to age and sex are different. Valleysiders and Punjabis also differ in the way they identify themselves. Punjabis, who freely and proudly call themselves Punjabi or Sikh, forthrightly assume an ethnic identity. Valleysiders, on the other hand, reject the idea that they have any ethnic identity. They may differ among themselves in religion, ancestral national background, and social class, but their identification is strongly and simply American. They see themselves as "the Americans" and other people, the minorities, as "ethnics." Several Valleysiders even wondered if they had a cultural tradition at all.

The Punjabis, the Jat Sikhs in particular, are a far more homogeneous group than the Valleysiders. These Jats come from one small area in the northwest of India and share the same religious and occupational traditions. Although their responses to interview questions clearly reflected a range of viewpoints, they also indicated a striking degree of similarity in attitudes and values. The perspectives of the Muslim and Hindu parents were little different.[6]

Preserving the Ties with Punjab

Within immigrant enclaves, traditional values are generally reinforced by orientation toward the native country. For some groups a myth of return serves this function (Anwar 1979; Bonacich 1973:586). In carrying out fieldwork among Punjabi Sikhs in Britain, Roger and Catherine Ballard found that most immigrants from India—as opposed to those born in England—maintained that they would return to Punjab "in a few years' time," even though few realistically expected to do so. The myth of return, the Ballards point out, is used by overseas Punjabis "to legitimize continued adherence to the values of their homeland and to condemn the assimilation of English cultural values as irrelevant and destructive" (1977:40–41).

In Valleyside, however, few of those we interviewed spoke of ever returning to India to live. The option remained if economic or social conditions in the United States became unbearable, but few thought this likely. Their children, moreover, whether Indian- or American-born, had little or no interest in living in India. It was other forces beyond a sojourning orientation that promoted community solidarity and adherence to Punjabi values.[7]

In India, where neither language, culture, nor race distinguishes them from other Punjabis, Sikhs have been able to maintain their separate identity despite persistent pressures from the Hindu majority to deny Sikhs their distinctiveness. For overseas communities, the protection of Sikh rights in India and the maintenance of Punjab as the Sikh homeland serve as symbols for sustaining group solidarity.

Wherever Punjabi Sikhs have settled, they have demonstrated great skill in resisting assimilation. A strong immigrant enclave, such as that in Valleyside, reduces the need for Sikhs to mix in the larger society. All Valleyside Sikhs have kin and village mates in the area and, thus, a ready network of relatives, friends, and acquaintances. The *gurdwara* also serves as a center of communal activity, not only religious but social, political and economic. Most immigrant Sikhs participate actively in *gurdwara* affairs, more actively than was the case back in

Punjab. Regular attendance at religious ceremonies, furthermore, helps them to keep in touch with India since the *gurdwaras* frequently host religious and community leaders from Punjab. These men and women bring word of the latest happenings in India and exhort overseas Sikhs to remain faithful to their Gurus.

A sense of opposition to the dominant group is critical to the continuation of the Sikhs as a separate people (cf. Anwar 1979:182; Bonacich and Modell 1980:258; Castile 1981:xix; Spicer 1971:797). Discrimination against Sikhs in India, as well as in Valleyside, contributes to group solidarity and a feeling of "us versus them." The political unrest that has plagued Punjab in recent years has strengthened the link between Sikhs abroad and coreligionists in India. It has also rallied emigrants behind the call for an independent Sikh nation.

Valleyside Sikhs stated strongly and repeatedly in our interviews that their own ways were best for them, better than those of the American majority. They were particularly convinced of the superiority of their core beliefs about marriage and family relationships. "If we just follow them, do what they do," one man explained, "then we are going to be lost. We will fail." Learn from the Americans, he said, but don't become like them. "If you try to copy them," another parent cautioned, "you only suffer later on." "We are Sikhs; we keep beard, [long] hair, and turban," said a third. "We cannot change. . . . Nor do we wish to."

Actually, Valleyside Sikhs—both conservatives and the more "Americanized"—often do cut their hair and shave their beards, especially the younger ones. Within a single typically close-knit and very respectable family, one may see three married brothers, the youngest of whom is clean cut, the middle brother sporting a dashing close-cropped beard and a movie-star coif, and the eldest, an *amritdhari* Sikh, with full beard and turban. Little boys with long hair usually cover their topknots with handkerchiefs, since the turban is not adopted until the boys are old enough to tie them themselves. By the time they are teenagers, all but the most recently arrived have short hair. Maintenance of Sikh identity reaches beyond this most visible marker, however. "Usually it doesn't matter if the man has his hair cut," one parent explained, "but when the ladies cut their hair, then we say that the whole family is American."

Punjabi parents spoke constantly of the drawbacks of American culture and its influence on their children. "When our children get together with the white children, they start doing things that affect the

Schoolboys at home in Valleyside.

family honor," one parent explained. Too much time with Valleysiders, most agreed, would alter their children's values. In general, however, parents believed the strength of the home culture would outweigh negative impact from the majority culture.

Central to the Punjabi Sikhs' system of cultural maintenance are traditional marriage practices and the importance placed on upholding family honor. Both are used effectively by Valleyside Sikhs to shape their children's behavior. Parents expected, without question, that their offspring would marry other Sikhs of the same caste background. They also stated explicitly that they preferred their children to marry someone fresh from India, although this was not an absolute rule. Parents recognized that young people raised in America were less tied to Indian customs and values and that arranged marriages were a primary mechanism for preserving the Punjab link and maintaining Jat Sikh values. Parents noted, furthermore, that because so many Indians were desirous of emigrating to America, they could make more advantageous matches for their children in India than was generally possible in America.

Some parents worried that the extended family, with its system of mutual obligations, was losing ground to American influence. The current emphasis in this country on the pursuit of self-fulfillment, even at the expense of family concerns, was one of the most troublesome aspects of American culture for Punjabi immigrants. They saw the typical American family as dangerously fragmented, and they vehemently warned their young not to adopt American values on love and marriage. Those who deviated too far from culturally appropriate norms, especially girls, were severely sanctioned. Communal gossip in most cases proved an effective device for social control.[8] Relatives were quite prepared to employ shame and guilt if necessary. Young people were reminded of their duty to the extended family and of the sacrifices their parents had made to assure their future.

Young people were also warned that those who abandoned their roots and tried to assimilate would inevitably discover that the majority group would not accept them. Nor would the children themselves be able to fit in, their parents assumed. "We laugh at such children," one man noted. Pulled in both directions, they seemed unable either to fall back or move forward. "They just hang in the middle," it was said.

Punjabi parents expressed deep concern about the Americanization of their children. An Americanized Punjabi was one who had cut off his or her ties to family, temple, and community, who mixed mostly with

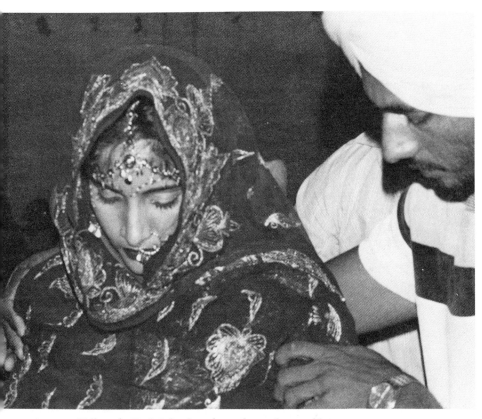

A recent Valleyside High School graduate during her wedding ceremony.

members of the majority group, and whose style of life resembled that of white Americans. Such a person became, in the eyes of these Punjabis, a caricature of all they disliked about the dominant culture. Those who made decisions on their own without listening to their elders, who married someone of their own choosing, and who ignored their obligations to family and community were undoubtedly destined to end up divorced members of a fractured and insecure society.

When young people appear in danger of adopting such traits, their parents often arrange an early marriage. This was the case for several girls in the core sample. Sons are given more latitude. When young people persistently refuse to comply with parents' wishes—as for example in marrying without parental blessing—they are cut off. So strong are the ties of Punjabi youth to family and community that this

[127]

ultimate sanction is rarely needed. All Punjabi young people know of such cases, however.

Life in America requires some change, the parents recognize, but they believe it should be gradual. A strong cultural tie is the only way, as they see it, to keep the family together. One Punjabi parent captured the feelings of most:

> If they forget [their heritage] then they will be neither like us nor like them. The whites will not let us catch up with them, nor will they let us join them. But these children think that they will be like them. We can never be like them, nor do we need to. Some intelligent sons and daughters do understand. The fools, they start thinking like them, doing the same things as the Americans. The most important thing for the children is that they receive a good education. Through education they will be recognized and respected.

The ideal, as here expressed, is to maintain family and community integrity but also to achieve success in the larger society. The former is seen as no impediment to the latter—in fact, just the reverse.

Parental Involvement in Schooling

Valleyside Punjabis expected their children to do well academically and taught them to be diligent in their studies. Schoolwork came first, ahead of housework, jobs, and especially social activities. "The main thing is to study," one mother said, "nothing else." Those we interviewed noted that they directed their children to do as teachers said, to follow the rules, and to get home without any criticism of their behavior. They urged their young to acquire the skills and credentials necessary for competing in mainstream society but warned them at the same time to do nothing that would shame their families. "Dress to please the people," they repeated, "but eat to please yourself." Accommodation without assimilation was their strategy.

Only rarely did parents directly involve themselves in school affairs. They were reluctant to visit the schools or to attend school meetings, nor did they see any reason why they should do so. Parents in India, they explained, were only asked to go to school when a child had refused to obey those in authority. Their responsibility as parents was to see that this did not occur.[9]

Most parents had little understanding of the American system of education. Few were able to help with homework or course selection. Newer arrivals, moreover, simply had no time to get involved in school matters. Their entire lives were consumed by the realities of sheer economic survival and by the myriad problems of adapting to life in America. Even longtime residents had little knowledge of what their children were actually doing in school and whether or not they were progressing satisfactorily. "We send the children to school and leave the strings to God," one farmer reported. Illiterate himself, this man relied on more educated family members to deal with school officials.

Although these parents practiced what may be termed a noninterventionist strategy vis-à-vis the schools,[10] and even at home were not much involved in either the substance or the mechanics of their children's schooling, they did make sure their children behaved in ways that would enable them to take advantage of their educational opportunities. They insisted, for example, on regular and punctual attendance. They expected their children to do homework daily and some— generally those with a secondary education themselves—would phone the schools to ask that more work be sent home. Equally regularly they reminded their offspring to do what was requested of them by their teachers and others in authority and to cause no discipline problems. Although most families had few books or even a daily newspaper, parents encouraged their children to bring books home from school and county libraries.

Furthermore, even if their parents had little formal education, Punjabi young people nearly always had access to educated individuals through their extended kin group or through the *gurdwaras*. Such individuals were held up as role models. Academic achievements were represented as what an individual could accomplish without parental wealth and education. Schools, moreover, were seen as serving a useful social function, in addition to their more obvious academic and vocational benefits. The Punjabi parents wanted their young to become proficient in the economic and vocational ways of the majority group, and they saw the schools as instrumental to this goal. Work hard in school, take up the good values of the majority culture, but ignore the rest, the parents counseled. They took great pride in their children's ability to speak English and to help them deal with the host society, *providing* the children also maintained strong roots within the Punjabi community. Parents, therefore, gave powerful support to schooling itself, yet discouraged their children from mixing socially with Valleysider peers outside of school.

[129]

While all parents wished their children to do well in school, they recognized that some had neither the interest nor the ability to excel in matters academic. They saw little point in keeping such children in school. "If the child does not wish to study, then what can the teacher do?" one parent asked. "Those that are only interested in play and clothes, or who wander around with the 'baddies,' cannot become successful," commented another. Punjabis rarely blamed the educational system or the teachers for a child's difficulties. Responsibility for learning, in the Punjabi view, rests with the individual. Those who wish to learn, will learn.

Parents were not naïve about the difficulties their children faced in school. They simply brooked no excuses for poor performance. Those who squandered their chances bore the consequences. With only a "simple education," children were reminded, they could expect only a "simple job."

In village Punjab, when a boy shows little progress in his studies, he is put to work on the farm and expected to remain there for the rest of his life. A similar set of sanctions was at work in Valleyside. One man recounted the fate of his nephew. Following a period of continued misbehavior in high school, the young man's parents and older relatives got together to discuss the offender's future. Deciding that he had had sufficient education, they withdrew him from school and arranged work for him in an uncle's orchards. As soon as an appropriate bride was found, the boy was sent to India to be married. Later he repented his misdeeds and wished to return to school. He was told, simply, that he had had his chance. This young man had found it unpleasant to take orders from farm "bosses" who had had no formal education, and he had secured a factory job in a nearby city.

In another case, a Punjabi girl was withdrawn from Valleyside College because rumors reached her parents that she had been seen hanging around with a male Punjabi student. The girl herself denied any interest in the young man, but gossip persisted. She was kept at home and plans for her marriage were speeded up.

All Punjabi young people could cite examples of culturally deviant students who had been withdrawn from school, first for a few days and then, if the misbehavior was not corrected, permanently. Punjabi youngsters realized that if they got out of line their parents might well arrange an early marriage and put them to work in the fruit orchards. Parents expressed it strongly and succinctly: "The fields are waiting."

Teachers' Perspectives

High school teachers remarked on the orientation of Punjabi students toward academic achievement: "They have goals and strive to achieve them—a sense of purpose and direction." Teachers also commented favorably on the respect Punjabi youths accorded them. Only very rarely did Punjabi students become serious behavior problems.[11]

Several school administrators observed that Punjabi parents, when called by the school, moved swiftly to take care of any problem related to a child's behavior. They noted, too, that Punjabi parents were less likely than Valleysider parents to side with their child when called in for a conference regarding student discipline. In addition, teachers cited the importance of peer pressure in bringing deviant students back into line. Punjabi students, one shop teacher observed, competed with one another for good grades, teased those who did poorly, and placed pressure on one another to uphold Punjabi standards of behavior.

Teachers also noted that Punjabi students did their homework more regularly than many Valleysider peers. In the senior sample, twice as many Punjabis as Valleysiders considered homework "very important" (89 percent to 41 percent). The difference was especially striking between the two groups of boys. While over half the Valleysider males said they "almost never" did homework, three-quarters of the Punjabi males reported doing an hour or more nearly every day. Punjabi students, on average, regardless of their age on arrival in this country, appeared to spend substantially more time on schoolwork than majority-group classmates.

Analysis of attendance patterns also revealed sharp contrast between the two groups. While no Valleysider students in the core sample had perfect attendance senior year, one in five Punjabis never missed a day. Only 11 percent were absent over ten days, compared with 57 percent of the Valleysiders. The median number of days absent for Valleysiders was fourteen; for Punjabis only three.

Elementary and junior high principals commented not only on how rapidly these students learned English but also on their generally serious orientation toward schoolwork. Several Valleysider educators noted that Punjabis appeared as desirous as other minority groups of maintaining their culture but that they were less demanding of the schools in this regard than some other groups. They noted, too, that Punjabi students adapted quickly to the school situation, doing what was required of them but, for the most part, remaining socially separate.

Teachers and administrators liked Punjabi students, for they worked hard, valued education, and followed the rules. At the same time, school personnel remained largely ignorant of Punjabi culture and were often quite negative about the Punjabis' resistance to assimilation. Many noted, moreover, that it was difficult to get Punjabi parents to come to meetings or other school functions and that Punjabis also discouraged their children from participating in extracurricular activities. Teachers believed that both parental involvement in school affairs and student involvement in extracurricular school activities were closely associated with success in school. The Punjabis provided a different model, one quite unfamiliar to most Valleysider educators.

Teachers also believed, as a rule, that it was possible to tell which parents provided strong support for education by looking at who came to back-to-school night or other such functions designed to bring parents into the high school. Indeed, examination of teachers' records did reveal a clear correlation between students' grades and their parents' attendance at back-to-school night. Those doing above average work had the highest rate of parent attendance. Those doing least well had the lowest turn out. But the relationship did not pertain to Punjabis.

Students' Perspectives

Punjabi young people said of their parents, "Every day they tell us: 'Obey your teachers. Do your schoolwork. Stay out of trouble. You're there to learn and not to fight. Keep trying harder. Keep pushing yourself. Do your homework. After you have done that you can watch TV.'" In interview after interview these students said the same, and in large measure, they heeded this advice. They, like their parents, believed that success in school would bring success in later life. They knew firsthand the realities of life as a farm laborer or owner, and this was not a future they chose for themselves. Said one farmer's son: "If it rains your crop is gone. Like right now, the crop is coming out and, if it starts pouring, it will cause all the peaches to brown. If it rains for a couple of days or so, your peaches won't have a very good chance at all. All year long you fertilize, spray it and disc it up, irrigate it, hoping it will come out all right and then, all of a sudden, you get this rain. It's just a big gamble." This young man knew the risks involved in orchard farming, and the hardships. His goal was four years of college, a business degree, and then a nine-to-five job with a steady income.

A majority of the Punjabi seniors, when asked how happy they would be to have the same kind of job or the same income as their parents, responded "Not happy at all." They wanted technical and professional jobs, occupations requiring postsecondary education. Three out of four said they hoped to finish at least two years of college. (My estimate is that about half actually did complete two years.) Almost two-thirds aspired to a four-year degree, girls as well as boys.[12] A few felt that racial discrimination would hamper their job prospects, but they also believed that a good command of English and a good education would enhance their opportunities.[13]

Punjabi high school students not only liked school, they had a definite sense that they were learning things valuable to their future. Most were satisfied with their grades. Most also believed that they had had a successful school experience. Punjabi boys, whether freshly arrived or American-born, felt the pressure not to squander their opportunities. Their parents' lives had not been easy, they knew, and they considered it their responsibility to help them in their later years. A few complained about their lack of freedom and believed their parents to be overly concerned about their doing "something out of their culture." Their indiscretions, however, were usually forgiven, and although these students found their parents strict, they were not so strict that a young man was denied his chance to get out with his friends.

Most newer arrivals, male and female alike, were firmly grounded in their Punjabi ways and expressed little desire to participate more actively in the "on your own" culture of American teenagers. The girls who had only recently come from Punjab used Indian standards to assess their lives in Valleyside. One newcomer, for example, when asked if she wished more freedom, replied: "I'm just satisfied where I am. I can do anything I want. But I just don't want anything." This was the typical response of girls who had grown up in India. A few noted, however, that their parents were more protective of them in Valleyside than back in Punjab. There, they said, they could play field hockey or meet after school with girl friends. Here, where many parents themselves felt less secure, girls were more tightly supervised.

The American-educated Punjabi girls had the most difficult time reconciling their two worlds, and this ambivalence was reflected in their appraisal of their school experience. Within the senior sample, half of those raised from early childhood in this country characterized their school experience as "not too successful." At school and through the media, they received one message. Be independent. Make your own decisions. Go as far as you can with your education. Postpone marriage and children until your career is begun. Their parents told them something else. Uphold Punjabi standards. Do nothing that will reflect poorly on your family. All our respect is in your hands. Many of the American-raised, American-educated young women were indeed pulled in two directions. They wanted more freedom to mix with friends, more support for their ideas, and more opportunity to pursue their educational and occupational goals.

These young women wanted to complete a four-year degree and perhaps a graduate degree also. Most believed, however, that their parents would never give them permission to go away to college. At the time of their interviews many seemed uncertain whether their parents would permit them even to attend Valleyside College. That decision seemed to them to depend in part on how they behaved in high school.

Some of the girls felt that whatever they did, they were criticized. They were faulted by Valleysiders for not dressing American and by their parents for dressing up. Their parents asked, "Why does she have to wear different clothes everyday and wear her hair out [as opposed to braided]?" "She's asking for trouble," they assumed. Before marriage a girl was to appear quiet and unassuming, in dress as well as actions. When boys took notice, the girls were blamed. They must have done something, their parents told them, to attract attention. Even Punjabi peers were critical when a girl's behavior deviated from conventional standards.

One American-born girl, whose parents, though quite conservative, permitted her a bit more freedom than was the norm among these village Punjabis, explained: "The Punjabi girls that go to the high school, I don't think I can mix with them because I know they don't like me. They think I'm too Americanized. . . . I know I'm just the same as other East Indians. It's just that I act more Americanized. That makes a big difference." This young woman was distinctly atypical.[14] She had few Punjabi friends. At school she mixed largely with Valleysiders and participated actively in a number of school activities. Occasionally, too, she attended the parties of Valleysider girl friends. She understood Punjabi but rarely spoke it. She wore her hair long but had cut her bangs. Although usually dressed in jeans and blouse, she said her parents permitted her, on occasion, to wear skirts and dresses. She rarely wore a *salwaar-kameez* even when attending functions at the *gurdwara*.

[134]

In a number of essential respects this young woman's behavior deviated from the standards advocated by the large majority of Punjabi parents. Most parents insisted that their children speak Punjabi at home, at least with them. While they allowed girls to wear Western clothes to school and when out with friends, their legs were to remain covered at all times. Their hair was to be pulled back and in braids. Cut bangs and skirts were symbols of becoming too Americanized.

Many other American-raised girls wished to do these same things, and some did, at times behind their parents' backs, but they maintained a central place for themselves within a Punjabi peer group and gave the appearance, at least, of being less Americanized. Some were frustrated with their lot and felt their parents were unsupportive of their views and needs. One girl, a bright and popular student, explained:

> My parents don't like my clothes, my hair, the way I talk. They don't like my future plans. They don't like anything about me. They don't like my philosophy about marriage. You should marry an East Indian, yes, but you should pick your own husband. . . . My aunt understands. She went to Valleyside High. But my parents say, "Don't talk to anybody; don't go anywhere; come straight home," and that's it. I don't know how I can get it through their heads that I want to go out with a guy if they won't even let me go out with a girl.

This young woman was especially bitter about the constant gossip and the pressures placed on her family to make her conform. " 'Don't let her cut her hair. Watch her closely. Keep her locked up.' I feel like I'm in jail. 'If she gives you a hard time, get her married. Don't listen to her. Don't let her go anywhere alone. Don't let her go to college.' " These were the kinds of things she said others in the community told her parents. Her parents had lived and worked for a time in England and, thus, were more familiar with the Western world than many of the Valleyside parents, but they were, nonetheless, equally protective of their daughter's reputation.

Another girl remarked upon how her parents were always saying, "You guys are becoming Americans." Her response: "We were born here. We've got to change a little. We can't help that." This girl, like many of her friends, felt that she had no choice but to do things behind her parents' back. She donned jewelry and makeup on the way to school. She cut classes to be with friends, male as well as female. She wrote her own excuses when she was absent. It was "too bad," she said, but "what are we supposed to do?" In school she was a moderately good student, obviously intelligent and articulate, quite ambitious in her choice of advanced academic courses, but the stresses and strains of her social position showed in her mediocre grade point average and her open clashes with her parents.

The girls who had been raised in Valleyside, as a group, were absent from school far more than any other subgroup of Punjabis. While the median number of days absent senior year for Punjabi boys was 2, and for the recently arrived Punjabi girls just 1, for the American-raised girls it was 8.5, closer to the Valleysider norm than to that of other Punjabis. School time, they said, was their only opportunity for social activities. One girl in the senior sample had also missed a week of school because her parents kept her home as punishment for her misbehavior.

Not all the American-educated Punjabi girls were upset by their situation. Some had worked out a modus vivendi satisfactory to themselves and to their parents. More of this group, nevertheless, felt the pull of opposing values than was the case among the other groups. "It's my life and I'm going to live it the way I want to," remarked one. "It's the people who have been exposed to both sides that want to have more control of what goes on in their lives," said another.

These were strong and determined young women. They seemed not so much to be "hanging in the middle" as to be forging ahead to create a Punjabi American identity. As one explained: "I don't want to be so American I lose my identity. I don't deny that I am Indian. I am proud I am Indian. I don't want to hurt my parents. I just want them to realize that I don't want to be so traditional. I wouldn't go out with just any guy. I will talk with them, but I won't run around. They don't realize that. It's hard for them. They're new here. They don't know what to expect." Her views were shared by many other Punjabis raised from childhood in this country, males as well as females. They wished to acculturate but not assimilate. Many wished to mix more with white Americans but felt their parents disapproved. While their parents, by and large, were uncomfortable with the majority culture and, therefore, wished to protect their children from what they perceived to be its negative influence, the students themselves were quite comfortable in switching between the two cultural systems.

These high school seniors, both males and females, liked life in America, and few could imagine themselves living in India. Those born in the United States or here since early childhood actually had little concept of the realities of life in village India—either its pleasures or its hardships—unless they had had opportunity to visit Punjab with their parents. Based on our observations of somewhat older Punjabis—often the older siblings of those in our senior sample—it appeared, moreover, that as Punjabi young people entered college and jobs after college they became more comfortable with their upbringing. Said one, who had been raised from childhood in America: "I think you are the richer because you are exposed to two cultures and you can pick the best from both. You have to make an adjustment, but I wouldn't choose it any other way. If I had a choice to start all over again, I would choose to do the same again." Although a more systematic study of Punjabis in their early to middle twenties would be needed to know how many share this young woman's views, it is quite clear that the seniors had a strong sense of their dual Punjabi and American identities and were proud of both.

Both boys and girls appreciated their chance to attend American schools and believed the education in this country was good. The girls, furthermore, were pleased that they would be allowed to work outside the home and in jobs of their own choosing. Follow-up data indicate, moreover, that their parents have listened to their views. Most of the girls did go on to college, at least for two years. Some have been able to marry young men raised in America or another Western country, typically Canada or Britain. After marriage, the frictions with their parents rapidly diminish.

Independence Orientation

To help probe apparent differences between the values of recent arrivals and those raised in Valleyside, we developed a "test" consisting of two sets of statements which reflected, on the one hand, the family orientation of the Punjabis and, on the other, the individualist orientation more characteristic of mainstream American culture. Valleysider and Punjabi students were asked to choose, for example, whether in making decisions about their future it was better to follow the advice of their parents or to do what they themselves believed best.[15]

The results, shown in Table 19, indicate clear differences between Valleysiders and Punjabis. About 70 percent of the Valleysiders reflected an "on-your-own" orientation, compared to 44 percent of the Punjabis. The results show differences, too, between males and females and between the more recently arrived Punjabis and those residing in America since elementary school.

Girls, it may be noted, picked the individualist responses more frequently than boys in all three subgroups. This may say something about the keeper-of-culture female role for Punjabis. If it does, however, it says the same for American culture. The general trend within American society for women to be independent, ready to support themselves and their families whether single, married, or divorced, has clearly had an impact on these students' responses.

The impact of American values becomes readily apparent when one compares the responses of Punjabi newcomers to those of Punjabis reared in the United States. The latter group picked the individualist responses twice as frequently as students raised in India. The opinions expressed by those raised in the United States came closer to those of the American majority than to those of fellow Punjabis freshly arrived in Valleyside and indicated a high degree of acculturation. The American-reared Punjabis expressed a desire to make decisions independently and to go off on their own following their education while newer arrivals expressed a stronger desire to involve their elders in decision making and to remain closely tied to their parents throughout their adult lives. The same trend was apparent for both boys and girls, although the girls picked the on-your-own responses more frequently than the boys.[16]

Persistence with Change

Informal interviews with the Punjabi students revealed further indications of their changing values. The second generation and those raised in the United States mixed largely with one another, not newcomers, and said, in fact, they did not know what to talk about with those recently arrived from India. Those raised in this country preferred English to Punjabi, and while most spoke Punjabi with adults, they more generally spoke English with their siblings and friends. Few could read or write Punjabi, although classes were offered through the *gurdwara* for this purpose. Their reference point was America, not India, and many, particularly the girls, were distinctly uncomfortable with the prospect of marrying someone who had grown up in Punjab.

These young people liked American clothes, music, and food. They chatted easily with members of the opposite sex. Quite a few had Punjabi boy friends and girl friends, but at the same time, most favored arranged marriages. Many found village Indian ways strange, backward even. While many expressed interest in learning more about

Punjab, few could imagine themselves ever living there. They had grown accustomed to their American ways. They ate at McDonalds and Pizza Hut. They loved sporty American cars and bought them if they had the money. They elected to visit Marriott's Great America for the Asian Club outing. They looked forward to Western-style honeymoons, not in India but in Honolulu or New York. They freely stated that they expected to give their own children more freedom than they had had.

Values were changing, but Punjabi young people remained firmly and squarely anchored in their Punjabi Sikh identity. Like their parents, they reacted negatively to the conformist pressures of the majority group. "Being in America," one student explained, means "you have to compromise a little," but "we are not saying that we want to become like whites." It is "best to remain separated," another remarked, because "so-called integration will cost the Punjabis much in terms of lost culture."

There is a direct and strong relationship between home and community forces and the school adaptation patterns of these Punjabi Sikh students. The focus here has been the role of family and community in promoting academic success, although we have also seen how traditional village values operate to discourage girls in their final two years of high school from pursuing the more advanced college-preparatory courses. In general, however, parents have high educational expectations for their children and see no reason their children should not do well in their studies. They assume that success is the result of hard work more than innate ability or prior advantages. Peer pressure, too, serves as a force for compliance with school norms, as does firsthand exposure to the drudgery of farm labor. Punjabi students invest more effort in their schoolwork than majority-group classmates not only because they wish a better, easier life for themselves than their parents have but also because of the honor their accomplishments bring to both family and community.

Punjabi children are taught to value formal education, to respect and obey their teachers, and to uphold their family's good name. They are taught also that no person is better than another and that an individual will rise, or fall, on his or her own merits and initiative. It is assumed that through hard work and cleverness any person can become a successful and important person, and all Punjabi young people know of such individuals within the Valleyside Punjabi community.

[139]

Within traditional Punjabi Sikh society great emphasis is placed on individual achievement, little on inherited status (Pettigrew 1972). The egalitarian principles of Sikhism act as an equalizing influence on the Sikh community and weaken the potential development of restricted educational categories and socioeconomic groups. Sikhs believe that all children should be entitled to the same education. They embrace the concept of intermixing with those of different caste, class, and racial backgrounds.

In India, however, Jat Sikh farm families have placed no similar emphasis on education for all their children. In many families only one or two sons were educated and the others not. And for daughters, education beyond the primary level has often been discouraged. Too much education, according to traditional village views, makes a woman too independent in her behavior and beliefs and contributes to the breakup of the extended family. In rural Punjab, furthermore, formal education for Jat women has had little function because there were, and still are, no jobs apart from the managing of household affairs, a complicated job but one requiring little schooling. Views are changing, and in recent years the more prosperous farm families have placed a higher value on educating all their children, but as the parents' own educational levels make clear, there is no long history of secondary and postsecondary education among the Valleyside Sikhs.

The Valleyside case points to the importance of contextual and situational as well as cultural variables in shaping school performance patterns. In America, many more employment opportunities exist, for women as well as men, than is the case in India, and Punjabi immigrants believe that, regardless of their minority status, they will have a chance to compete for jobs based on their skills and credentials. In such an environment, formal education has far more practical value than it does in rural Punjab. Schooling, furthermore, is more readily available and generally of a higher quality than in India. Children can attend high school and community college without leaving home. Older students, by holding after-school and summer jobs, can even pay their own expenses.[17] In rural India, students have no similar opportunity to be wage earners.

Important, too, is the Punjabis' situation as voluntary immigrants. They come here quite consciously because America holds greater opportunities for them and their children than India. They are willing to work hard to realize their economic goals. Their reference point is India. Their comparative perspective helps them to see the many advantages of life in this country.

[140]

The parents want their children to become proficient in the ways of white America but to maintain a strong anchor within the Punjabi community. Such a balance is not always easy to achieve. The parents see their young as acculturating too rapidly and fear that they may find themselves marginal in both Punjabi and Valleysider worlds. The students insist that acculturation without assimilation is both possible and desirable. The two generations agree, however, that Punjabis should not be pressured into changing, that if a girl wishes to wear a *salwaar-kameez* or if a boy wants to keep his long hair and wear a turban, they should not be teased and made to feel they must conform to the majority standard. Both generations are disturbed, moreover, by the climate of prejudice that pervades the school experience of all Punjabi young people attending Valleyside High.

[8]

Barriers to Achievement

Our children dislike being teased and picked on. They cannot
concentrate on their education, and the whole day is wasted. They
cannot concentrate on their schoolwork, and we feel concerned
about this.

Punjabi mother, Valleyside

For Punjabi students the most frequently cited difficulties faced at
Valleyside High were three: racial hostility, limited proficiency in
English, and the pressures to conform to majority-group ways. We
shall consider each of these areas in turn.

Racial Prejudice at Valleyside High

A climate of prejudice permeates the high school experience of all
Punjabi students. While no Valleysider students said Punjabis caused
difficulties for them personally, many Punjabi youngsters cited the
prejudiced attitudes and actions of Valleysiders as their main problem
at school. Punjabi parents were troubled by the negative social climate
and its impact on their children's development. "If you are always
worried in case some white child is going to say something to you," one
parent observed, "then obviously it is going to interfere. You are not
free from worry." Another noted that when children are picked on they
become "upset psychologically." Still another commented that "instead of the child being successful, he becomes weak and afraid, saying
'Why study?' and goes to work in the fields or the factory."

Without exception, every Punjabi student we interviewed recounted examples of Valleysider hostility. Verbal jibes, such as "you stink,"
"you God damn Hindus," and "get out of our country" were common,
as were mild forms of physical abuse, such as food throwing and

[142]

crowding into line ahead of Punjabis. Much of the trouble occurred at lunchtime or on the school buses. One second-generation Punjabi girl, fluent in English, described an incident that had occurred at lunch the day we interviewed her: "We were coming from a meeting of the Asian Club and white students threw oranges at us. Before that we had been standing in the hall and the supervisor kicked us out. So we went outside and they threw oranges. So there is nowhere to go. Sometimes we play volleyball at lunchtime. And the white students come and take the ball and throw it on top of the boys' gym." Punjabis also reported more serious but less frequent occurrences, in which Valleysider students spit at them, stuck them with pins, and threw lighted cigarettes in their direction.

Those very few Punjabi boys who wore their hair long and in a turban, in keeping with Sikh teachings and parental wishes complained of being constantly teased. An interviewer questioned one Punjabi man about his son's experiences at Valleyside High:

Father: Concerning education, he did not have any difficulties, but the atmosphere at the school is not good.

Interviewer: In what ways?

Father: With the American children. They hate our children. They keep on calling them, "Hindu, Hindu." They should be told that we are not Hindus, that we are Sikhs. Secondly, pulling off someone's turban, or spitting, this is really bad.

Interviewer: Does your son wear a turban?

Father: He did before. Just after he started at the high school a group of white boys got together and took off my son's turban. He was very upset about this. The boys ran away.

Interviewer: Did it happen again?

Father: Two boys took his turban off when he was walking home from school. . . . Then last summer he had his hair cut.

Interviewer: [To the boy, who was also present] Did you take off your turban because of this pressure?

Son: Yes.

Interviewer: What do you think about this now?

Son: Everyone has their turbans off. Most of the boys have had their hair cut.

Interviewer: Is it mainly the ones with turbans that have the problems?

Father: No matter whether they are clean shaven, they hate us all. Someone with a turban on will get more harassment. They call the turban a diaper. They say you have a diaper on. The boy gets really upset.

[143]

To most Valleysiders turban snatching seemed little more than a childish prank. To Punjabis it was a deliberate attack on their honor.

Two Punjabi seniors reported falling prey to more serious acts of racial hostility, one a criminal offense. In the first case a girl's long hair was deliberately set on fire: "I was walking along with a friend of mine after I finished my class and a [white] boy lit my hair with a lighter. I had to cut a lot of my hair off. . . . One girl who was coming behind me quickly put my hair out with her hands. If she hadn't done that, all of my hair would have been burned." The girl, a limited-English speaker, had been in the United States for only two years. In the second case another girl, again a recent arrival and limited in English, was put off a school bus taking students to their summer employment at the nearby air base. The bus driver, a Valleysider, later reported that some non-Punjabi students had told him the girl had head lice. The girl was simply put off the bus miles out of town and without explanation, because the bus driver believed she had lice. When questioned about the impact of prejudice on her high school experience, she noted: "If something has happened to you once, for example when they told me to get off the bus, all of the time you are afraid and lack self-confidence. You are afraid that something will happen again." Other students had similar apprehensions.

Most of the harassment of Punjabis took place during lunch, between classes, or while students were traveling to and from school, often on buses. But problems also occurred during class, usually out of sight of teachers or in those classes where the offending students believed they could escape disciplinary action. One member of the research team, for example, observed a Valleysider student walk into an ESL class, deliver a note from the school office, and then, on leaving, announce in a loud voice, "Pee-U," to the amusement of friends standing in the hallway. In another case, a Valleysider was observed refusing three times to comply with an office worker's request to deliver "call slips" to the ESL classrooms. "I'm not going to take them. All the Hindus are there," she announced, and threw the slips on a table. To avoid such hassles high school staff generally asked Punjabi students to deliver messages to ESL classes.

Some Valleysider youths spoke freely about their actions. One explained how, "just for the hell of it," he and his buddies hassled the "Hindus." Another boy told of throwing food at Punjabis to make his friends laugh. He also described how a classmate used to pass by a bunch of Punjabis where they were sitting during lunch hour and "slap each of them on the head." His reaction: "It was pretty tight, but it was pretty funny." No Punjabi student reported amusement at such antics. All Valleysider students recognized that Punjabis were given a hard time. While only a relatively small minority of Valleysiders actively participated, the majority either condoned their classmates' behavior or felt powerless to alter the situation. Most (83 percent) thought that Punjabis *should* change their way of life when they came to live in America. Furthermore, negative attitudes about Punjabi culture pervaded every segment of the Valleysider student body.

Valleysiders preyed upon new arrivals the most. Newcomers stood out in terms of speech and dress. They were generally weak in English and unable to identify their assailants. Those who had grown up in Valleyside knew their Valleysider classmates and were known by them. They also had learned to fit in with the crowd and were able to respond to verbal cracks with quick comments of their own.

In spite of all the troubles, Punjabi students felt little ill will toward Valleysiders as a group. "Not all Valleysiders are prejudiced," Punjabis explained. "A lot are nice." Most Punjabi seniors (72 percent) responded in the affirmative to the question, "Do you have any non-Punjabi friends in high school?" The friendships, moreover, were not only in the minds of the Punjabis. Two-thirds of the Valleysider seniors said they had Punjabi friends.[1] Many of these friendships were of a casual nature. Few saw such friends outside of school. Some students did not even know their friends' names. But still there was a sense of friendship across the ethnic boundary. Valleyside High was not a battle zone or a tense place to attend school. Casual observation, supported by interviews, indicated that most Punjabi students enjoyed school.

The undercurrent of prejudice, however, was never far from the surface. It was easy to uncover. During the course of fieldwork a social studies teacher, at my request, replicated a study he had carried out in 1967. He asked world history students to participate in a survey "to find out current thoughts, information, or feelings about East Indian people." Students were told it was "a chance to make [their] thoughts clear." Out of more than seventy essays, written by both fast- and slow-track students, most of them Valleysiders, not one described positive or likable traits about Punjabis. A few said they had Punjabi friends or thought Punjabis provided them an opportunity to learn about a different culture, but often these same students went on to note a negative characteristic—for example, that many Punjabis "smell bad." Some said Punjabis were "just people, like everyone else" and that they deserved equal treatment and equal opportunity. A few wanted more mixing between the groups, a comment more frequently made by girls than by boys. Some felt sorry for Punjabis and uncomfortable with all the rude comments. A few took exception to the assignment or had nothing to say. Taken as a whole, however, the tone of the essays was strongly negative, considerably more negative than the set collected in 1967 when Punjabis were only 1 percent of the student body.

Also at my request, the female Punjabi research assistant on the project, in a conscious effort to see what might occur, walked through the central part of the high school campus one day while students were eating lunch. It was an area where the Quaddies hung out, the "popular" students, those in the demanding academic classes, the campus leaders. She was accompanied by two other Punjabis, both school employees. They walked casually, chatting with one another. All were young and it was possible to mistake them for students. The Valleysiders pelted them with french fries.

Punjabi Response Patterns

Most Punjabi students believed they had little choice but to live with the hostility. Their parents, in spite of their obvious concern about the situation, urged them to say "never mind," to forget about the troubles, and to avoid fights. They counseled them also against collective action or getting involved in one another's problems. Such responses, parents feared, would only cause Punjabi youngsters to be viewed as troublemakers, further contributing to their difficulties in school. One man, a long-term resident of Valleyside, explained his views: "A child who is intelligent, no one bothers him or her. No one bothers a good child. The children who are bothered are bothered because of the way they behave. If I am sitting at a desk and I am studying and someone comes, don't answer back. Quietly keep working. He will go away." This was a strong and consistent belief.

So deep was some Punjabis' conviction that "good" children could stay out of trouble and that those who deviated from traditional norms were sure to suffer, that one parent even suggested improper behavior as cause for the incident in which the girl's hair was burned:

I haven't attended any . . . meetings at the school, but I did hear that someone lit a Punjabi girl's hair on fire. This girl was walking with her hair

[146]

loose [unbraided], like the white girls do, and they put a match to her hair. [With resentment in his voice] Our children don't look nice with their hair open. If they have it loose like the whites, copy them, then obviously they are going to be mocked by the whites. The girls with braided hair, their hair looks nice. They won't light their hair. Because it was open, they lit it.

Few parents took such an extreme stance, but just as many Punjabis believed they could avoid conflict by staying away from bars and other public places, a majority of the parents believed that their children, by their response to racial incidents, could keep the problems from escalating.

If pushed too far, however, parents realized their children were bound to react. One mother explained: "We usually say that she should not say anything. She should ignore it. Not get involved. Stay away from trouble. Leave it. Forget about it. Someone can keep quiet once, twice. But if something continues, then the third time the child is obviously going to say something back." In keeping with their parents' advice, most Punjabi youngsters tried simply to ignore the hostilities. Immigrants, said one Punjabi senior, "don't want to cause any trouble. They want to adjust. They want to get ahead and they want to learn something. They tend not to be aggressive. They tend to overlook things. . . . They are not cowards, they are just in a new society. The last thing they want to do is fight. . . . They don't want to rock the boat." This particular student, a boy who had grown up in Valleyside, believed the only way to stop the harassment was for Punjabis to join forces to protect their rights. He contrasted Punjabi and Mexican American response patterns. Mexican Americans, he said, "are more aggressive mainly because they have been in this country for a long time. They know the environment, know the culture, whereas the East Indians have been here [only] ten years or so. They haven't adjusted to the culture." Valleysiders agreed that Mexican American students at Valleyside High would not "stand for being put upon" and that they stuck together in a confrontation.

One Punjabi, a self-confident young woman who had grown up in Valleyside and had graduated from Valleyside High a few years earlier, described an incident with a Valleysider peer who sought to provoke a fight:

Young woman: If they want to fight, I let them have it. I stand up for my rights. I went to the vice-principal and said, "If someone fights me,

what am I supposed to do?" He told me "Don't come and bring tales."
The teachers say that, too. "Don't come and tell us about it, okay?"
Then, if we get into a fight, they want to kick us out of school. What the
hell are you supposed to do? That made me mad. I told him, "You don't
want me to come and tell you anything, and I have a good record. I
have never been in to tell you anything. I have never been in any
trouble and I'm supposed to ruin my record getting into fights?" Mr.
M. said, "No. Tell me the name of the girl." So I told him. She [the
provoking Valleysider] had been in trouble and had been kicked out of
school before.

Interviewer: So she was trying to get you in trouble?

Young woman: Yes. Well, lots of times, if you are a Hindu, you are not
supposed to say anything back, right? I turned around and called her a
"Fucking Honky!" [Laughter from family members present for the
interview.] Well, I was mad. Honestly, I turned around and let her
have it. I'm glad that some of the kids are fighting back now.

Every Punjabi knew of students who had been suspended for fighting
back.

Second-generation students and those raised in Valleyside from
early childhood, while disagreeing with their parents' approach, generally heeded their advice. They knew that to fight, or even to stand
together, would lead to disciplinary action, first by school authorities
and then by their parents. "If you get in a fight [with a Valleysider],"
one boy explained, "the principal will suspend you both and when your
parents find out, they get mad." Their parents, Punjabi students explained, always assumed their children were at fault if they got in
trouble at school. Nonetheless, Punjabi youths, particularly those born
and raised in Valleyside, showed a willingness to defend themselves,
by force if necessary, and to bear the consequences. Punjabi boys kept
hockey sticks in their lockers and were not afraid to use them if pro-
voked to fight. One even brandished a revolver, kept in his father's
truck, in response to some racial insult made by Valleysiders in a
passing car.

The Need for Change

No one was comfortable with the racial tensions. All—be they students or teachers, Valleysiders or Punjabis—agreed that there was
considerable need for improvement. On our standard questionnaire,
respondents were asked to rate relations between Punjabis and non-

Punjabis on a scale ranging from "very good" through "good" and "fair" to "poor."[2] The query was designed to ask not only how things were, but also the amount of improvement that was needed, if any.

Responses to the query are presented in Table 20. As expected, teachers, Punjabi students, and Valleysider students all rated ethnic relations heavily on the low end of the scale. The most strikingly united response came from Valleysider students. Over three-quarters of them chose the lowest possible alternative ("needs lots of improvement"), and not one rated relations with Punjabi students as "good" or "very good." Neither teachers nor Punjabi students approached this degree of negativity. From the relatively objective view of the researchers who put the question, the Valleysider students' response seemed closest to the reality. Theirs was, moreover, a request for change and improvement in race relations.

The modal response for teachers drew much more to the middle of the scale, with over half responding "needs some improvement" and several responding that Valleyside High rated "good" to "very good" in the area of ethnic relations. Positive responses, however, were characteristically qualified with comments like "as compared to other places" and "at the present time." One even went on to predict that the situation, while "good now," was a "time bomb" for the future.

The response pattern of Punjabi students merits comment, for it was they who responded most frequently on the positive end of the scale. Clearly, this response was not meant to be a denial of prejudice, for in other parts of the questionnaire and in their interviews, they stated repeatedly that Valleysider hostility was their major problem in school. Rather, their response reflected both the strong Punjabi desire to fit in and the operation of the Indian reference point. The latter involved their parents' appreciation of the excellent public school facilities in this country, as compared to India, and the relatively good ethnic relations in Valleyside, as compared to Britain. They liked America and had no wish to be critical. Like their parents, also, these Punjabi adolescents believed that in any group there were the good and the bad. They sought here to work with the good.

Valleyside Faculty

Teachers varied in how they dealt with prejudice. Some reported that they tried to "shield" Punjabis from rude remarks and called offending students aside to tell them their behavior was unacceptable.

Some talked to students about cultural differences. Some said they "simply insisted on respect." Others said they "ignored" the cracks, unless they got really out of hand. Regardless of their approach, most believed that the problems were beyond their ability to solve.

Administrators recognized the explosive nature of the situation— their concerns, in fact, were impetus for initiating the current re- search—and they tried to deal swiftly and firmly with the most serious offenses. They were less effective, however, in addressing the underly- ing causes of the problems or in bringing a halt to the constant petty acts of annoyance which plagued Punjabi students. Administrators, like the teachers, appeared resigned to the status quo and felt power- less to change it.

Teachers and administrators pointed out that prejudice originated in the larger society. One observed: "American kids call each other Baljit and Gurdip [common Sikh names] like calling each other nigger. Kids pick this up by the time they're three or four. They call each other Hindus." Valleyside was "redneck country," teachers explained, and students' attitudes were shaped by the larger community.

Punjabi parents and students were disturbed by school administra- tors' reluctance to deal more sternly with the troublemakers but ex- pressed no similar concerns about teachers' attitudes and behavior. Teachers, in their view, were "good and capable people" who treated all students the same. When questioned specifically about whether some teachers were biased, Punjabi students said they did not think so. Informal interviews with high school teachers and staff revealed, how- ever, a strong and unmistakable undercurrent of prejudice.

Many faculty members shared the widely held belief that Punjabis smelled bad. So insistent were they about this that the researchers found themselves sniffing in the classrooms. It soon became clear, however, that teachers' complaints were simply a reflection of the widespread racial prejudice in Valleyside.

One teacher called me into her office and confided that some Punjabi students smelled so bad that she could not stand to be near them. Others noted that Valleysider students would throw open the windows on entering class, pointedly request to have their seats moved if they were placed next to a Punjabi, or complain out loud of the "smell." One teacher said, "I have to ask [the Valleysiders] to be compassionate." Others offered more scientific rationalizations, suggesting that the Punjabi odor stemmed from diet and the lack of deodorants. Accord- ingly, Punjabi students were counseled by teachers on personal hygiene, sometimes in group meetings. Not one faculty member ever suggested that Valleysider prejudice was, in fact, the underlying problem.

Valleysider teachers, no less than Valleysider parents and students, readily recited a variety of prejudicial Punjabi stories. They told of ways Punjabis tried to cheat the system to make an extra buck, such as including a lot of dirt when weighing in their peaches. They maintained that the new wave of immigrants were from a lower class than the earlier group. They asserted that large numbers of Punjabi students were here illegally.[3] They insisted on calling Sikh students Hindus. They remained confused about the Sikh system of names, first, middle and last. They told a joke about a Punjabi buying a new camper with an automatic shift, starting down the highway in it, and getting up from behind the wheel to go to the bathroom supposing it would drive itself.

A few teachers were extremely well informed about Sikh history and culture. More, however, were ill informed and uninterested. Most believed that ethnic hostility was inevitable when immigrants arrived in a community in large numbers. Only time, as they saw it, would ease the tensions. Time would allow the Punjabis, like other immigrant groups before them, to blend into the American "melting pot."

Most teachers believed that it was best to treat all students the same, without regard for cultural differences. The difficulties inherent in such a policy were highlighted in gym class. One physical education teacher described how students were expected to wear shorts for class and to participate in all required activities, including square dancing. He realized some Punjabis were uneasy with these requirements but explained his position: "We expect the kids to be Americanized. I tell the parents this. . . . A great portion of them want to change. That's why they're here. I tell the parents to go elsewhere, back to India, if they don't like these things." Rules were rules, he said, and the Punjabis simply had to accept them like everyone else. Other teachers also noted that they could not attend to Punjabi cultural preferences where they conflicted with school norms and practices. To do so, they said, would create a "double standard." In their view it was the responsibility of Punjabis to make the adaptations.

Learning English was a case in point. Valleysiders, both teachers and students, said that if Punjabis would only learn to speak English, then there would be more mixing across ethnic lines and less friction. Punjabi students, on the other hand, said it was the prejudiced attitudes and behavior of Valleysiders that deterred them from mixing and, in the process, restricted their opportunity to learn English. Limited-English speakers were fearful, they said, whenever Valley-siders spoke to them, always wondering if some remark was in fact an insult. The ESL program at Valleyside High, together with the overall system of sorting students into instructional tracks, inadvertently contributed to newcomers' difficulties.

The ESL Program at Valleyside High

In 1975 the Valleyside School District began an English as a Second Language program at the secondary level. Over the next five years the program expanded rapidly, from just four classes a day to twenty-two English classes, plus additional classes in other subject areas. The district instituted the ESL program to meet the needs of all those so weak in English on entering Valleyside High that they could not compete in mainstream academic classes. This group included almost all the newer arrivals from India and other foreign countries, most notably Mexico, as well as a significant minority of those who had immigrated to this country before fifth grade. Our research findings raise a number of questions about the unintended effects of the ESL program.

At Valleyside High for much of the school day students designated as limited-English-proficient and non-English-speaking were segregated from the rest of the student body. The NES students, usually those who had just arrived from India or another foreign country, were placed in the ESL 1 track. They received five periods a day of ESL instruction, three in English and two in other subject areas. Only for one period each day, usually for physical education, did they have an opportunity to mix with non-ESL students. All NES students, regardless of age, grade level, previous preparation or ability were placed in the same classroom.

The ESL 2 track was for LEP students whose test scores showed them to have a third- or fourth-grade command of English. Students placed in this track received three periods a day of ESL instruction, two in English and one in another subject area. During the remaining three periods they attended "regular" classes. ESL 2 included students who had been in ESL 1 the previous year, as well as some students who had been living in the United States for as much as five years.

According to a ruling by the Office for Civil Rights, U.S. Department of Education, students attending Valleyside schools were required to receive a minimum of one hour of ESL instruction per day until they could demonstrate that they were fluent in reading, writing, and speaking English and were able either to score above the 40th percentile on a standardized achievement test or to maintain a C average in all regular classes. Thus, students' performance in regular classes, together with their scores on standardized tests and on an English proficiency test, determined whether they continued with ESL 2 for another year, progressed to ESL 3 (one period of more advanced English instruction), or moved out of the program altogether. Since many of the students who had arrived from India after fourth grade could not meet these requirements, they continued to receive at least one hour of ESL a day. ESL instruction could not be waived by a student's parents. The large majority (76 percent) of the ESL students at Valleyside High were Punjabis.

The ESL program provided a protected environment where students felt free to make mistakes, ask questions, and request assistance in ways that were not possible in other classes. With twenty-five or more students in the regular academic classes, teachers simply were not able to provide instruction geared to the needs of NES, or even most LEP, students. New arrivals commented positively about the special help they received, both from their teachers and from instructional aides assigned to the ESL program. Many of these students, however, also described the ESL classes as far "too easy," easier some said than the English instruction they had previously received in school in India. They also noted that the ESL classes, unlike classes in India, required little in the way of homework.

Many ESL students appeared willing to work harder. Some felt their classes were geared to the less able or less interested students and complained of being held to the slower pace. Some believed they spent too much time covering material they already knew. Some simply concluded that American schools were far less demanding than those in India.

A number of ESL students believed they would have learned more in regular classes. They knew more English, they said, than their test scores indicated. They wanted an opportunity to compete at the higher level. If unable to keep up, they could then move back to ESL. "You can go from higher to low," one newcomer explained, "but not low to higher." This student, an intelligent and industrious young man who had arrived from India in tenth grade, expressed concern that he would

[153]

graduate from high school without taking the courses he needed for college. The system, as then set up, made it virtually impossible for such a student to move at his own pace.

Students received full high school credit for all ESL classes. Thus, for example, two years of ESL English could be substituted for English 1 and English 2. Immigrants also received full transfer credits for their foreign instruction. District policy was designed to permit language-minority immigrants to be placed in the same grade as their age-mates and to progress through school in the same time span regardless of whether they had received an equivalent level of instruction.[4] Many of the more recent immigrants earned 70 or more of the 220 credits required for graduation through the ESL program. Most of their other credits came from a combination of general education and vocational classes. These students were moved along through the system with little chance to take either solid basics or college-preparatory classes.

A number of Punjabis were sharply critical of the ESL program. One said bluntly that the low reading level of ESL materials, which he called this "dog in the park stuff," just "won't do." Another expressed outrage that Punjabi students received good grades and high school credit for classes that did not prepare them to be competitive in the job market. "Our children are placed in ghettos and remain there for the whole time spent in school," he said. A few Punjabis accused school officials of "racist" intentions, noting that the outcome of the current program was to "perpetuate second-class status for Punjabi students." Others felt that the ESL track had become an unintentional "trap."

Teachers explained that success in even the slower-paced mainstream classes required at least a sixth-grade command of English. Students arriving from India with little or no English, no matter how bright and well prepared, simply could not make the transition from Punjabi to English in one or even two years. Teachers also pointed out that some of the Punjabis, although of high school age, had received only the most rudimentary education in their village school back in India and were totally unprepared for high school–level work. Separate classes for new arrivals was the best solution, most teachers believed.[5]

Teachers noted additional difficulties with the ESL program, including their own lack of specialized training for teaching LEP/NES students and the scarcity of proper instructional materials. Most of the ESL materials were written at a very elementary level and were not stimulating for secondary students. Some teachers, furthermore, were said to "baby" the ESL students and, instead of encouraging competition and self-reliance, they created an environment in which the limited-English speakers came to rely on extra help. Teachers also cited as a fundamental problem the absence of an overall ESL curriculum at either the high school or district levels.

Punjabis agreed that those with limited proficiency needed special help with English, but they believed, too, that they needed more chance to interact with non-Punjabi classmates. "The whites hate the [Punjabis] all the more because they are being kept separate," one Punjabi man observed. When we asked Punjabi seniors to select from a range of options the best approaches to teaching English, they overwhelmingly (thirty-three of thirty-six) rejected the option of "separating non-English-speaking students from others until they have mastered English." Yet both the formal curriculum and informal instructional milieu tended to do just that.[6] The high school tracking system for mainstream students was part of the problem, as was the pervasive negative attitude toward recent arrivals from India.

The Tracking System

The high school also tracked all non-ESL students for their English, math, science, and social studies classes. Students moving up from ESL were generally placed in the remedial or the average track. Until they had overcome their language handicap, one teacher explained, they simply could not keep up with the pace of the fast-track classes, no matter how smart they were. Others pointed out that in the slower-track classes teachers provided more in-class assistance and supervision. They also placed comparatively more emphasis on skills development, repetition, drill, and rote learning in slow-track classes and less emphasis on abstract concepts and inquiry skills. For all these reasons the slower-track classes were considered a more comfortable learning environment for students still trying to master English. For a number of other reasons, however, the slow-track classes provided a potentially negative environment for the Punjabi students.

In response to our inquiries about the different tracks, teachers explained that in their faster classes they devoted comparatively more time to problem solving, independent thinking, and originality. Fast-track students they characterized as "goal-oriented," able to grasp new ideas quickly, and "self-motivated." The slow-track students they described as generally "lower ability" and "not college bound." It was difficult, some said, to require homework in the slower track. Many students simply did not do the assigned work. A lack of parental involvement in the educational process, teachers believed, was an underlying problem. Teachers noted that parents of slow-track students had much less contact with the high school and were less aware of their children's academic progress.

Some teachers expressed concern that slow-track students were poor role models for the Punjabis. While teachers commended Punjabis for their regular attendance, hard work, and motivation, as well as their ability to memorize required materials and master factual information, they found a high percentage of Valleysider youngsters in the slower track to be unmotivated, lax in attendance and study habits, and, in general, "turned off by school." Slow-track students, furthermore, were felt to be less tolerant of Punjabi classmates than students in the tougher classes. "It goes back to rednecks, the poor-white-trash types looking for another group to put down," one teacher explained. Teachers recognized, then, that the slow track was a less than ideal learning environment.[7]

Punjabis agreed that it was the "low-level" students who picked on them the most. One American-educated Punjabi, himself a top student, also observed: "Once you are in a harder class, they [Valleysiders] start identifying you with a hard class and say, 'He knows a lot. He's just like us.' They won't bother me as much as they will someone from the ESL class." This young man, and others like him, however, were not free from problems. He explained: "A majority of people in my school did not accept me for who I was. They thought that since my English was good and I had difficult classes, I should act like an Anglo-American." Almost all Valleysiders assumed that assimilation was the goal.

Cultural Barriers and the Press to Americanize

All Punjabi students were faced with conflicting sets of expectations regarding appropriate behavior, one set applicable to their Punjabi world and the other to the world of school. At home, for example, Punjabi young people learned to defer to their elders and to remain respectfully quiet in their presence. When Punjabis first entered American schools, whether as small children or teenagers, they were reluctant to speak in class except to respond with factual information to a teacher's direct question. Punjabi students were especially uncomfortable with the American technique of "brainstorming," one elementary teacher observed, and fell silent when expected to express their own ideas. High school teachers made similar observation. "'I don't know,' is their answer almost before the question is asked," one English teacher responded, when asked if Punjabi students participated in class discussions. It was rare, said another, for Punjabi girls "to be outgoing enough to initiate conversation in class." Part of the difficulty stemmed from the coeducational nature of American high schools.

In village Punjab teenage boys and girls traditionally avoid conversation with one another and even eye contact. In Indian schools, girls are not faced with the necessity of mixing with boys or speaking up in their presence. Classroom interaction is structured differently and, in most cases, secondary schooling is segregated by sex. At Valleyside High the Punjabi girls, including those born in America, participated only with great reluctance in coeducational activities, especially those that appeared competitive, such as physical education classes. They did not wish to draw attention to themselves in the presence of the opposite sex.

Just talking to boys could pose difficulty, particularly for the newer arrivals: "A family that has just come over gets really upset if they see their [teenage] daughter talking to some guy," one student explained. Even for the American-educated students informal conversation between the sexes did not always come easily: "When I came here [to the high school] from eighth grade and saw girls talking to guys I thought, 'Oh my God, what are you doing?' I had never thought of myself doing that. And if a guy came I'd go the other way." Most Punjabi girls did talk to boys at school, we discovered, but not in front of their parents. One student explained in an interview:

Interviewer: Does it bother your parents if you just speak to fellow students who are guys?
Girl: A lot of guys . . . come by [my house] and say "Hi, how are you?" I tell them not to stop [by] . . . because my mom and dad would get mad. They say, "Okay, we understand." I talk to guys here at school, and if my parents were to find out they would probably kick me out of school.
Interviewer: Just for chatting with them?
Girl: They are afraid . . . the guy might start liking me.

[157]

Interviewer: How do they feel about your making friends with American
girls?

Girl: They don't say anything about that, just as long as I stay away from
boys and going out on dates.

Interviewer: So you can mix with all kinds of girls?

Girl: Yes. . . . I enjoy talking to everybody. I even like to talk to boys.
I've always been shy, but I enjoy talking to them. . . . If you don't talk
to people they might say, "She thinks she's too good." I don't consider
myself too good to talk to anybody. I think everybody is equal.

Interviewer: It must be awfully hard on the girls when they know their
parents would really get upset.

Girl: Just about every girl here [at the high school] talks to everybody. If
their parents were to be with them, they would have to face the other
way. It's like in India. You hardly can look at anybody at all.

Punjabi students had learned to behave one way at home, another at
school, but even in school the separation between the sexes remained.
In sharp contrast to Valleysider social patterns, Punjabi boys and girls
were never seen walking or sitting together. In group meetings, such
as a get-together of the Asian Club, girls and boys sat separately. Most
girls also refrained from speaking up in these sorts of gatherings, not,
they said, because they felt incompetent to do so, but because it was
their way of showing respect for the opposite sex.

Coeducational schooling posed the most obvious difficulties for Punjabis, but the constant attention given to preparing young people to go
off on their own and to make decisions in accordance with individual
rather than family wishes provided equal cause for tension. The entire
high school curriculum carried an implicit emphasis on teaching students that they had both the responsibility and the right to make
decisions independent of their elders' views. So strong was the individualist orientation that it had become formalized in a social studies
course titled "On Your Own." This course or one similar to it was
required for graduation.

In this class students learned how to rent an apartment, get married,
plan the family budget, and even arrange a funeral—all on their own.
Punjabi students were distinctly uncomfortable with this class, which
from start to finish presumed white, middle-class values. Lessons dealing with marriage and family life, always taught from a Western point of
view, were embarrassing to Punjabi adolescents, as were units dealing
with contraception, abortion, and divorce, particularly in the coeducational setting of the American classroom. Outside of class Punjabi girls

[158]

were teased by Punjabi boys for having to pair off with members of the opposite sex for some of their assignments, in accordance with the teacher's instructions. In spite of their discomfort with this and many other class assignments, however, the girls reported that "whatever the teacher says, we have to do."

Even some Valleysider parents expressed concern about the heavy emphasis by school personnel on independent decision making for young people. The high school, they felt, was undercutting parental authority, teaching students, for example, not to believe something just because "your parents believe it." Some objected to the message that at age eighteen the child, then legally an adult, could "do as he pleases, at school, at home, or any place else, and the parents don't have anything to say about it." Those Valleysiders who wished the schools would do more to support parental authority were also those who reinforced the legitimacy of school authority. In this respect, some Valleysider parents sounded very much like their Punjabi counterparts.

Most Punjabi students in time learned to juggle the different demands and expectations of home and school. There were occasions, however, when Punjabi girls resisted complying with class requirements, even at the risk of losing credit. Physical education raised the most difficult problems. Two years of physical education were mandatory for high school graduation. Students received full credit if they attended class regularly, changed into gym clothes (short shorts and shirt), and made reasonable effort to do what was asked of them. Although requirements seemed straightforward to Valleysider teachers, for many of the Punjabi girls in the senior sample they were simply beyond the pale. "Our children cannot change for sports," said one Punjabi parent; "this is against our culture." Almost no Punjabi parents wanted their daughters to expose their legs in the presence of boys or men. Some girls wore street clothes to class until they realized they would fail. Then they changed to sweat pants, no matter the temperature.

Quite a few Punjabi parents were opposed to all sports for adolescent girls, especially if they were expected to run around in the presence of boys and men. In village Punjab only little girls played outside. An older girl, one man pointed out, would be seen "walking with her head low." Right or wrong, he concluded, Punjabi parents wanted the same from their daughters in Valleyside.

Some parents recognized that they had to adapt to American customs and, moreover, that physical exercise was necessary for physical health. They would have been more inclined to support full participation by their daughters in sports, however, if they had played out of sight of boys and if their physical education teachers were all women. Ironically, the implementation of Title IX regulations, designed to bring about equal opportunities for women in sports, and all other aspects of education, worked to the disadvantage of Punjabi students. Among the goals of Title IX are "the elimination of within-class segregation" and the inclusion of "role models of both sexes."[8] To comply with the letter and the spirit of the federal regulations when they were first mandated, Valleyside High instituted coed physical education classes, except for contact sports. Coed sports, however, caused many girls, Punjabis in particular, to participate in gym activities even less than before.

Teachers and students provided a number of examples of Punjabi girls refusing to take part in required gym activities. In coed classes, one teacher observed, the girls would not practice cardiopulmonary resuscitation. In an all-girls section of the same class they did participate. Any activity that required dancing in mixed company also created problems. One Punjabi woman said: "We do not want them to dance naked [with exposed legs]. They do ask them to dance a lot of times. . . . They shouldn't dance." Respectable women, in the Punjabi view, simply do not dance in the presence of men, legs bared or not. Other Punjabi parents complained about a physical education unit that involved girls in wrestling: "[My daughter] told me that the teacher wants her to wrestle. I don't think that it is a good idea for a girl to wrestle. . . . I said, 'Forget it. Don't take that class,' even if she has less credits." Two-thirds of the Punjabi girls in the core sample received less than full credit for PE classes taken in ninth and tenth grades. In order to graduate, they had to make up the lost units as juniors and seniors. By then, as it turned out, the high school had made wrestling an elective and coed gym classes had been abandoned, since, the teachers reported, they simply did not work.

Another problem for Punjabi youngsters, male as well as female, related to standards of modesty. Punjabi youngsters had been taught not to undress in the view of others, but the openness of the locker rooms at Valleyside High made this difficult. For privacy some changed in the toilet stalls. Valleysider classmates became annoyed by the inconvenience. Punjabis "used to bug me," one explained: "Like in PE and stuff, some are a little strange. They go and change in the bathroom

[160]

stall and no one can go to the bathroom. This is kind of irritating. Everyone else changes out where they are supposed to." Student interviews revealed many other examples of Valleysider annoyance when Punjabi behavior did not conform to majority expectations.

Valleysider students said they believed in religious freedom and the right of every individual not to conform, but in practice they penalized those whose standards were different. Sikh students were even pressured to abandon unshorn hair, turban, and steel bangle—all outward marks of their Sikh faith and identity. "We have numbers on our side," explained one Valleysider senior, a bright, popular student and a class officer. "Numbers means power, and you get 100 Anglos and 10 Punjabis, and you know that the Anglos can overpower the Punjabis. So they can say that my way of living is right and yours is wrong and get away with it." To this Valleysider youth, being American meant "acting like white people."

Most Valleysiders, high school faculty and staff included, viewed acculturation as a one-way, linear process. It would take time, they said, two or three generations perhaps, but Punjabis would eventually adopt the ways of the majority group. A cafeteria worker whose daughter attended Valleyside High declared: "The main thing is that they need to learn American ways. The older folks don't want them to change. They don't want them to become advanced. When they first started coming here, they wore those little things on their heads, their funny clothes. But they are learning." Like most Valleysiders, this woman believed that majority-group ways were best for everyone.

The Punjabi system of arranged marriages proved particularly difficult for many Valleysiders to accept. One teacher expressed surprise that "enlightened and intelligent" young people would permit their parents to arrange their marriages. Others spoke even more strongly. "They don't deserve that," said one. "This is a horrible thing; it's just unbelievable they are doing this to her," said another. Both were referring to Punjabi girls who had expressed considerable apprehension about their future, because they were unsure of whom they would marry and feared they might find themselves incompatible with a mate raised in India. The period just before marriage can be a time of stress and worry for Punjabi girls in India, as well as in Valleyside, but for some of the American-educated girls the anxieties were heightened by the majority-group presumption that enlightened and intelligent young people should insist on finding their own mates.

School administrators sometimes seemed more concerned with how

Punjabi students were fitting into the campus social scene than with how they were doing academically. Even though most Punjabi students adapted quickly to the formal demands of the instructional program, they rarely participated in team sports or clubs or attended such functions as Homecoming, Senior Follies, or the senior class picnic. School administrators were troubled by the Punjabi students' reluctance to get involved. Extracurricular activities were considered integral to the life of the school and the overall education of students. Those few Punjabis who did participate, even in minor ways, were almost always those who had been raised in Valleyside and almost always boys.

Many different forces worked together to deter Punjabi students from taking part in nonessential school affairs. First of all, as one student explained, "most of the activities turn into social situations and we think we won't fit. No one actually comes out and says, 'We don't want you.' It's just the way the Punjabis feel." Several students noted lack of self-confidence and insecurity as impediments to their involvement in school activities. A sense of not being welcome, coupled with the fear of actual harassment, discouraged many students.

Punjabi parents, furthermore, objected to participation in activities that might detract from studies or that would involve situations viewed as culturally inappropriate. Overnight trips and school dances were particularly discouraged. In spite of the best efforts of school officials, almost no Punjabi students received parental permission to attend the week-long nature camp held each year for all sixth graders. Nor did Punjabis join in the two overnight field trips organized each year for eighth graders, one to make plans for the year and the other an outing to San Francisco. Elementary and junior high principals noted, moreover, and with considerable frustration, that they could not even get Punjabis involved in the soccer league, 4-H, or Scouting.

In high school, where heavy involvement in extracurricular activities was the norm for Valleysiders, Punjabis were conspicuous for their absence. "Most of the clubs here are social types," one Punjabi student noted. "A lot of the clubs have dances and the parents say 'No dancing,'" another explained. Punjabis were also reluctant for their sons to play team sports at school. While they encouraged boys to be physically active and showered praise on good athletes, they believed varsity sports required too much time and too many trips away from home. In early fall and late spring, moreover, boys were often expected to help out with farm work after school.

[162]

Forces for Ethnic Enclavement

The more the schools pushed Punjabi students, especially girls, to take part in extracurricular activities and to make decisions on their own, the more closely Punjabi parents supervised their children's lives. Girls complained that even in Punjab there were more opportunities to mix with friends and participate in sports and social activities. As an example, one girl noted that in India she had been able to play field hockey for her school team, but that in Valleyside she could not. Another complained that in Valleyside she was not permitted to ride a bike, though in India she had. The Valleyside context, however, was different. In India not only were high schools segregated by sex, but in the villages all boys were like brothers, not potential mates. Everyone was known and everyone adhered to a common set of cultural standards. Parents had far less reason to worry that their children would get into trouble or be tempted to behave in ways considered inappropriate. The Valleyside setting required additional vigilance.

Many Valleyside Punjabis were wary of fellow Punjabis who had become westernized. Such individuals, especially if they were teachers, were perceived as a potentially dangerous influence and efforts were made to undermine their standing. When, for example, one Punjabi teacher had asked two Punjabi students, a boy and a girl, to shake hands following a disagreement, the girl's father complained: "Boys and girls, men and women, do not touch one another." Such was the animosity toward this teacher that members of the community pressured the high school for her dismissal. Others among the more westernized Punjabis living in Valleyside were the focus of similar controversies.

Peer pressure was another force for social conformity. Those who socialized too much with Valleysider classmates attracted gossip. "They say something like, 'Look at her. She thinks she's white,'" one senior, a girl born and raised in Valleyside, explained. She felt that she had been forced to choose between groups. Another second-generation student observed that peer pressure caused most Punjabis to stick with their own. "You don't want to be an outcast from your own people," she said.

Boys, too, commented on the pressures to pick between groups. It had not always been so, as one student explained: "It has to do with the size of the Indian community. . . . When there were not too many East

Indians here we had to socialize with the Anglos. Right now . . . the majority of East Indians at the high school, if you go around with the Anglos, will say, 'He's Anglo, or he thinks he's white. He's not one of us.' So there is pressure [now] to stay with us." This young man had both Punjabi and non-Punjabi friends. He believed it was possible to mix across ethnic lines without losing one's cultural identity and noted that he had benefited from so doing. He recognized, however, the pressures brought to bear by most parents and the community at large, as well as peers, to discourage too much social contact with non-Punjabis. He recognized, too, that boys had more opportunity to mix socially with Valleysiders than did girls.

In response to the question "Is it possible for a student to be accepted by non-Punjabis and Punjabis?" one girl replied:

A boy can and a girl can't. A girl can be willing to mix, but her parents must be willing to let her go out with American girls, at night or during the day, over to their house, have them come to our house. Our parents won't let this happen. Even my little sister—she's about ten years old—my parents don't want her to go next door to play with the neighbor's children. I can't mix with American kids. I'm ready to, but my parents won't let me. That's the whole thing.

Many of the Punjabi girls, especially those raised in Valleyside, were uncomfortable with the social separatism on the high school campus. Many said they wanted to mix more. They found it difficult to do so, however, given all the problems.

Punjabi parents in this study were not unmindful of the difficulties their children faced in school. But they chose to play down the problems, urging their children to get on with their studies and to ignore as best they could the hostile actions of those who pressured or oppressed them. Punjabi parents well realized that they, and their children, were operating from a position of weakness, and their response to prejudice stemmed from this realization. They adopted a deliberate and conscious strategy of putting education first, believing that a situation of response and counterresponse would only escalate the troubles and detract from their central purpose in sending their children to school. Punjabi Sikhs are not merely accommodative. Sikhs, throughout history, have shown their toughness and their willingness to stand firm in the face of abuse. There is a strong Sikh military tradition and outward symbols of it in religious and personal life. Sikh males, in

Valleyside no less than India, are instructed to defend their honor and that of family and community. This is at their cultural core. "Turn the other cheek once, twice," Sikhs say, "but the third time defend yourself." The current activist Sikh resistance in India, no less than the militant nationalism of California Sikhs earlier in this century (Juergensmeyer 1982; Singh 1966b), show the Sikhs' readiness to resist their oppressors, with force if necessary, when they feel no other means exist. There is, moreover, a growing awareness on the part of American-born Sikhs that accommodation to racism serves only to perpetuate the status quo.[9] It may be anticipated that newer arrivals will join with the second generation to actively resist racism if they find themselves barred from moving forward economically.

There was little agreement among Valleysiders and Punjabis regarding the causes of the problems or the solutions. Teachers tried to meet the needs of all their students but were hampered by their own beliefs that immigrant students should conform to the cultural standards of the majority group. The teachers' sense of powerlessness to alter the climate of prejudice stemmed in part from their conviction that cultural assimilation was the ultimate solution to the ethnic hostilities. They believed that Punjabi parents placed their children in a bind by discouraging their participation in all but the essential instructional activities, yet teachers seemed quite unaware of how they themselves contributed to the students' difficulties by promoting a definition of school success that hinged on participation in mainstream social activities. This preconception, coupled with the presumption that Punjabi ways were inappropriate in America, made even the most academically able Punjabi students seem social failures, unless, of course, they succumbed to conformist pressures.

Some tension was inevitable as Punjabis sought to maintain a separate identity and way of life, but the problems were greatly exacerbated by the social climate at the high school. Punjabi parents wanted their offspring to get along with majority-group students and to learn from them the skills they would need to be competitive in American society, but they were strongly opposed to cultural assimilation. The more, it seemed, that Valleysiders pressured Punjabi students to conform to majority ways, the more the Punjabi community pressured their young to limit contact with members of the majority group.

In spite of all the pressures and counterpressures, Punjabi students made every effort to meet the demands of the formal curriculum, only rarely refusing to comply with a teacher's demands or school regulations, and then only in matters perceived to affect family and community honor. This was true even though Punjabi students often found the values of the classroom incompatible with those advocated by their parents. The easy give and take between the sexes and between students and teachers, the emphasis on individual decision making and on asserting one's own ideas, and the underlying assumption that majority-group norms should prevail were examples of home-school discontinuities with which all Punjabi students had to contend and with which, in fact, they were successfully contending, by working out a multicultural modus vivendi.

Punjabis did not view compliance with school rules or doing what one must to succeed academically as symbols of majority-group conformity, and they rewarded those who excelled in school. Diligence in matters academic and the acceptance of school authority were not equated, in the Punjabi view, with "acting white" or "like the Americans." Furthermore, although Punjabi teenagers condemned peers who acted "like whites," they enjoyed American burgers, wore designer jeans, and, if they could possibly manage it, zoomed down a highway standing on the seat in an open Trans-Am.

[9]

Immigrant Minorities and Schooling: Some Implications

Education opens new worlds.

Punjabi folk saying

The Sikhs of Valleyside can be viewed as a special case, an exceedingly interesting one and worthy of documentation for this reason alone. They can also be viewed as one example of an immigrant minority group whose school-adaptation patterns can help shed light on two questions of pressing concern within the field of education. First, what are the problems faced by recently arrived immigrant students who have begun their schooling in another language, and how might they be alleviated? Second, why do immigrant youths often work harder and remain in school longer than nonimmigrants, both majority and minority? In particular, what is it that enables children of immigrants to overcome, to the degree that they do, the problems associated with low socioeconomic status, a home language other than English, and the prejudice and discrimination embedded in American society?

Punjabi children, both American-born and those who arrive in this country during their preschool years, do comparatively well in school and, by a number of different measures, are as successful in school as their majority-group classmates. *Their success, however, offers no cause for complacency.* All face substantial difficulties in school. All could do significantly better and enjoy their education much more were the barriers to their success eliminated or reduced. Newer arrivals, moreover, do far less well because the barriers in many cases simply prove too great to overcome. Some of these barriers lie beyond the purview of school officials, but others relate directly to matters of school policy and practice.

[167]

The Comparative Success of Immigrant Minorities

The comparative success of the American-educated Punjabi Sikhs and other immigrant minorities forces us to take a fresh look at some of our theories and assumptions regarding the school performance of minority students. Many of these theories have originated in an effort to explain minority failure and have been generated without sufficient attention to cases of minority success. They have been tested, for the most part, on involuntary or nonimmigrant minority populations. When applied to immigrant groups, particularly those that have demonstrated considerable success in transcending cultural discontinuities and the influences of low socioeconomic background, the theories are found wanting.

The Theory of Cultural Congruity

Students of Asian origin have been said to do better in school than involuntary minorities because of congruity or harmony between their cultural traditions and those of the white majority (Caudill and De Vos 1956; Kleinfeld 1979:127; Sanday, Boardman, and Davis 1976). The assumption is that because their own values and standards of behavior are embedded within the American system of education, Asian American youth have an edge over those minority students whose cultural traditions conflict with those of the majority group and, thus, the schools. In such a fashion Asian American school success is explained by the absence of the problems that have been identified as contributing to the poor school performance of many involuntary minority youngsters.

Other researchers, pointing to areas of strong conflict between traditional Asian values and those of the dominant white majority take exception to the cultural compatibility explanation of Asian success (Sue and Sue 1971). The Punjabi example has provided further evidence of such conflicts. In fact, newly arrived Punjabi immigrants face far more situations of cultural discontinuity in school than nonimmigrant minorities who have been exposed to the majority culture for generations.

The Theory of Anglo Conformity

A related explanation for Asian American school success points to Anglo or majority-group conformity (Sanday, Boardman, and Davis

1976:87). Asian Americans themselves note that cultural assimilation is the price exacted by the white majority for upward mobility within American society and that their educational and economic success, to the degree that it exists, must be weighed against its cost in lost identity (Chun 1980; Kim 1975:58). Punjabis, too, feel the intense pressure to Americanize, particularly in school. They try to find ways to meet the demands and expectations of Valleysider peers and teachers, but their adaptation strategy is far from conformist.

Punjabis, as we have seen, resist assimilationist pressures. They refuse, for example, to join in most nonessential school activities. The more the schools pressure them to conform, the more tightly their parents supervise and restrict their behavior. Peer pressure comes into play. The price of assimilation is high; few teenagers will risk being ridiculed by fellow Punjabis for socializing too freely with white peers.

The Theory of Cultural Discontinuities

While compatibility between home and school cultures has been represented as contributing strongly to success in school, discontinuity and conflict between the two settings have been seen as impeding classroom learning. Clearly, those who come to school lacking the skills and values required for educational success are at a disadvantage compared to those who arrive in school already possessing such skills. However, the theory of cultural discontinuities fails to explain the considerable success evidenced by immigrant minority youngsters of working-class and non-English-speaking backgrounds in competing academically with white, middle-class peers.

In analyzing the impact of cultural differences on school performance, it is useful to distinguish between the formal curriculum and the informal curriculum. Punjabi teenagers, as we have seen, are more comfortable with the formal authority structure of the school than are many Valleysiders, but they are far less comfortable with the informal curriculum. The easy give and take of the American classroom, the importance given to coeducational activities, the general informality of the instructional process, and the emphasis on independent decision making and preparation for life "on your own" cause many difficulties for Punjabi students, but they do not result in poor school performance. Rather, these very differences provide partial explanation for their academic success.

[169]

Theories of Immigrant Ethnic Enterprise

Research on the economic adaptation patterns of immigrant minorities has identified a number of situational factors that, in interaction with cultural and contextual variables, promote a high frequency of entrepreneurship (Boissevain and Grotenbreg 1986; Bonacich and Modell 1980; Lieberson 1980; Light 1984; Nee and Wong 1985; Turner and Bonacich 1980; Wilson and Portes 1980). I have focused on three major situational factors, all prominent in the literature, which interact with elements of the Punjabi Jat Sikh culture and with general characteristics of U.S. society. These are, first, the Punjabis' relative sense of satisfaction with life in the United States, second, a high degree of family and communal solidarity, and third, a strong orientation toward India and Punjab, which, together with their custom of endogamous arranged marriages, helps to sustain a Punjabi Jat Sikh identity and culture from one generation to the next, even in overseas settings.

I have shown how these factors work together in the Valleyside setting not only to promote economic enterprise but, similarly, to promote educational enterprise. The Punjabis' success in school appears to stem less from cultural attributes per se or from conformity to the majority culture than from diligence and persistence in their schoolwork, combined with a strategy of accommodation and acculturation without assimilation. While the parent generation tends more toward accommodation and the student generation more toward acculturation, both agree that proficiency in majority-group ways will enhance the younger generation's ability to get ahead in American society. Both generations concur, moreover, in their desire to maintain a separate Punjabi identity. Their strategy is one of *multilinear acculturation* in which young people acquire competence in the dominant culture of this country while also maintaining their primary social identification within the Punjabi group. I shall return to this point presently.

Valleyside Sikhs as a Special Case

The Punjabi Sikhs' strategy stems in part from their experiences in pluralistic India, a country where seventeen major languages are spoken and where all schoolchildren routinely study Hindi and English in addition to their provincial language. Sikhs also have a distinct and self-conscious history, replete with heroes, martyrs, and religious leaders,

[170]

and they have effective institutions for preserving, honoring, and teaching this history. They have, moreover, long experience as a minority group and have well-developed strategies for maintaining their ethnic and religious identity within a heterogeneous, competitive, and highly stratified society. They are an example of what Edward Spicer has termed an enduring or persistent people (1971, 1980; see also Castile 1981).

Even though they are in actual fact simple rustics, low skilled and with little formal education, they call themselves *sardar;* each one is a "leader" in a sense endowed with rich historical connotations. Their strong and positive sense of cultural identity, even superiority, protects them to some extent from pressures to Americanize. Their high self-esteem and self-confidence also help to shield them from the most negative effects of prejudice and discrimination (see Parekh 1983:114). Although subordinated by the white majority, these Punjabi immigrants do not perceive themselves a dominated or subordinated group.

Among the new wave of immigrants—those who have arrived in the United States since 1965—few have settled in rural America. The Valleyside setting thus is itself a special one in the context of recent American immigration. Punjabi immigrants have come from one farming community to another. It is, as they say, like moving from home into a home. Even with limited job and English skills, they are able to find immediate, albeit low-wage and back-breaking, employment. Teenagers, too, can work alongside their parents during the summer months. Punjabi teenagers and their families, furthermore, are to a large degree spared the hardships faced by many minorities, who must settle in inner-city ghettos beset by problems of gang violence, drugs, high unemployment, and the anomie of street life. Such problems inevitably compound the difficulties faced by minority youngsters in American society.

Nor do Valleyside Punjabis face the problems that often accompany residential segregation, where minority and poor white students end up in separate schools, frequently inferior to those serving middle-class peers. All students in Valleyside attend a common high school. All have the same teachers. Although students are tracked in some of their subject areas, the teachers are not similarly sorted, with more gifted instructors assigned to more gifted or privileged students. Nor is discipline a major problem at Valleyside High, as it is in all too many urban schools today. Rich and poor, majority and minority receive essentially the same instruction.

Asian Americans are said to do well academically, in part at least,

[171]

because of cultural traditions that promote success in school. Such a case may certainly be made for Valleyside Punjabis. Cultural and religious values, together with the particular nature of the Valleyside setting, help Sikhs adapt to the demands of their new environment and overcome many of the hardships they encounter in school. These forces alone, however, are insufficient explanation for the educational achievements of Punjabi students raised from early childhood in this country. While Punjabi Sikh children in Valleyside persist in school longer than white American peers, there is no strong pattern of school persistence among rural Punjabis, even of the Jat caste. Within our core sample of forty-five Punjabi high school seniors, more than three-quarters persisted with their education to the community college level and well over one-third of the boys went on to pursue a four-year degree.[1] This represents a radical shift within a single generation.

Punjabi students were confident that they would find employment far more to their liking than their parents' occupations. Further research is needed to determine how successful these Punjabis are in achieving their occupational goals, but research on Punjabi Sikhs in Britain indicates a significant degree of upward socioeconomic mobility occurring within a single generation (Ballard 1986; Bhachu 1985b; Brown 1984; Gibson and Bhachu 1986).[2] In 1979 South Asian–born students in Britain held 6.2 percent of all first-year university places in medicine and other medical-related subjects, even though they constituted only 2.9 percent of their age cohort (Ballard and Vellins 1985; Vellins 1982).[3] While 61 percent of the white students gaining places in medical school came from a professional or managerial social class background, only 36 percent of the South Asian parents held professional or managerial jobs. The British data suggest not only that Asian Indian students are highly successful academically but that they are better able to transcend class barriers than whites (Ballard and Vellins 1985). Ballard observes: "Sheer persistence *does* produce results, however adverse the odds."

In America there are a great many more employment opportunities for women as well as men and for persons of all educational levels than in India (or even in Britain). Employment in this country, furthermore, is more open than in India, and Punjabi immigrants believe that, regardless of their minority status, their children will have greater chance to compete for jobs based on their skills and credentials than is the case in India. In such an environment, formal education has far more practical value than in Punjab. Schooling, furthermore, is far more readily available and generally of a much higher quality than in rural India. In Valleyside, children can attend high school and even community college without leaving home.

Punjabi Sikhs welcome, too, our egalitarian values, the overall fairness of our institutions, and the laws safeguarding individual rights. Their ability to shrug off prejudice and discrimination, to the extent that they do, must be understood in comparative light. Most Valleyside Sikhs do not view the prejudice and discrimination they experience as a threat to their livelihood or their identity. Although they are troubled by the hostility, particularly as it impinges on the lives of their children, they see no advantage to be gained, at this point, from escalating into more open conflict.

The Punjabis' response to prejudice in this country is influenced not only by their experiences in India but also by their status as immigrants. Because they consider themselves better off here than back in India or, for that matter, in most other countries where Sikhs have settled, they are more willing than indigenous and other involuntary minorities to minimize the impact of the prejudice. They maintain a positive attitude toward America and white Americans.

The Valleyside Sikhs are a special case, but they are only one among many immigrant minorities that have responded in a similar fashion to the hostility of the majority group. They are but one example of an immigrant minority that has exhibited a high degree of enterprise in both economic and educational spheres. They are but one example of a minority group that has pursued accommodation and acculturation without total assimilation.[4] And they are but one case of an immigrant group that has demonstrated considerable success in using formal education as an avenue to middle-class occupational status.

The Immigrant School-Adaptation Pattern

There is mounting evidence that immigrant youths of working-class and language-minority backgrounds do comparatively well in school, if they receive all their schooling in their new homeland. In many cases they do better academically and persist in school longer than native-born majority-group peers of similar class backgrounds or, frequently, even of the middle class. So pronounced is their success in using schooling as an avenue to higher socioeconomic status that one must question the applicability to immigrant minorities of theories of social

[173]

and cultural reproduction (Bourdieu 1974; Bowles and Gintis 1976; Willis 1977). According to these theories, schooling helps reproduce class status. For many immigrant groups, however, just the reverse appears true. Schooling provides the avenue to middle-class status for children of working-class backgrounds. Greeks in Australia, Italians in Canada, South Asians in Britain, and Central Americans in the United States are such examples. Researchers have documented similar examples among Japanese and East European Jewish immigrants to the United States in the early decades of the twentieth century (Cohen 1970; Sowell 1986; Tyack 1974).

Comparative ethnographic research points to an immigrant school-response pattern that appears to contribute directly to success in school. Not all immigrant groups share this pattern, because of differences in their histories and current circumstances—a point I will return to—but enough do that the pattern merits examination. Many of the studies of immigrant minorities have focused on students of Asian origin, contributing to the stereotype of Asian Americans as a "model minority." Yet the pattern here described is characteristic not only of many Asian Americans, including Valleyside Punjabis, but of non-Asian immigrant groups as well (Blakely 1983; De Vos 1983; Gibson 1983c; Guthrie 1985; Lee 1984; Matute-Bianchi 1986; Peng et al. 1984; Suarez-Orozco 1986; Sung 1979; Tsang and Wing 1985).

Educational and Occupational Aspirations

Immigrants, on the whole, have higher educational and occupational aspirations than indigenous groups, majority as well as minority, and are more determined to use education as a strategy for upward social mobility than nonimmigrants of comparable class background. Immigrant parents and children assume that education can enhance opportunities to compete for jobs. High expectations and assumptions about the value of schooling appear to have far more impact on the immigrant child's decision to persist in school than either family background or actual school performance.

Effort and Persistence over Innate Ability

Not only do immigrant parents expect their children to do well in school, they are more likely than majority parents to assume that effort is the key to school success. Majority-group parents and teachers, on the other hand, including many of those interviewed in Valleyside, are more likely to believe that academic achievement is largely a matter of innate ability. Such an assumption erodes students' incentive to work hard.[5] In keeping with their view that effort will be rewarded, immigrants invest more time and energy in their schooling than nonimmigrants, whether majority or minority. They devote more hours to homework and are less likely than indigenous students to shy away from classes they find difficult. They assume not only that education requires hard work but that it is effort well invested. So strong is their conviction that there will be some return for their labor, that they persist in school almost regardless of their ability. Anticipated rewards, moreover, may extend beyond strictly economic ones into such areas as the enhancement of family reputation and the arrangement of more advantageous marriages.

Many immigrant minority youngsters, whether American-born or recently arrived, face substantial barriers to their success in school. Limited English skills, racial hostility, home-school cultural differences, and the pressure to conform are problems common to many immigrants. Newcomers generally suffer most, and for many the impact is severe. In spite of their difficulties, however, immigrants typically complete more years of schooling than nonimmigrants. Comparative research in Australia, Britain, and Canada points to similar patterns of school persistence among immigrant groups.

Respect for Teachers

Teachers, for the most part, like teaching immigrant students because they appear to have a sense of purpose and direction. Their attendance and general classroom behavior are exemplary. They are respectful of their elders and cause few problems. They comply with school regulations and teachers' requests. They play by the rules set forth by those in authority, even when they may feel these rules work to their disadvantage.

Immigrant parents instill in their children a respect for teachers and will discipline their young if they find that they have misbehaved or not been properly attentive or courteous. Most immigrant pupils, in keeping with their parents' attitudes, appear to hold teachers in high regard, and this deference may well give them an advantage in the classroom. Teachers respond positively to those who show them respect and appear eager to learn. Students who respect their teachers may also be more receptive to their instruction than classmates who do not hold their instructors in similar high regard or who feel themselves to be the victims of discrimination.[6] Many studies show that the micropolitics of the classroom impinge directly on the teaching-learning processes. In some situations, although such a pattern is infrequent among immigrants, students simply refuse to learn from the teacher (Erickson 1984; Gibson 1982; Giroux 1983; Kramer 1983; McDermott and Gospodinoff 1979; Willis 1977).

Family and Community Forces

Home and community play major roles in shaping the school-adaptation patterns of immigrant students. Children of recent immigrants often feel intense pressure to do well academically and to accept the authority of the school, even when they are made to feel uncomfortable by its rules. Their success, they are told, will justify the sacrifices their parents have made. And, as we have seen in the Punjabi case, both positive and negative sanctions work together to produce academic success.

Children are taught, furthermore, that responsibility for success or failure in school rests with the individual. If they do poorly, they are told they have no one to blame but themselves. They did not work hard enough. "Those who wish to learn, will learn," Punjabis say. "If the child does not wish to learn, then what can the teacher do?" Although family and community support are critical ingredients in school success, it is, the parents recognize, the individual student who must exert the effort. Parents recognize, too, that not all children are interested in schoolwork or especially good at it. From their perspective, there is little point in keeping such a child in school.

Parental Involvement in Schooling

Many immigrant parents, like those in the present study, are directly and strongly involved in assuring that their children have a positive response to their schooling. Teachers notice this and credit the parents for their children's academic achievements. Curiously, however, many immigrant parents, particularly those who themselves have

[176]

little formal education and do not speak English, do few of the things that researchers and educators commonly equate with parental involvement in education.

Punjabi parents who have little or no formal education are unable to help with their children's homework or even to read to their children at home. Few of the parents in the present case ever visited the schools unless expressly requested to attend because their child was having a problem. Nor did they volunteer for any of the myriad activities that seem to be the mainstay of public elementary schools in middle-class neighborhoods in this country today.

The pattern is not unusual to the Punjabis. It is a familiar one in many parts of the world where parents see no need to intervene directly in what they see as the school's business and the teacher's authority and expertise. It is standard among recently arrived immigrants in this country. These parents adopt what may be characterized as a noninterventionist strategy (Bhachu 1985b), which, this study and others would seem to indicate, can be as effective as its opposite. Nevertheless, it is the latter, an interventionist strategy, that educators and researchers generally equate with school success.

Educators frequently assume that minority parents, immigrant and nonimmigrant alike, need to be encouraged to emulate the interventionist strategies of middle-class, mainstream Americans. It is supposed that adoption of the mainstream model will help solve the problems faced in school by lower-class and minority children even though many poor and minority children actually do quite well in school without interventionist parents. There is evidence, moreover, that "dramatic changes in children's academic progress" occur when parents who otherwise feel alienated from the schools are given a sense of empowerment. Cummins explains the relationship: "When educators involve minority parents as partners in their children's education, parents appear to develop a sense of efficacy that communicates itself to children, with positive academic consequences" (1986:26). Such findings are extremely encouraging. We need to be cautious, however, about their generalizability or applicability to all minority groups and subgroups. If school programs are so structured that parental intervention becomes a prerequisite for student success, we may actually penalize children with noninterventionist parents. For example, if homework is set up in such a way that parents must take an active part in its accomplishment, the children of poorly educated or non-English-speaking parents may be penalized. If the mainstream middle-class

[177]

model is imposed on these families, it may actually become more difficult for their children to use schooling as an avenue for upward mobility. No single model of parent and family participation in the educational process can fit all groups.

The Role of the Peer Group

There is increasing evidence that the peer group can act as a force for resistance to school authority (De Vos 1982:112; Erickson and Mohatt 1982; Gibson 1982; Giroux 1983; Philips 1983; Willis 1977), but among immigrant students the peer group more frequently serves to reinforce a positive school-adaptation pattern and to support compliance with school norms. Some minority students find it difficult to conform to school demands while gaining and maintaining peer respect. Their peer subculture exerts strong pressure not to accept school rules and identifies those who conform to classroom demands as "acting white" or "acting Anglo" (Fordham and Ogbu 1986; Matute-Bianchi 1986). While Punjabi teenagers exert direct pressure on one another not to act white, they do not view acceptance of teacher authority as white behavior. No Punjabi teenager ever complained of being labeled white or Anglo for going along with school rules or for excelling academically. Quite the reverse. Punjabi students often tease one another for poor grades or inappropriate school behavior. We need further comparative research on the role of the peer group in shaping school-adaptation patterns.

Teachers' Expectations and Immigrant Success

There is much evidence to show a strong relationship between teachers' expectations and students' actual performance. In Valleyside, too, high school teachers had very different expectations for fast- and slow-tract students, and they tailored their instruction in accordance with their expectations. Teachers' views undoubtedly influence their treatment of students, and in turn, this treatment to a certain extent influences students' performance.

This relationship has often been cited to help explain the poor performance of some minority students (Leacock 1968; Mercer 1973; Rosenthal and Jacobson 1968; Rist 1970; Rosenfeld 1971; Sieber 1978)

[178]

and, likewise, to explain the high achievement of others (Troike 1984; Wong 1980). While teachers' expectations undoubtedly do affect students' performance in school, in both positive and negative ways, their behavior is not the basic cause for the disparities that emerge between various minority groups and subgroups (Leacock 1982:47). Teacher expectations and prejudices are only one of the many forces shaping school-adaptation patterns and, in the Punjabi case, do not appear as critical as home, community, and peer forces.

A similar finding emerged from my research in St. Croix. Many of the native Crucian teachers viewed immigrant West Indians, "aliens" in the teachers' terminology, as an economic and social threat to Crucian interests. They were firmly opposed to admitting alien children into the public schools and did so only under court order. They described the immigrant West Indians as "overage, underprepared, and ruining the schools." Yet these very children, males in particular, had more successful school-adaptation patterns than their native-born Crucian male counterparts. The immigrants received better grades, were far more likely to be assigned to the fast track in junior high and, in the case of the males, were far more likely to persist in school than their Crucian peers (Gibson 1983c). The Crucian students' own explanations for these disparities were that the immigrants worked harder and were more willing to accept teacher authority.

We need to study not only how teachers' expectations of students are formed but also how students' expectations of teachers are formed. Much of the literature points to teachers' behavior as a major, perhaps the major, causal factor for minority students' resistance to learning. We need also to explore the role of peer, family, and community forces in shaping students' expectations about teachers and schooling and students' behavior in the classroom, for students' behavior shapes teachers' expectations as well as the reverse. Most Valleyside teachers have little understanding or appreciation of Punjabi culture, and many harbor negative attitudes toward Punjabis as a group. At the same time, they respect the Punjabis' industry in the classroom, welcome their respect, and have generally high expectations for their performance.

The situation is clearly a dynamic one and merits additional research on intergroup differences and on the variations within a single ethnic group. Peer subcultures exert a major influence on school adaptation (Matute-Bianchi 1986; Troyna 1978). We need, in particular, to know more about why some minority students associate with peers who advocate resistance to teacher authority, while other student subgroups from the same ethnic group are more willing to accept teacher-established rules for classroom behavior.

Coping with Racial and Ethnic Hostility

Immigrant minority parents, especially those recently arrived, Punjabis included, rarely blame the school system or the teachers if their children experience academic difficulty, even when their children are subjected to ethnic and racial hostility. It was the Punjabi parents' perception that in class teachers treat all children alike. The Punjabi students generally concurred, although they were disturbed by the teachers' inability or unwillingness to discipline majority-group students who were actively hostile toward Punjabis, and they were frustrated by teachers' lack of attention to creating a climate where understanding rather than prejudice was the norm.

First-generation immigrant adults, no less than more established minorities, are deeply concerned about the impact of racial and ethnic prejudice on their children. But their response to prejudice is tempered by their relative satisfaction with life in America, their past experiences in other countries, and their recognition that they have little power to alter the situation. Their strategy of playing down racism is also intended to avoid open conflict with the majority group and the ill will they fear it would engender. A situation of response and counterresponse, in the Punjabi view, would only distract their children from their studies.

The Relationship between Schooling and Jobs

Immigrant minorities often recognize that they do not enjoy the same opportunities in the job market as members of the majority group. They also recognize that educational credentials can only enhance their chances in competing for employment, and statistics bear them out. Minorities generally earn less than white Americans with comparable years of schooling (U.S. Bureau of the Census 1984c). Within each group, however, income increases as years of schooling increase (D. Taylor 1981; Young 1983). College graduates can expect to earn more than high school graduates. There is, in other words, a monetary return for remaining in school. Unemployment also decreases as education increases, although, again, the return for education is not equal across groups. Unemployment continues to be higher for minorities than for white Americans, much higher among black Americans under age twenty-five, even when years of schooling are held constant.[7]

While native-born Americans, both majority and minority, often take free public education, well-prepared teachers, and well-equipped schools for granted, immigrants, depending on their prior experiences, may see these in a very different light. Immigrants, on the whole, value the relative openness and fairness of American institutions, including the schools, however imperfect they may be. They welcome the opportunity to compete in school and at work on the basis of objective criteria, even if the system promises greater fairness than it delivers. When immigrant minorities encounter discrimination in the workplace, they do not always evaluate their situation in racial or ethnic terms. They may assume they were passed over because they are foreigners or because of their inferior education and training. They may also note that discrimination is far worse in other countries.

The immigrants' comparative frame of reference and relative satisfaction with life in America influences their perspectives on the educational and economic opportunities in this country. Immigrants compare their new situation to the one left behind. While indigenous minority groups tend to focus on the persistent inequalities within American society and problems embedded within our system, immigrants see America as providing far greater opportunities than those available to them in the old country, or in most other parts of the world. For a generation or two at least, they also use different criteria to evaluate economic success, judging their progress in comparison to other members of their ethnic group. Family income may be small in comparison to that of the white middle class, but as they see it, they earn far more than relatives in the homeland. They anticipate, moreover, an even brighter future, if not for themselves, then for their children, and there are role models in the group to prove it. Nonimmigrant minorities, on the other hand, along with better-educated and better-established members of immigrant minorities, tend more frequently to associate success with parity and to note that minority groups in this country clearly have yet to achieve parity.

Perceptions of opportunity, as well as perceptions of discrimination, appear to have a strong influence on minority response patterns. Why

[181]

some groups give more emphasis to the opportunities available in this country, while other groups give greater attention to the persistence of discrimination within the society, relates, research would suggest, to the historical context of the contact between the minority and majority groups (Lieberson 1980).

Future Generations

Throughout this book I have focused on first-generation immigrants. Future generations will see their situation differently. In the Punjabi case they will not have such close ties to India or the firsthand experience of living in Punjab. Even within a single generation, values and attitudes are changing rapidly. Children raised from early childhood in America, although foreign-born, have little memory of the old country and no similar comparative perspective to draw on in forming opinions about life in America. Even more different are the experiences and perspectives of the second and third generations. Their attitudes about American culture, white Americans, ethnic relations, education, and the opportunities available to them differ sharply from those of recent arrivals.

School-performance patterns now emerging indicate that second-generation Punjabi students will accommodate themselves to the demands of the classroom and perform well academically. Not all will excel scholastically, and some may well be influenced by an American peer subculture that places little emphasis on academic diligence and persistence, but the group pattern, it may be anticipated, will be one of educational success. Increasing numbers of the next generation will pursue advanced professional and technical training, females as well as males. British research on second-generation Punjabi Jat settlers, as well as the American research on second- and third-generation Chinese and Japanese Americans, plus the latest census data on urbanized Asian Indians, support such an expectation.

The next generation of Valleyside Punjabis will also have an easier time in school because their parents will be more westernized, urbanized, and educated. More parents will be familiar with the American system of education and fluent in English, thus making it somewhat more likely that they will assume an interventionist strategy of parental involvement in education. Such is the case in Britain (Bhachu 1985b). More of the children will enter school already fluent in English. Pun-

[182]

jabi children growing up in Valleyside will also have more role models who are products of the American educational system and who hold a wide variety of jobs; thus, their course selections in high school will range more widely.

The next generation of Punjabis will also continue, I predict, to pursue a strategy of acculturation without assimilation. There will be variation within the group, some few withdrawing from the Punjabi community altogether, others resisting as best they can many of the forces for acculturation. As a group, however, they, and their parents, will be more comfortable about mixing with non-Punjabis and participating in school activities. Like their British counterparts, most will maintain strong roots within the Punjabi community and will continue to accept marriages arranged by their parents, although with increasing voice in these arrangements.

A shift may also be anticipated in the area of minority-majority relations. As more Punjabis become acculturated to the dominant American culture, they will encounter fewer frictions with the majority group, but they will also be less likely to turn the other cheek to those they do encounter (Portes, Parker, and Cobas 1980; see also Portes and Bach 1985).

Minority Status and School Performance

Although immigrant minorities do well in school more frequently than indigenous and other involuntary minorities, there are clear variations within and among groups. Not all immigrant groups do equally well, and some have poor academic records and exhibit few of the characteristics I have depicted as an immigrant school-adaptation pattern. In Britain, for example, clear distinctions emerge among the various groups of South Asians, with East African Indians—Muslims, Sikhs and Hindus—meeting with a notably high degree of academic success and the Bangladeshis, the Pakistani Mirpuris, and the Bhattra Sikhs doing significantly less well in school. The academic performance of West Indian students in Britain, moreover, falls far short of national norms (Swann Committee 1985; M. Taylor 1981; Tomlinson 1983). Studies show similarly poor academic performance among Turkish children in West Germany (Castles 1984; Skutnabb-Kangas 1981) and Finnish students in Sweden (Paulston 1982:40; Skutnabb-Kangas 1979). Yet my own fieldwork in the U.S. Virgin Islands showed West

[183]

Indian migrants to be doing comparatively well academically, and far better, in the case of boys, than the native West Indian population (Gibson 1982, 1983c). There are also studies indicating that children of Turkish and Finnish origin in Australia may be doing better in school than their immigrant counterparts in Germany and Sweden, although age on arrival proves a critical variable (Inglis and Manderson n.d.; Troike 1984:50).

Recent evidence also suggests that age on arrival is important in the German case. The Turkish children who begin their schooling in Germany at a young age do significantly better academically than those who start their German schooling at an older age (Mehrlander 1986). Most of the Turkish families now settled in Germany came originally as guest workers not permanent immigrants. Many left their smaller children in Turkey, arranging for them to come to Germany in their late primary or early secondary years. Upon entering schools in Germany they faced many of the problems described for Punjabi newcomers of similar age in Valleyside: home-school cultural discontinuities, no proficiency in the dominant language, and a high degree of prejudice on the part of the native white population. The West German government, furthermore, not only segregated the Turkish students from their German peers but operated on the assumption that these young people, like their parents, were temporary residents and would soon be returning to Turkey. Neither the German government nor the migrant families themselves made the learning of German or proficiency in the dominant culture a priority.

In Australia, on the other hand, both the societal context and the immigrants' situation within it are different. Turkish families come not as guest workers but as settlers, and they therefore recognize the necessity for their children to master English and become skilled in the ways of the Anglo-Australian majority. The policies of the Australian educational system, moreover, promote both the acquisition of English as a second language and support for cultural differences (Inglis 1986).

The specific nature of the relationship to the dominant group plays a critical role for immigrants, no less than for nonimmigrant minorities. So, too, do the immigrants' folk beliefs about the probable return for investing time and effort in schooling. The Bhattra Sikh settlers in Britain do not generally view schooling as a means to economic and social mobility and, typically, place less pressure on their children to excel academically than do Jat Sikh families (see Ghuman 1980). The clash between cultures is also more extreme for some immigrant groups than others. Many Muslim families in Britain refuse to permit

[184]

their adolescent daughters to attend coeducational institutions and have exerted strong pressures on their local school districts to continue single-sex secondary schools. Some Mirpuri immigrants, fearful of the influence of Western values on their children's development, send their teenage children back to Pakistan to ensure that they receive a proper Muslim and Pakistani-style education.[8]

Comparative research on the school-adaptation patterns of various immigrant groups in various settings and situations will yield further insight into the interrelationship among cultural, contextual, and situational variables and contribute to our emerging theories about why minority students, both immigrant and nonimmigrant, perform in school as they do. Existing research suggests, however, that minority groups that have experienced and continue to experience disproportionate school failure are generally those that have also experienced long histories of subjugation and degradation at the hands of the dominant group in the host society (Ogbu 1978, 1983). The Finns in Sweden are such a case. Yet when a formerly dominated group migrates to a new country, patterns of school success may emerge, as is the case among Finns in Australia (see Troike 1984). The West Indian immigrants in St. Croix provide another example of this type.

The West Indian Case

In the mid-1970s, when I carried out fieldwork in St. Croix, immigrant British West Indians constituted about 40 percent of the student population within the island's public schools, native Crucians 30 percent, and students of Puerto Rican origin (both immigrants and second generation) another 30 percent. The Crucian and British West Indian students were of similar racial, cultural, and class background. They shared, furthermore, a common historical experience of slavery and a continued dependence on a colonial power. All were black, all lower class. Recent immigrant status was the one significant variable that distinguished British West Indians from Crucians. Yet in school performance the two groups differed sharply, although gender differences emerged as an important variable as well. More of the girls in both groups finished high school than boys.[9] But immigrant girls did somewhat better academically and had a higher rate of school persistence than native girls. And immigrant boys did far better on all measures of school success than native-born males.

Ethnographic data strongly suggested that the students' school-ad-

[185]

aptation patterns were shaped not only by the objective realities of their subordinate position and unequal opportunities but also by their subjective evaluation of their status and chances to get ahead in society. The native males described manual labor as "slave work" (Gibson 1976), just as West Indian youths in Britain have been found to reject jobs that they perceive to be the "shit end" of the labor market (Brake 1980:133). Lacking the educational qualifications for skilled positions and refusing to accept work they consider degrading, many of these youths, in St. Croix and in Britain, opt instead for unemployment. The immigrant West Indian males in St. Croix, however, welcomed the economic opportunities available in this American territory, including jobs requiring hard physical labor (Gibson 1983c).

The response patterns of each group had been shaped not only by their historical experience of slavery and colonization but also by their particular situations in the host society and their relationship to the dominant white group. The West Indians who migrate to St. Croix— locally called "Down Islanders"—come because of depressed economic conditions back home in the formerly British West Indies. They see in St. Croix, one of the three major islands that make up the American Virgin Islands, a chance to get ahead both educationally and economically. In their home islands schooling was neither universally available nor free. In the mid-1970s, moreover, it was not uncommon for a Down Islander refinery worker to be earning ten to fifteen times what he could have back home in Antigua or St. Lucia, had he any work at all. Much like the Punjabis in Valleyside, the Down Islanders in St. Croix were willing to endure the host society's prejudice and discrimination so long as they were not cut off from educational and economic advancement.

While many young Crucian males of lower-class background had come to view both white "Continentals" (persons from the mainland United States) and members of the Crucian middle and upper classes as their oppressors, the Down Islanders bore no comparable grudges. It made little difference whether the Down Islanders were permanent residents or temporary workers.[10] In their view, the opportunities for schooling and for jobs were far greater in the U.S. Virgin Islands than in their native islands. The Crucians, however, felt increasingly threatened by the encroachment of outsiders—Continentals, Puerto Ricans, and Down Islanders—into nearly every segment of the local economy. Although proud of their American citizenship, they were acutely aware of their dependency on the United States and their inability to determine their own affairs. Laws governing the flow of aliens into St. Croix,

[186]

permanent residents and guest workers alike, were set in Washington, not locally. The Continentals, furthermore, like the Haoles before them in Hawaii, felt that they had every right not only to establish residence in the territory but to open the island to the American tourist trade and to their other lucrative business interests.[11]

During the early 1970s, as economic competition mounted, natives increasingly referred to Down Islanders as "aliens," or even "garots," treated them rudely, and accused them of stealing the island's resources.[12] For the Crucians, too, there was a growing resentment toward Continentals bred from the island's status as an "unincorporated territory" of the United States. The Down Islanders, as newcomers and outsiders, felt far less oppressed by the island's political status and social structure than did the lower-class natives.

The differing situations and perceptions of the immigrant and native groups in St. Croix were reflected in students' school response patterns. At school, the immigrant males found it easier to accept the authority of their Crucian and Continental teachers than did Crucian males. "Teachers like aliens," one Crucian teenage boy told me, "because they can get them to do what they say—kiss their asses" (Gibson 1983c:188). Teachers, he said, tried to get Crucian students to comply with school authority but could not "get away with it." Classroom observation supported his views (Gibson 1982).

The oppositional behavior exhibited by the Crucian males is strikingly similar to that of "the lads" in Britain (Willis 1977). It also appears to resemble that of many West Indians in British schools. The parents and grandparents of these young West Indians migrated to England from the Caribbean, but their geographic relocation did not free them from their historical relationship with their white British colonizers. They came expecting a new beginning, but instead, they found themselves subordinated by the same dominant group that had once enslaved their ancestors. For generations whites in Britain have defined black West Indians as inferior. Their situation, thus, is more like that of an involuntary minority group, such as blacks in the United States, than that of voluntary immigrants. This historical reality affects the way the white British treat black West Indians, and it also influences the West Indian response (Allen 1971:7). Many West Indian youths in Britain today feel that in order to survive they must resist white authority both within the schools and in the larger society (Mullard 1982:131). The situation of response and counterresponse has a direct impact on West Indian students' academic performance.

Not all West Indian youths, however, become absorbed into a peer subculture that emphasizes resistance to school authority. In a high school where he carried out fieldwork, Barry Troyna (1978) distinguished three different perspectives and adaptation patterns, which he labeled "mainstreamer," "compromiser" and "rejector." The mainstreamers did well in school and sought to acquire skills in the dominant culture. To do so, however, they had to disassociate themselves from the oppositional features of the West Indian community and from their peers in lower academic tracks—the rejectors. Troyna notes that the rejectors felt alienated from mainstream society and strongly believed that racism in Britain prevented them from getting ahead. The *"perception* of racism and discrimination as salient restraints of life chances" was, according to Troyna, the most significant factor in shaping the students' reactions to their schooling and to life in Britain generally (406, emphasis original). Ethnographic research among adolescents of Mexican descent points to a similar relationship between school performance and students' perceptions of racism and discrimination.

The Mexican American Case

By all measures of school success the Valleyside Mexican Americans *as a group* did less well than either the Punjabis or the Valleysiders. Yet a subgroup of Mexican Americans were among the top students in the high school. A number of recent studies explore the variations in Mexican American perceptions and performance. Sylvia Valverde (1987), in a controlled comparison of high school graduates and dropouts, found that a higher percentage of the graduates were immigrants from Mexico, while more of the dropouts were native-born. She also found that more of the dropouts than graduates spoke English as their first language, or were classified as fluent-English-proficient. In other words, the immigrants persisted in school in spite of their language handicap. Both groups of students were from families of low income and low educational background. Valverde's conclusion was that the peer group played a primary role in shaping the differing school-adaptation patterns.

In another comparative study of immigrant *Mexicanos* and native-born Mexican Americans, Harriet Romo (1984) found sharp differences in the way families perceived the school experiences of their children and once again, the immigrant families had far more positive attitudes toward the U.S. school system. The *Mexicanos*, in general, like many other immigrant groups, believed an American education and proficiency in English would provide the avenue to a better life for their children. The second-generation U.S.-born Chicano family, on the other hand, had "acquired heightened sensitivity to subordination and discrimination" which, according to Romo, had resulted in alienation from the schools and skepticism of school encounters. Both sets of parents were unskilled workers, although the Chicano parents had some secondary education and spoke both English and Spanish, while the immigrant *Mexicanos* spoke only Spanish and were usually illiterate. *Mexicanos*, moreover, were residing in the United States without benefit of legal status and were constantly worried about avoiding apprehension by immigration authorities.

Maria Matute-Bianchi has found similar disparities in both perceptions and performance between Mexican immigrants and native-born students, but she has also documented sharp differences within the native-born group itself relating to differing perceptions of discrimination. Students who identify themselves as Chicanos are more likely to perceive a high degree of discrimination and to feel alienated from mainstream society than those who identify themselves as Mexican Americans and *Mexicanos* (Matute-Bianchi 1986). Matute-Bianchi found that both the native-born students who identified themselves as Mexican Americans and the Mexican immigrants tended to do better in school than those who saw themselves as Chicanos. As was the case with the "reactors" in Troyna's study and with the Crucian males in St. Croix, the Chicanos in Matute-Bianchi's study often made fun of their peers who were good students and accepted the rules of the school. In Chicano parlance such students were "Wannabees," those who "want to be white" or "want to be Anglo" (240).

Linear versus Multilinear Acculturation

Comparative research suggests that immigrant minorities are more likely than nonimmigrants to view acculturation in a positive rather than a negative light. They see the acquisition of skills in the majority-group language and culture in an additive rather than a subtractive fashion, leading not to a rejection of their minority-group identity and culture but to successful participation in both the new cultural system and the old.[13] While involuntary minority students often appear to equate school learning with acculturation and acculturation with assimilation, immigrants more frequently distinguish the acquisition of cultural competencies in the ways of a new group from their own social identification with a particular group. School learning thus is not viewed as a threat to their identity.

These differing conceptions of acculturation may help to explain why immigrant minority students, more frequently than involuntary minorities, tend to play down ethnic, racial, and social class boundaries in classroom settings. Immigrants appear more willing than indigenous and other involuntary minority youths to set aside ethnic, class, and racial differences in their interactions with teachers. While immigrant minority parents may strongly discourage their children from embracing the school's assimilationist agendas and instruct their young outside of class to resist unwarranted pressures to change their culture, as we have seen is the case in Valleyside, they may equally strongly instruct their children to set aside ethnic differences in the classroom and to play down ethnicity in any strategic or instrumental sense in their interactions with teachers.[14]

If immigrants do distinguish school learning from Americanization and assimilation, it may be easier for them to accept school authority and to apply themselves wholeheartedly to their studies than it is for involuntary minorities. If members of a minority group seek to resist assimilation but see schooling as leading to assimilation, they will be ambivalent about or even resistant to school learning. It would follow that those who view education and acculturation as a linear path to assimilation, and who reject assimilation as a goal, would have a more difficult time in school than those who regard acculturation as a multilinear process opening the door to multiple cultural worlds.[15] It would also follow that those who adhere to a linear or subtractive model of acculturation will emphasize their ethnic identities and boundaries within the classroom setting as a means of protecting their ethnic interests. On the other hand, those who embrace a multilinear or additive form of acculturation will see less need to emphasize ethnic identities and boundaries within the classroom setting and will feel more free to compete as individuals rather than as groups (see Banton 1983).

Neither Punjabis nor Down Islanders equated school learning with "acting white," which to many minority students, including both the Punjabis and the Down Islanders, is equivalent to forgetting one's roots and rejecting one's identity. Within classroom settings these immigrant students tended to minimize ethnic differences and to compete on an individual basis. Such a strategy appears to contribute to their academic success. On the other hand, there is increasing evidence to suggest that involuntary minority-group students frequently equate school learning with "acting white" and that to do well in school involuntary minority-group youngsters may be forced to disassociate themselves from their ethnic group or to find strategies for disguising their serious academic effort (see Fordham and Ogbu 1986; Gibson 1982; Ogbu 1981). Further research can shed light on these processes. In particular, it would be useful to know if the involuntary minority-group students who have become academically successful themselves equate education with assimilation, or whether they, like may immigrant youths, consciously embrace a strategy of acculturation without assimilation.

Language Proficiency and School Success

The immigrant educational strategy, as presented here in the Punjabi example, helps minority students to transcend some of the barriers to their success in school, but it does little to alter the basic inequalities within the American system of education. Prejudice and discrimination continue to be major barriers for minority students, including, as this study shows all too clearly, students of Asian ancestry. Furthermore, while many immigrant minority youths do well academically, at times surpassing the national norms, many others do poorly, achieving far below their obvious potential.

The Valleyside study reveals a very close relationship between academic success in high school and English proficiency. Those Punjabi students who are strong in English do about as well academically as majority-group classmates. Those who are weak in English do far less well; many of them are simply unable to keep up in high school level (as opposed to remedial) academic courses. Many go through high school as part of a remedial academic track, taking almost no high school level academic classes and barely meeting minimum graduation standards. Particularly at risk are those who arrive in their late primary and junior high years without prior exposure to English.

Age on Arrival

Age on arrival in the United States (or in English-medium schools in another country) proved the single most influential factor in determining which students became fluent in English. Punjabi students who

[191]

received all their education in the United States, regardless of birthplace, were four times more likely to be classified as fluent-English-proficient in high school than students who arrived in this country in grades five, six, seven, or eight. Even after five to seven years of American education, the English proficiency and level of academic performance of these older arrivals remained far behind that of the Punjabi students who had received all their education in this country. The same pattern emerged for students of Mexican origin. Many other studies, both in the early part of this century here in America and more recently in other parts of the world, point to a similarly strong relationship between age on arrival and school performance. Language-minority students who arrive in the new country by age six or seven do better academically by high school than older arrivals (Allen 1971:128; Cummins 1984:133–35; Dumon 1974, 1979; Little, Mabey, and Whitaker 1968; Masemann 1975; Mehrlander 1986; Ramsey and Wright 1974; Rutter et al. 1974; Tyack 1974; U.S. Immigration Commission 1911).

In the Punjabi case, the striking differences in performance between the younger and older arrivals would appear to suggest a much stronger relationship between age of arrival or age of entry into U.S. schools and school success than between length of residence in this country and school success, especially if students arrive not only weak in English but also with weak academic preparation *and* are thrust into regular academic classes with little or no special assistance. This was the case for many of the Punjabis who arrived in grades five through eight. They started behind and fell farther and farther behind as they moved into the higher grades.[16]

The Punjabi students' ability to gain sufficient proficiency in English to be academically competitive at the high school level does not appear to be closely related to their proficiency in Punjabi.[17] The older arrivals, although more proficient in Punjabi than those raised from early childhood in the United States, had more difficulty than the early arrivals in mastering English. Explanation for their difficulties, as I have shown, involves social and cultural factors, as well as linguistic ones.

The Need for ESL

The Punjabi students who received all their schooling in America managed to learn English and to become competitive academically through what may be characterized as an all-English submersion program.[18] The fact that they survived academically in such a program does not mean, however, that this is the best approach either for Punjabis or for other groups of language-minority students (see Cummins 1984:158). In spite of their record of achievement in school, the American-educated Punjabis, as a group, second generation as well as foreign-born, continued to suffer an English language handicap throughout their high school years. One in five of these students was still classified as LEP during high school. Moreover, standardized tests given to these students in grades seven through ten showed them to be considerably weaker in English than majority-group classmates. For example, twice as many Punjabis as Valleysiders scored below the 25th percentile and only half as many above the 75th percentile on a nationally normed reading and writing test. Although the American-educated Punjabis appeared to be conversationally fluent in English, they still lagged behind native English speakers in their command of academic English.[19]

My findings suggest that even when students are highly motivated, receive all their schooling in this country, and embrace an additive model of bilingualism, they still need specialized "English as a Second Language" training if they are to become fully proficient in English. Language-minority students who arrive at an older age or who adhere to a subtractive model of bilingualism are even more in need of formal ESL instruction.

The Punjabis favored the concept of ESL, newer arrivals in particular expressing gratitude for their small classes and the special assistance they received from the Punjabi-speaking teachers and aides, but at the same time they pointed to serious drawbacks in the ESL program as it had come to be constituted at Valleyside High. They wanted a more rigorous curriculum and expressed concern about receiving high school credits for watered-down classes. They objected to the heavy reliance on standardized test scores for determining placement in mainstream classes. They observed that they should be given opportunity to try to compete in mainstream classes, rather than being insulated in ESL. They complained in particular that the ESL program segregated Punjabis from non-Punjabis, thereby contributing to racial hostilities on the high school campus. The ESL program was like a ghetto, they said, a trap from which Punjabi students could not escape. They felt they could progress more rapidly in English and in their academic subjects if given greater chance to mix with non-Punjabi students, speak English, and attend regular classes.

Graduation requirements at Valleyside High had been established to permit immigrant students to complete high school in the same number of semesters and at the same age as native students, almost regardless of the immigrants' prior academic preparation in foreign schools or their facility with English. Students could graduate with as much as one-third of all their high school credits coming from ESL classes, the primary purpose of which was to impart a basic knowledge of English rather than to provide a high school education. Some ESL students graduated without ever taking even one high school level class in English, science, or mathematics. District policy has subsequently been changed and all students are now required to meet the same graduation requirements. In recognition of the fact that some immigrants (and nonimmigrants) may require a longer period of time to meet the common standard, students attending Valleyside High are now permitted, if they so choose, to stay in high school for more than the customary eight semesters. This seems a sensible policy and one that will help meet the goal of providing equal opportunities to all students.

Bilingual Education

Like many recent immigrants, the Punjabi parents placed much higher priority on their children's learning English in school than on their studying their mother tongue (cf. Guthrie 1985). Most Valleyside Punjabis were opposed to bilingual instruction for their children as part of the formal school program and were quite specific in their preference for an all-English curriculum, for in their view school hours devoted to Punjabi were school hours taken away from mastering English. This was a pragmatic response. Parents felt that children raised in America needed, first and foremost, to be strong in English. They saw little need for the schools to teach oral Punjabi—their children learned this at home. Nor did the parents see it as the school's role to teach the younger generation to read and write Punjabi. Those who wished to could attend the special Punjabi language classes offered at the *gurdwara*.[20]

Immigrant minorities are less likely than involuntary minorities to favor bilingual education as an integral part of the regular instructional program of the public schools. This difference relates in part, it seems, to their differing models of acculturation and their differing perceptions of the majority group. Those who equate an all-English curriculum with forced assimilation and Anglo conformity, favor bilingual-bicultural education. These same groups tend also to be those that feel most exploited by the dominant group and that view majority-group teachers with suspicion. Those who support bilingual education generally see it not only as a linguistically sound pedagogical strategy but also as a potentially effective means for changing the general instructional climate. Bilingual education gives status to the minority language and culture, in the process perhaps promoting a new attitude on the part of majority-group teachers and administrators toward the minority language and culture. At the same time, it may reduce the alienation of minority parents and students, making them more receptive to the formal instructional process. In sum, bilingual-bicultural education may be one strategy for helping both majority-group educators and minority-group students and their families move away from a linear model of acculturation to a multilinear model. Future research needs to explore these relationships more fully.

The Press to Americanize

At the opening of this century schools were seen as a primary vehicle, perhaps *the* primary vehicle, for absorbing immigrants into the American mainstream. By 1911, 57.5 percent of all public school students in thirty-seven of America's largest cities were of foreign-born parentage.[21] Many educators feared that foreign cultures would adversely affect the American way of life. Accordingly, educational programs were designed "to suppress or eliminate all that was conceived of as 'foreign' and to impose upon the immigrant a cultural uniformity with an American pattern" (Covello 1967:411, cited in Cordasco 1976: 36–37). Such a policy was explicitly stated by school administrators early in this century. Ellwood Cubberley, sometime superintendent of schools in San Francisco, wrote in 1909 that the goal of the schools was essentially one of enforced assimilation. "Our task," he asserted frankly, "is to *break up* [immigrant] groups and settlements, to assimilate and amalgamate these people as a part of our American race, and to implant in their children, so far as can be done, the Anglo-Saxon conception of righteousness, law and order, and popular government" (1909:16, cited in Cordasco 1976:26). Like Cubberley, most educators of this period viewed immigrants as in need of change; few saw need for change in the schools themselves or in the standard concept of Americanization they embodied.

Although schools in the 1980s explicitly advocate a respect for cul-

[195]

tural differences and give immigrant students far more specialized assistance than was generally the case at the turn of the century, the goal in the minds of many majority-group educators remains assimilation. Administrators and teachers worry that the immigrants' behavior is out of step with current American standards and values and feel that newcomers must be urged to adopt an "American life-style" as rapidly as possible. Thus, it is still the immigrant child's culture that is viewed as in need of change, rather than the dominant group's assumptions regarding acculturation and assimilation.

In Valleyside, although most majority-group parents, students, and teachers strongly stated their belief in the right of the individual not to conform, in practice they condemned Punjabi teenagers for failing to join in extracurricular activities and for resisting, as best they could, the pressures to adopt the ways of the majority group. Many high school teachers equated "fitting in socially" with a successful school experience. Accordingly, they often seemed more conscious of the Punjabis' apparent resistance to mixing socially than to their academic diligence. While Punjabis viewed extracurricular activities, such as clubs and sports, as extraneous to the formal academic process and even, at times, in direct conflict with their beliefs about proper adolescent behavior, teachers saw participation in these and other school affairs as a primary measure of school success. From the teachers' perspective, moreover, the Punjabi parents put their children in a bind, as in fact they do, by discouraging them from assimilating. Few teachers seemed aware, however, that they themselves contributed to the immigrants' difficulties by insisting that assimilation was the appropriate and desirable goal.

The focus of education in America today, as has been noted for the secondary level in particular, has more to do with general social conventions than with academic achievement (Collins 1979:19). Thus, immigrant minority students, no matter how diligent in class, outside of class are labeled un-American because their behavior deviates from majority norms. A definition of school success that essentially hinges on assimilation contributes to the problems of minorities in America's schools.

Once in America, it is up to immigrants, as the Valleysiders see it, to replace their foreign ways with American ones. Not to do so is considered unpatriotic and un-American. To most Valleysiders, and indeed to most Punjabis as well, Americanization means assimilation, or what nonimmigrant minorities frequently refer to as "Anglo conformity."

[196]

(The several terms—"Americanization," "Anglo conformity," "assimilation"—seem almost indistinguishable in common usage.) Many of the Punjabi students, particularly those who had been raised from childhood in America, had, in fact, become quite proficient in the ways of the dominant culture. Yet, at the same time, they insisted on their right to maintain a separate identity. Their reluctance to assimilate contributed to majority-group prejudice and hostility.

Punjabis have to cope with pervasive prejudice aimed at the very cultural essentials that enable them to achieve success both in school and in the marketplace. Valleysider youths abuse them both verbally and physically. In school, the offending Valleysiders may refuse to sit next to Punjabis in class or may crowd ahead of them in line. They may throw food at them, stick them with pins, tell them they stink, or worse. Punjabi students who defend themselves are labeled troublemakers. Schoolteachers and administrators may decry this atmosphere of prejudice, but often they tacitly support it.

In one way or another Punjabi students are told almost constantly that India and Indian culture are inferior to Western and American ways. Punjabis are criticized for their diet, their dress, and their hair style. They are faulted for deferring to adult authority, placing family ahead of individual interests, accepting arranged marriages, and believing in group decision making. Their success in the classroom, wrought by hard work and strong parental support, counts for little.

It is hardly surprising that most Valleyside Punjabi adults see what they call Americanization as undesirable. To them this means not only forgetting one's roots but adopting the most disparaged traits of the majority group. It means weakening the family and inviting divorce; it means weakening the community and inhibiting economic success; it means losing a Punjabi Sikh identity and destroying a useful sense of pride and belonging. And yet Americanization, in a more general sense, continues apace. Punjabi teenagers enjoy the latest pop music and youth-culture slang. They wear designer jeans and Vaurnet sunglasses. They love french fries and ice cream. They watch the Super Bowl on television. They visit Marriott's Great America and Marine World U.S.A.

Majority and minority in Valleyside agree that ethnic relations are poor and need improvement, but their perceptions of the problems and their solutions differ sharply. The majority, unquestioning in its view that Punjabis must change their ways, believes ethnic relations can only improve as the immigrant group becomes assimilated. This

[197]

will take time, they say, some two or three generations. Teachers and administrators express the majority view, and so, although uncomfortable with ethnic relations as they exist at Valleyside High, most feel quite powerless in the short run to turn things around. They deal with the most serious racial offenses but give little attention to the underlying causes. Someday, they hope, when the new wave of immigration has ended, the situation will improve.

In the view of most Punjabis the ethnic hostility stems not from their unwillingness to adapt or to mix with whites but from the deep-seated and active prejudice of many Valleysiders toward those whose values and way of life differ from theirs. The second and third generation Punjabis resent the suggestion that they are less American because their cultural traditions differ from those of the dominant group, and all Punjabis, immigrant and nonimmigrant alike, resent the presumption of their inferiority. Parents firmly instruct their young to add what is good from majority ways to their own but not to lose what is significant about their Punjabi heritage. Young people, for their part, adopt more of the majority group's values than their parents would like, but still they resist assimilation and, like their parents, resent the pressures on them to change.

Educational programs need to address this oppression of those who demand the right to be different. Immigrant minorities, at least for a period of time, seem able to withstand the pressures to assimilate without erosion of their identity or sense of academic self-esteem, but these pressures nonetheless exert a strong negative influence on the instructional milieu. At present, Punjabi young people do not see the classroom as an arena for ethnic competition. This can change. If the pressures become too great or the return too small, they may be expected to pursue new alternatives.

A Strategy for School Improvement

We need to consider not only how schools can better meet the needs of immigrant pupils but also how immigrants can contribute to the schools. Many other countries are now surpassing the United States in terms of educational achievement, especially at the high school level. So serious is the situation that in 1983 a National Commission on Excellence in Education declared this nation "at risk," asserting that "the educational foundations of our society are presently being eroded by a rising tide of mediocrity that threatens our very future as a nation and a people." The report and many other studies since published have brought about a national mandate for educational improvement. Reform efforts typically emphasize what schools must do to raise academic standards, and clearly, there is a great deal they can and should do. Nevertheless, the fundamental causes of our educational malaise, it would appear, lie not with the schools per se but in the society at large. We appear to have lost our commitment to educational excellence. It is this commitment that many immigrants bring to our society and our schools.

In the course of this research some Valleyside educators suggested that the values and behavior of the Punjabis were anachronistic in terms of current American standards. The educators referred specifically to the Punjabi sense of purpose, diligence, commitment to family, and belief in pulling themselves up by their own bootstraps. Rather than faulting immigrant students for not adopting the norms of the average American teenager, for whom book learning and academic excellence come low in the order of priorities, schools need formally to recognize these students for their educational industriousness.

Some change in perspective is taking place. High school students are being required to take more academic courses and to spend more time in homework. Many teenagers, however, feel stressed by the new demands because the present structure of their lives allows very little time for serious academics. Their lives in school are filled with sports, clubs, and other extracurricular activities. Outside school there are jobs and an active social life. Some students understandably feel strained if they must add more demanding classes and more homework to their already busy schedules, and this, all too often, without real parental support. The balance needs to shift. Students need to be encouraged to cut back on their after-school work and social lives and to view schooling as their primary responsibility during their teenage years. Parents may expect too much of their children socially, and too soon. The student interviews in this study show a great preoccupation with getting out "on your own" when high school is finished, or even during the high school years, ironically to the detriment of studies. All too many American teenagers appear to flounder when left to choose their own courses.

Immigrants seem better able to cope with academic pressures. Immigrant parents place stricter controls on their children's use of "free" time and they expect teenagers to devote substantial amounts of time to homework. Immigrant students, if properly rewarded for their hard work and exemplary behavior, might provide a model for the mass of American teenagers seeking new ways to budget their time. If schools were to cease lending support to the conformist pressures and begin rewarding immigrant industriousness with "You're good for this school and this country," academic achievement would be reinforced all around. The basic reason for such a policy ought to be American principles of liberty and equity, but the major advantages would be for the mass of society, middle class no less than blue collar.

The issue for educators is not whether immigrants change their ways of life or how fast but whether schools foster an instructional and social climate that helps students pursue their educational and vocational goals. By pressuring minority students to conform to majority social standards, with all the concomitants of traditional racial prejudice, schools devalue these students' cultural traditions and contribute to an oppositional climate, a sense of "us versus them" (and "they stink too"), which can do much to undermine the instructional process. Minority students would accommodate themselves more readily to the formal demands of the school curriculum were their identities not challenged in the process.

Pressures to assimilate and problems of prejudice, as they exist at Valleyside High, differ little from what may be found in many American high schools. While most majority-group students do not actively harass minorities, most are quite unaware of their own cultural assumptions and demonstrate a cultural parochialism that schools would do well to address. These problems can be alleviated if educational programs are dedicated to providing students with a cross-cultural perspective. Here, too, immigrants can provide a most valuable resource to any classroom discussion or educational program.

Many involuntary minority students and their families see conformity as the price required for school success because this is the model set by schools themselves. Instead, schools need to foster learning environments where students are given full opportunity to participate in the mainstream of American society while also, if they so choose, maintaining their separate identities, so that the concept "mainstream" itself comprehends multiple cultural identities. The American system of education has much to gain from the immigrant model. A policy of supporting accommodation and acculturation without assimilation will benefit all, majority and minority alike.

[200]

Notes

1. Introduction

1. I use the term "South Asian" rather than Indian because the Muslim students attending Valleyside High, or their parents—unless they arrived prior to 1947— have migrated to Valleyside from Pakistani Punjab, not Indian Punjab.

2. Caste, in the Indian context, refers to "interdependent, hierarchically ranked, birth-ascribed groups," each of which is culturally distinct. Castes are usually endogamous and are usually associated with a traditional occupation (Berreman 1972:389).

3. The 1980 Census reports that 10.8 percent of Asians and Pacific Islanders, ages eighteen to twenty-four, have completed four or more years of college, compared to 7 percent of whites, 3.2 percent of blacks, 2.6 percent of Hispanics, and 1.8 percent of American Indians (U.S. Bureau of the Census 1983c).

4. California Postsecondary Education Commission 1985. This survey of 1983 graduates from California high schools shows that 26 percent of all Asian American graduates meet the eligibility requirements for attendance at one of the campuses of the University of California, compared to 15.5 percent of whites, 4.9 percent of Hispanics, and 3.6 percent of blacks. Of those eligible, 60 percent of the Asian American students actually enroll at the university, compared to 35.5 percent of the whites, 32.7 percent of the Hispanics, and 44.4 percent of the blacks.

5. Much of the recent literature on the economic success of Asian immigrants deals with such advantaged groups. See, for example, Chiswick 1979; Hirschman and Wong 1981; and Min 1984.

6. I place Asian Indians within a discussion of Asian Americans not because of any necessary sense of shared ethnicity—most are first generation, and feelings of Asian American unity and identity occur more commonly among the second and third generation—but because they are Asians and their adaptation patterns in this country merit comparison with other groups of Asian ancestry.

7. Many studies concerned with the educational performance of minority stu-

dents in this country simply omit Asian Americans from the analysis because their performance *as a group* meets or exceeds national norms. The unfortunate result is a paucity of research that seeks either to investigate the nature of the difficulties encountered in school by Asian American students or to explain their comparative academic success.

8. The 1980 Census reports that 44.8 percent of Cuban Americans, aged twenty to twenty-one, were enrolled in school, compared to 33.6 percent of non-Hispanic whites, 28.4 percent of blacks, 21.7 percent of Puerto Ricans, and 18.9 percent of Mexican Americans (U.S. Bureau of the Census 1983c).

9. So striking is the general pattern of success among students of South Asian origin in Britain that a government-appointed committee has recently asked what it is that enables South Asian young people to surmount, to the degree that they do, both the influence of prejudice and discrimination and that of low socioeconomic status (Swann Committee 1985:86). See also Taylor and Hegarty (1985) and Tomlinson (1983) for reviews of current research on the educational performance of Indian students in Britain.

10. This research design was worked out in collaboration with Punjabi community leaders and school district administrators. For a more complete discussion of the research methodology see Gibson (1983a, 1985). All interview schedules and other data collection instruments appear in Gibson (1983b).

11. The following discussion of the development of Sikhism and the Sikhs as a separate and self-conscious community draws on a wide variety of sources. See specifically Banga 1978; Fox 1985; and K. Singh 1953, 1966, 1976. For additional references to the origins and evolution of the Sikh religion, see the bibliography included in Juergensmeyer and Barrier 1979.

12. I draw much of my discussion from Murray Leaf's (1985) analysis of the political and economic conditions giving rise to the current crisis.

13. The archives, including copies of sacred literature written by the Gurus themselves, were destroyed not during the assault on Bhindranwale and his followers but the day after they had all been routed or killed. Sikhs worldwide interpreted this as a deliberate attempt on the part of Gandhi and her government to destroy the Sikh religion.

14. Overseas Sikhs report in February 1987 that support for Khalistan is growing among Sikhs in Punjab. Reports from Punjab remain impressionistic, however, since access to Punjab by outside observers, including members of the foreign press, continues to be tightly controlled by the government of India.

15. No Sikhs were safe in Delhi following Gandhi's assassination. What started as a wave of anger soon took on "a dangerous form." According to M. Akbar, "the urban lumpen, the poor, suddenly discovered that they had been given a licence to attack and loot. When they tasted loot, they began searching for blood. A nightmare descended in Delhi. For the first time since partition, Sikhs became the target of the kind of horrible, unbelievable communal violence that this subcontinent had witnessed in 1947. Sikhs were sought and burned to death. Children were killed, shops looted, cars burnt, markets destroyed, houses gutted. . . . The police were either spectators, or in fact participants" (Akbar 1985:208–9; see also

A. Singh 1985b). Many of the Sikhs who lived in the riot-torn areas of northern India were given refuge by their Hindu neighbors and friends.

16. For further analysis of the Punjab crisis and the factors leading up to it see Ballard 1984; Gupte 1985; Kapur 1986; Nayar and Singh 1984; A. Singh 1985a; G. Singh 1984; P. Singh and Malik 1985; Tully and Jacob 1985; and Wallace 1986.

2. An Emerging Theory of Minority School Performance

1. See, for example, de Lepervanche's 1984 study of Punjabi Sikh farmers in Australia and Desai's 1963 study of Sikh settlers in Britain.

2. See Chancellor 1983; Dworkin 1980; Fisher 1980; Ghosh 1979; Hossain 1982; Leonhard-Spark and Saran 1980; Minocha 1984; Nandi 1980; Saran 1985. All describe a privileged group of Indians who arrive in this country fluent in English, possessing skills in great demand in the American job market, and familiar with Western life-style and values, all of which enhance their acceptance in United States society (Saran and Eames 1980:136).

3. The 50 percent estimate comes from local farmers interviewed by the author, as well as representatives of the Cling Peach Advisory Board (Diana Richards, Personal Communication, March 17, 1986, Marysville, Calif.).

4. Research on cultural discontinuities has been the stimulus for more applied work that seeks to encourage "positive transfer" between home and school settings (see, for example, Au and Jordan 1981; Barnhardt 1982; Jordan 1984, 1985).

5. A special issue of the *Anthropology and Education Quarterly* (18[4], Winter 1987) presents the different theoretical positions and discusses this need for synthesis.

6. In some societies, such as South Africa, the subordinate group is in fact the numerical majority and the dominant group the numerical minority. In the United States, however, and in the other countries referred to in this book, the majority group is also the dominant or superordinate group.

3. Asian Indian Immigration to the United States

1. Personal communication, Nicholas MacNeil, American consul, New Delhi, and members of his staff, 29 Feb. 1984.

2. The 1980 Census (U.S. Bureau of the Census 1983b) placed the Asian Indian population for the bi-county area at 2,764, but based on ethnic census data available from area public schools, the 1980 population of Asian Indians was probably closer to six thousand. Some Punjabi community leaders themselves estimated that as many as eight thousand Indians were settled in the bi-county area.

3. Many, in fact, migrated from British Columbia to California after Canada halted immigration from India to Canada in 1909. For more extensive accounts of the early history of Sikh immigration to British Vancouver and to California see Buchignani and Indra 1985; Chadney 1976; Jensen, in press; Johnston 1979; La

Brack 1980; Mayer 1959; Ramakrishna 1979; and Santry 1982. The most complete source of references to the history of South Asians in North America is an annotated bibliography compiled by the Center for South and Southeast Asia Studies at the University of California, Berkeley (1988).

4. Today's Punjab is divided into three areas—Majha, Doaba, and Malwa. People from Doaba are referred to as Doabis. *Doab* means, literally, two waters and is the Punjabi term for the land between two rivers. *Punjab* itself (or *panjab*), means land of five waters; it was named for the five rivers that ran through the province prior to its partition.

5. For accounts of the socioeconomic factors contributing to the emigration of Sikhs from the Jullundur Doab, see Ballard 1983; Desai 1963; Helweg 1979; Kessinger 1974; Pettigrew 1977.

6. This is not to say that caste differences have ceased to have import among Sikhs. In spite of the teachings of the Sikh Gurus, the caste system has persisted among Sikhs both in India and abroad (Bhachu 1985a; Singh 1966b). Caste endogamy remains a prominent part of Sikh marriage arrangements, and caste groups are thus perpetuated. In Valleyside, however, where the overwhelming majority of all Sikhs share a common Jat background, caste position plays little role in daily interaction.

7. These statistics do not reflect the large numbers of Japanese and Chinese who returned to their homelands.

8. The first legislation to bar immigration based on national origin was passed in 1882. The Chinese Exclusion Law remained in effect until 1943.

9. Punjabis also continued to be much concerned with conditions back in India. Not only were their families still there, but they themselves expected to return home within a few years. Many of these early migrants rallied to the cause of an independent India. Mark Juergensmeyer describes their efforts to overthrow British rule: "The Punjabis who organized it called their movement *Gadar*. . . . The name means 'mutiny' or 'revolt,' and their mounting publicity actually led to such an attempt in 1915. Five boats, loaded with weapons and propaganda, set sail from various ports in California, financed by the German war effort. Alas, most were soon intercepted by the British. Those that landed were met by British authorities, and many leaders were hanged. Others were put on trial by the American government and many of them were deported" (1982:48). *Gadar* activities represented a combination of ethnic anger and nationalist pride. The movement, which continued through the 1930s, formally came to an end only with the independence of India.

10. Gary Hess (1982:31) estimates that some three thousand Indians returned home between 1920 and 1940, most of them voluntarily.

11. Harold Jacoby (1956:12), through interviews with early immigrants, was able to identify only seven Indian women who lived on the West Coast in the period 1907–14. Karen Leonard's search of California county records for the period 1913–46 turned up only nine marriages by Indian men to Indian women, all but one of these occurring in the northern part of the state. During this period, 80 percent of the marriages of Indian men were to Hispanic women. Many of the men who

settled in San Joaquin, Sacramento, Sutter, and Yuba counties remained single until after 1946, when they could arrange marriages back in India or bring over wives left behind in Punjab (La Brack and Leonard 1984:528).

12. See Ballard and Ballard 1977; Desai 1963; and Helweg 1979 for studies on the development of Punjabi Sikh settlements in Britain. Britain has also became home to large numbers of East African Indians, the majority of whom migrated there in the late 1960s, others following in 1972 after their expulsion from Uganda by General Idi Amin. Their story is told by British social anthropologist Parminder Bhachu (1985a), herself an East African Sikh, in a book appropriately titled *Twice Migrants*.

13. For a review of the major developments in British immigration law and their "catastrophic effects" on South Asian and other minority communities in Britain, see Gideon Ben-Tovin and John Gabriel's article (1982:145–71), "The Politics of Race in Britain, 1962–79."

14. Gardner, Robey, and Smith (1985:5) place the 1985 population of Asian Indians at 525,000. By my estimate the total was closer to 575,000, assuming an average of thirty thousand new immigrants arriving each year since 1980, two-thirds born in India, one-third elsewhere, plus an increase in the American-born population of approximately fifteen thousand per year. This figure also assumes a fertility rate for Asian Indian women, ages eighteen to forty-four, of 67.3 births per 1000 women (Bachu 1984:9).

15. Of the 1970–80 arrivals from India who are age sixteen or older and employed, fully half (50.5 percent) are classified as professionals and managers and another 28 percent as technical, sales, and administrative support (U.S. Bureau of the Census 1984b).

16. The median family income for *all* Asian Indians in 1979, both immigrant and native-born, was $24,993, making them one of the most affluent groups residing in the United States. The median family income for whites that year was $20,835 (U.S. Bureau of the Census 1983c).

17. Only 1.7 percent of all Asian Indians in the U.S., age five years or older, speak no English and only 6.7 percent are limited-English speakers (ibid.). Because of the large number of languages spoken in India, English is the medium of communication in universities, government, and industry, and all university-educated Indians speak English.

18. In 1981 a total of 17,728 immigrant visas were issued at consular offices in India, 4,653 in New Delhi, 9,129 in Bombay, 2,911 in Madras, and 1,035 in Calcutta (U.S. Department of State 1981:13). See Leonhard-Spark and Saran (1980) for a more detailed demographic profile of Indians living in the New York metropolitan area.

19. In January 1984 the waiting period for visas to be granted under the second preference was ten months (U.S. Department of State 1984:2).

20. In January 1984 the waiting period for fifth-preference visas from India was more than three years (ibid.).

21. Bruce La Brack's (1980) doctoral dissertation provides a detailed account of the reconstitution of the Punjabi Sikh community in the Sacramento Valley.

22. The number of passports issued by the government of India to Punjabis rose almost fivefold in the period 1973–78. The demand for passports became so great that in 1979 the Indian government opened a passport office in the Jullundur District (Sharma 1981:27).

4. From Punjab to Valleyside

1. Our technique of including all Punjabi families with children in twelfth grade was readily explained both to the parents and the students, and all forty-two families agreed to participate. As is typical for this sort of research, some individuals became much more involved in the study than others.

2. Both the Punjabi and English versions of the parent interview schedule are included in the Punjabi Education Project, Final Report to the National Institute of Education (Gibson 1983b).

3. Because only four families in the core sample of forty-two were non-Sikh, the analysis necessarily centers on the Sikhs. Within the high school population as a whole, grades nine through twelve, 14 percent of the Punjabi students were of non-Sikh background (10 percent Hindu, and 4 percent Muslim).

4. Within the core sample, four families had lived in England, two in Fiji, none in East Africa.

5. By the early 1970s, 44 percent of landowning households in Punjab owned ten acres or less; 21 percent owned from ten to thirty acres; and 35 percent owned more than thirty acres, but only 2.5 percent of these had holdings of fifty acres or more (Sharma 1981:23). When the smaller farms are divided, the next generation will be unable to make ends meet.

6. Even this has changed in recent years, with more and more small farmers falling into debt. Many small farmers are being displaced, contributing to current tensions within Punjab (see Helweg 1986).

7. Punjabis refer to white Americans either as "whites" or as "Americans."

8. Chamars, the traditional leatherworkers in India, are one of the lower castes that bear the stigma of "untouchability." In many parts of Punjab Chamars constitute 15 to 25 percent of the village population and are employed by Jats to work their fields.

9. In the rural areas, where 76 percent of the population lives, only 1.3 percent of women were in the labor force in 1971. For urban areas the figure was only 3.0 percent (Singh 1979:3).

10. A *salwaar-kameez* is the traditional Punjabi dress of baggy trousers and loose tunic or shirt reaching to the knees, worn by both men and women in Punjab. Women also wear either a shawl or *dupatta* (a "scarf," about three yards long) around their shoulders or over their heads. In English a *salwaar-kameez* is often referred to as a "suit." Women make their own, or have them sewn by an Indian tailor.

11. For similar observations on Sikh settlers in Canada and in England, see Chadney (1980:47) and Desai (1963:87).

12. In some cases, the father had been settled in the United States longer than his children, although in recent years almost all Punjabi men have arrived together with their families. The four non-Sikh Punjabi families in the core sample all lived in rented housing. Two had lived in Valleyside for more than ten years, one for six years, and one for four years. In general, the Hindu and Muslim families who had settled in Valleyside lacked the same sort of extensive family and friendship networks that contributed to the Sikhs' economic mobility.

13. Punjabis readily make no-interest loans to close relatives.

14. See also La Brack's (1982b) "Occupational Specialization among Rural California Sikhs," which gives particular attention to the interplay of cultural and economic variables.

15. I have limited my analysis here to the thirty-eight Sikh families in the core sample. Only one of the four non-Sikh fathers in the core sample worked in farming, and he was a farm laborer.

16. One knowledgeable informant, a person directly involved in peach production surveys, estimated that in 1979 somewhat more than 60 percent of all peach farmers in the Sacramento Valley were Punjabis, up from 30 to 35 percent in the late 1960s.

17. Approximately 40 percent of all cling peaches—those commonly used for canning—are grown in and around Valleyside, an area including Yuba, Sutter, and Butte counties. The statistics on the decline in peach farmers come from the Cling Peach Advisory Board's Orchard and Production Surveys for the years 1979–80 through 1984–85.

18. As a result of this price differential, the sale of imported peaches rose from only sixteen thousand cases in 1981 to 1.2 million cases by 1984 (*Sacramento Bee*, 22 Sept. 1985).

19. In this same period, the value of U.S. canned fruit exports declined from $6 million to only $126,000 (*Sacramento Bee*, 4 Dec. 1985). Some relief may be in sight from a 1985 court-ordered agreement which called for the European Economic Community to reduce subsidies to processors by 25 percent in 1986 and to stop them altogether in 1987 and beyond (Personal communication, Diana Richards, Cling Peach Advisory Board, Marysville, Calif., 17 March 1986).

20. Edna Bonacich and John Modell (1980) provide an excellent overview of the literature on middleman minorities and a discussion of the theories used to explain the persistence of this phenomenon worldwide. For illustrative case studies see Bonacich, Light, and Wong (1977) on Korean small businessmen and Light (1972) on the relationship between informal financial cooperation among Chinese and Japanese immigrants and their financial success. For more recent articles discussing the importance of economic enclaves to the socioeconomic mobility of minority groups in this country, see Kim and Hurh 1985; Model 1985; and Nee and Sanders 1985.

21. In his study of minority businesses in London, Peter Wilson (1983) found that Asian Indians in 43 percent of the cases studied relied on family members for help with the initial costs of setting up a business. Roger Ballard (personal communication, 22 Dec. 1986) notes that Sikhs feel obliged to make interest-free loans

to their relatives, but by so doing also enhance their status and power within the extended family. In addition to family loans, Wilson found that British Indians relied heavily on bank loans in the start-up stage of their businesses (47 percent of the sixty cases studied).

22. Burton Benedict (1968) also found that family ties may play a more important role in the early stages of business development than in later stages for Indians in East Africa.

23. Marie de Lepervanche's (1984) account of the rapid development of a Punjabi Sikh enclave in Australia shows many parallels with my findings. There, Punjabis entered banana farming in the 1950s and 1960s, and within twenty years had established themselves as a successful farming community.

5. Ethnic Relations

1. For students' views see Chapter 8.

2. Bonacich and Modell (1980:253–59) note a similar pattern among other immigrant minorities in the United States.

3. The majority group in Valleyside may be viewed as unhyphenated Valleysiders or unhyphenated Americans (cf. Lieberson 1985).

4. Valleysiders generally refer to Punjabis as East Indians, a term that, until recently, has been commonly used in America to distinguish Asian Indians from American Indians. The term has no pejorative connotations, but it does lead some Valleysiders (and even some Punjabi young people) to suppose that East India is a separate country or perhaps a region, as in "I have never been to East India."

5. Lacking knowledge about how malaria is spread some Valleysiders worried that they could become infected through contact with Indians.

6. This observation is based on comments of some second-generation Punjabis who have observed the changes and on a comparison of sets of essays written by Valleysider high school students in 1967 and 1981. In both years students were asked to participate in a survey "to find out their current thoughts, information or feelings about East Indian people." The essays were unsigned and ungraded. Those written in 1981 were far more negative in content than the earlier sample.

7. Similar myths have been invented about other immigrant minorities, such as the Koreans in New York.

8. As noted in the previous chapter, some passages are exact quotations from single interviews. Others are pieced together from several interviews in order to provide as full a response as possible to specific topics.

9. Many Punjabis do in fact send some money back to India, most frequently to their parents and grandparents, if they are still alive, and capital from abroad has had a substantial impact on villages in Punjab (cf. Helweg 1983). Remittances may be used to improve the family home or pay for a relative's wedding, a trip to the United States, or, in recent years, tube wells and tractors. However, since few Valleyside Punjabis expect to return permanently to Punjab, their major business investments are in the United States and their remittances to Punjab are generally small.

10. So heated is the controversy over affirmative action that riots broke out in 1985 in the Indian state of Gujarat when the state government raised the proportion of jobs and college places reserved for "backward" castes from 31 to 49 percent (Scully 1985).

11. A similar pattern has been found to exist in Britain, where Asian Indians are less likely than whites or other minority groups to believe that an employer "would refuse a job to a person on racial grounds" (Brown 1984:171). Indians in Britain also express faith in the capacity of the British police to protect them against racial attacks, in spite of an increase in the frequency of attacks by whites on Indians and the Indians' general concern for their safety (ibid., 257).

12. In addition to the strategy of direct physical confrontation, Sikhs have proved themselves very effective in using local politics to advance their interests both in Punjab and abroad. See, for example, David Beetham's (1970) study of how Sikh bus conductors in Britain used local politics to press for the right to wear turbans instead of the regulation cap. Sikhs are also quick to hire lawyers to represent their interests and will press for their rights in court if they feel they have a case.

13. The recent conflicts between Sikhs and Hindus in India represent a situation very different from that between Sikhs and Valleysiders.

14. See Parekh (1983:114) for a similar observation with regard to Asian Indians settled in Britain.

15. De Vos observes that in some immigrant minorities—he cites the Japanese as an example—we see "a capacity for deferment of goals of higher status as a culturally available psychological tactic which does not injure one's self-assessment, while providing a means for accommodating to subordinate status" (1975: 33–34).

16. A much stronger "myth of return" has existed among Punjabi Sikh migrants to Britain than to California (see Ballard and Ballard 1977:40–41).

17. Communal tensions and the political upheaval in Punjab today would make reemigration more difficult, but the symbolic option remains.

6. Academic Performance at Valleyside High

1. In 1965 there were fewer than thirty Punjabi students in grades eight to twelve, or roughly six per grade level (Wenzel 1966). That number had doubled by 1970 when, by one report, 150–200 students of "East Indian descent" attended Valleyside schools, grades kindergarten through twelve (Bradfield 1971). By 1980, there were more than eight hundred Punjabis enrolled districtwide, or about sixty per grade level.

2. The district appointed a female administrator the year after fieldwork.

3. In 1983–84, the average score for Valleyside High students was 508 in math and 434 in English. Only 28 percent of Valleyside seniors took the test, however, compared to a statewide average of 39 percent.

4. Four years of English are not necessarily equivalent to four years of high school English because remedial classes are also counted in the totals. At the time

of fieldwork less than one-fourth of the Valleyside High students took "senior" English (see Table 14). Since 1981, because of educational reform efforts statewide and tougher curriculum entrance requirements at California State University, more students in Valleyside and throughout the state are enrolling in advanced English classes. Only since 1984 have four years of English been required for admission to one of the nineteen CSU campuses. Beginning in 1988, high school graduates will also need three years of math to gain admission, up from the two-year requirement adopted in 1984.

5. Students who had previously lived in England or Fiji had attended school in English. English is also taught as a subject in all public schools in Punjab, beginning at the junior high level, and is the medium of instruction in most private schools in India. Several of the students in grades nine, ten, and eleven may have attended English-medium, private schools in Punjab, judging by their proficiency in English at the time of their arrival in Valleyside.

6. Graduation standards have subsequently been changed. All data reported in this chapter pertain to the time of fieldwork (1980–82).

7. Valleyside High records show 463 students enrolled in twelth grade in June 1981 compared with 670 students enrolled in ninth grade in June 1978. A recent California survey of 335,000 students entering ninth grade in 1979 revealed that one in three did not finish, twice as many as in 1970 (*Sacramento Bee*, 1 Oct. 1985). The U.S. Department of Education reports an even higher dropout rate for California: 39.8 percent for 1982 and 36.8 percent for 1984 (*Sacramento Bee*, 21 Feb. 1986).

8. Attrition estimates are based on a combination of ethnic census data and overall enrollment figures for grades nine through twelve from 1977–78 through 1980–81.

9. "Special Education" placements were especially difficult to make in the case of Punjabi students, because of the lack of appropriate diagnostic tests written in Punjabi. No students, Punjabi or non-Punjabi, placed in special education classes by the school district were included in our analysis of school performance.

10. These differences were not subjected to tests of statistical significance, but they held for each of the subgroups examined.

11. Although we had academic achievement data for all 231 Punjabi students attending Valleyside High, we had detailed family background information, including parents' occupations, only for the seniors.

12. Spring semester 1981 the average grade given in ESL English classes was 2.45, compared with an average grade of 2.18 given in all other English classes. The cumulative grade point average for LEP students in the class of 1981 was 2.42.

13. See Cummins (1981:9) for his reference to age on arrival and length of residence as critical variables in interpreting the school performance of language-minority immigrants. I return to these points in the concluding chapter.

14. Because both the Punjabi and Mexican American samples were small, the findings need to be tested against larger samples.

15. By the spring of 1981, all elementary schools with concentrations of Punjabi-speaking students had one Punjabi teacher and the high school had two.

[210]

16. Analysis of the other courses taken by Punjabi, Mexican American, and Valleysider students attending Valleyside High is included in "Home-School-Community Linkages: A Study of Educational Opportunity for Punjabi Youth" (Gibson 1983a).

17. These findings are based on an analysis of student enrollment in the advanced academic classes spring semester 1983, compiled at my request by the high school principal. The course enrollment lists used to make the Valleysider projections shown in Table 14 did not specify the sex of the students.

18. Tests were first administered in Oct. 1978, when the class of 1981 was beginning tenth grade, the class of 1982 ninth grade, and the class of 1983 eighth grade. Students in the class of 1984 were first tested in April 1979, as they completed seventh grade. We examined test scores for all Punjabi and all Mexican American students in these four classes, and the scores of a random sample of all other students, stratified by sex. The Valleysider sample included approximately forty-five students from each class. As might be expected, students in the upper grades received higher scores, on average, than the younger students.

19. The School District used three versions of the competency tests in rotation.

20. Continuation high schools are designed to meet the needs of students who, for a variety of reasons, are unsuccessful in the large, comprehensive high school environment. Some are discipline problems, some are unmotivated, and some are simply floundering in the large mass of two thousand students and more than 150 different classes.

21. Many studies have reported a 40 to 45 percent dropout rate for Mexican American students (Brown et al. 1980; National Commission . . . 1984; Steinberg, Blinde, and Chan 1979:115; *Sacramento Bee*, 13 Dec. 1984, 1 Oct. 1985). In some California school districts the Hispanic dropout rate is reported to be as high as 60 to 70 percent, beginning in seventh and eighth grades (*Sacramento Bee*, 11 Aug. 1985).

22. I have no hard data on absenteeism for the elementary and junior high levels. Nor do I have data on parents' occupations. It is my impression, however, that the large majority of Mexican Americans lived year-round in the Valleyside area and that only a small percentage actually migrated seasonally. Further research is needed on which subgroups of Mexican American students experience the greatest difficulties in school and why.

7. Community Forces and Schooling

1. This description applies primarily to village schools. Government schools in urban areas are generally better equipped. India also has many private schools, some excellent.

2. Indian school statistics, it must be noted, are internally inconsistent and can only be accepted for overall patterns. For example, the "Fourth All-India Educational Survey," from which I drew the statistics for Table 18, reports that in the state of Punjab in 1978, 73 percent of males and 55 percent of females, ages eleven

to thirteen, were enrolled in school. Even though these percentages are for the total state and not just rural areas, they appear to suggest a far lower attrition rate than that indicated by Table 18. My impression, however, based on visiting village schools, is that the attrition rate is, indeed, very high.

3. In Punjab some women from the lower castes do work in the fields but not the women of Jat background. Most of the harvest workers are migrant workers from other states, not Punjabis.

4. A few of the very recently arrived Punjabi families, we were told, kept their teenage daughters at home rather than enrolling them at Valleyside High.

5. Punjabi Sikhs are nowhere near so restrictive with respect to their daughters as are Punjabi Muslims. Sikhs take self-conscious pride, furthermore, in giving social equality to women and see no conflict between their principle of sexual equality and their customs regarding teenage girls.

6. There were too few non-Sikh Punjabi families in our core sample—only three Hindu and one Muslim—to explore systematically either the similarities or the differences among the groups.

7. So, too, among East African Sikhs in Britain, few of whom express any desire to return to Punjab or to East Africa. Some do talk, however, of migrating to the United States or Canada (Bhachu 1985a:45).

8. Those Valleyside Punjabis who were willing to buck community norms and withstand the inevitable gossip were generally the better-educated, more urbanized members of the community.

9. More educated and more westernized Punjabis often take a far more active role in their children's schooling.

10. Bhachu (1985b) notes that a noninterventionist strategy is typical of rural Indian immigrants in Britain who have not been exposed to Western education.

11. We interviewed more than fifty Valleysider educators, some at length and on several occasions, including elementary school principals as well as secondary level teachers, aides, counselors, administrators, and staff. High school faculty members also shared their views on a written questionnaire.

12. In response to the question, "If it were in your power to control everything, how far would you like to go in your education before leaving school?," 64 percent of the Punjabi seniors compared to 45 percent of the Valleysiders responded either "graduate school" or "four-year college."

13. Somewhat more than a third of the Punjabi seniors felt that jobs were not equally available to all ethnic groups. A number of these respondents, however, pointed to English skills and education as the barrier, not racial discrimination.

14. There were other girls who were even more Americanized, but their parents tended to be among the small minority of urbanized and westernized Sikhs.

15. As part of a longer questionnaire administered to the senior sample, we asked students to choose from pairs of statements the ones that best represented their ideas. The statements were as follows:

    1. a. It is important to do what you think is best even if others disagree.

       b. It is better to listen to those who are older than you and to do as they suggest, even if you think your way is better.

2. a. It is important for young people to stay nearby their families.
   b. It is important for young people to go off on their own when they finish their education.
3. a. Young people should be able to count on their parents or relatives to help them out as long as necessary.
   b. Young people should learn to be independent and not rely on their parents or relatives to support them.
4. a. When you are making decisions about your future, it is better to follow the advice of your parents since they are older and wiser.
   b. When you are making decisions about your future, you're the one who knows what's best for you.
5. a. When I am old I hope to live on my own.
   b. When I am old I hope to live with my children.
6. a. When people grow old they should be able to count on their children to help support and care for them.
   b. When people grow old it is better if they can support and care for themselves.

16. It must be noted that the Punjabi sample was extremely small when divided both by sex and length of time in the United States, particularly in the case of boys raised in this country, of whom only four are represented. Not every student in the Punjabi core sample responded to these questions because a sheet was missing from some of the questionnaires. The family orientation pattern of the more newly arrived Punjabi students was supported, however, by a pilot test of the questionnaire with some sixty ESL students in grades nine through eleven. Interview data from Punjabis raised in the United States provided further evidence of their shift toward the individualist orientation.

17. Many Punjabi parents discourage their children from holding after-school jobs, believing that they will interfere with a child's studies.

8. Barriers to Achievement

1. The data reported here come largely from student questionnaires, given to our core samples of Punjabi and Valleysider students and from follow-up interviews with the same students.

2. Both the student and faculty questionnaires are included as an appendix to the Punjabi Education Project, Final Report to the National Institute of Education (Gibson 1983b).

3. In the course of fieldwork we heard of Punjabi men, usually young and unmarried, who were working in the fruit orchards without proper papers, but we found no indication that whole families were living in Valleyside illegally and sending their children to school.

4. In her research on Chinese immigrants in New York, Betty Sung (1979:68) also found that students were generally placed in school according to their age, not by previous preparation in the home country.

5. It should be noted that a few of the Punjabis who had arrived from India as high school students seem not to have been similarly handicapped. These students had both sufficient academic preparation and sufficient exposure to English— English is a required subject in Punjab from grade seven on—to transfer directly into mainstream academic classes. This pattern merits further analysis with a larger sample of students.

6. Punjabis were almost equally opposed to receiving instruction in Punjabi, even as a foreign language at the high school level. Both students and parents wanted an all-English curriculum.

7. See Sung's (1979:86) study for a similar observation about the slow track as a poor learning environment for recent Chinese immigrants.

8. Quoted in "Complying with Title IX Regulations" (Clearinghouse on Urban Education 1981).

9. Alejandro Portes et al. (1980) note, with respect to Latin American immigrants, that the greater the immigrants' level of education and familiarity with life in the United States, the greater their perception of discrimination. This is true in the Punjabi case as well. Long-term, better-educated residents also have greater resources for combating discrimination and are more aware of the pragmatic economic and social utility of active resistance.

9. Immigrant Minorities and Schooling

1. Based on informal follow-up data.

2. I have no systematic follow-up data on the forty-five students in the core sample, beyond their performance in community college.

3. Not all of these students are Jat Sikhs or even Punjabis. Many are Hindus and Muslims, but Punjabi Jat Sikhs represent one of the largest and oldest subgroups of South Asians in England.

4. See, for example, Hurh and Kim (1984); Kurokawa (1970:133); and Rosenthal (1960) for discussions of similar minority adaptation strategies among Korean, Japanese, and Jewish Americans.

5. Three recent studies sponsored by the National Academy of Sciences point to a serious disparity between the mathematical ability of American schoolchildren and their counterparts in other industrialized countries. A primary reason for the disparity is that American students invest less effort in the learning of mathematics. This lack of effort, according to one of the researchers, psychologist Harold Stevenson, is related to the attitude that native ability more than hard work is the key to mathematical achievement (reported in the *Sacramento Bee*, 11 Jan. 1987).

6. Sung (1979:101) notes that if students do not respect their teachers, neither will they respect the knowledge the teachers seek to impart.

7. In 1981, almost half (48.3 percent) of all blacks, ages sixteen to twenty-four, who had completed less than four years of high school were unemployed, compared to 22.7 percent of whites of comparable age and education. The rate of black unemployment declined steadily, however, as years of education increased, falling

to 29.6 percent for high school graduates, ages sixteen to twenty-four, 22.5 percent for those finishing one to three years of college, and 8.3 percent for those completing four years of college (Young 1983:30).

8. While visiting secondary schools in Pakistan in 1984, I met Mirpuri students, boys as well as girls, who had been raised in Britain and were fluent in colloquial British English, whose parents had sent them to Pakistan for their high school education.

9. At the time of fieldwork few Puerto Rican students, males or females, persisted in school through twelfth grade (Gibson 1982).

10. Only about half the Down Islanders enjoyed the security of permanent residence status. The remainder held temporary working papers.

11. Much of the island's shoreline had been badly damaged by spills from a large American oil refinery.

12. Robert Dirks notes that the native Virgin Islanders' use of the term *garot* "calls to mind the garot bird, a creature that flies from its home to other islands, stripping them clean of food before moving on again" (1975:105). Whether or not Crucians had the garot bird in mind, there is no doubt that they considered the Down Islanders to be predators.

13. See Lambert (1975:67) for his distinction between additive and subtractive forms of bilingualism.

14. See Cohen (1969) and Vincent (1974) for their discussions of ethnicity as strategy.

15. Ward Goodenough notes that "just as individuals can be multilingual they can also be multicultural, the particular culture that is to be regarded as *theirs* as when we talk of a person's culture being determined by considerations of social identification rather than simply of competence (although obviously the culture of the group with which a person identifies himself is inevitably one in which he is highly competent)" (1971:37). See also Goodenough (1976), McFee (1968), and Polgar (1960) for their discussions of "biculturation" and "multiculturalism as the normal human experience."

16. These findings regarding age on arrival and length of residence seem to contradict the body of research that shows "older immigrant children make more rapid progress than younger children in acquiring L2 [second language] proficiency" (Cummins 1981:31–32; Skutnabb-Kangas 1979). The work of Skutnabb-Kangas and others, however, has focused on the role of primary language development in promoting academic success. Here I have given almost no attention to students' proficiency in Punjabi and its effect on such areas as "cognitive flexibility and linguistic abstraction," areas where bilinguals have been found to have an advantage over monolinguals (Troike 1981:499; cf. Cummins 1984:108; Lambert 1975:67).

17. See Paulston (1982:49) for similar findings in Sweden.

18. A submersion program is one that makes "virtually no concessions to the child's language or culture" (Cummins 1984:156).

19. These findings lend support to other studies indicating that it takes a minimum of five to seven years for language-minority students to perform as well in

academic English as native English speakers (Cummins 1984:133–35; Ramsey and Wright 1974).

20. Second- and third-generation Punjabi parents may become more concerned about the maintenance of Punjabi if their children cease to speak the mother tongue at home, but building on the British data, it does not appear that they are likely to pressure the schools to assume this responsibility. Rather, it is more likely that they will increase their support for Punjabi instruction in after-school classes organized and run by the Punjabi community itself. A similar pattern has occurred among Chinese Americans, although some second- and third-generation Chinese also support bilingual instruction in the public schools (Guthrie 1985).

21. *Abstracts of the Immigration Commission Reports, The Children of Immigrants in Schools*, (Washington, D.C.: Government Printing Office, 1911), 2:1–15, cited in Cordasco 1976:27.

Tables

Table 1. Immigration into the United States, 1965–1980: Number of immigrants admitted and relatives as a percentage of total immigrants

	1965		1980	
	Number	Percent	Number	Percent
Total	296,697	100.0	530,639	100.0
Exempt from limitations	197,316		241,160	
Immediate relatives	32,714	11.0	151,131	28.5
All others	164,602	55.5	90,029	16.9
Subject to limitations	99,381		289,479	
Relative preferences	13,082	4.4	216,856	40.9
All others	81,313	29.1	72,623	13.7

SOURCES: U.S. Bureau of the Census 1970, 1985.

Table 2. Immigrants from Asia, as a percentage of total immigrants to the United States, 1951–1981

	Total immigrants	Asians	
		Number	Percent
1951–60	2,515,500	157,100	6.2
1961–70	3,321,700	445,300	13.4
1971–80	4,493,300	1,633,800	36.4
1981	596,600	264,300	44.3

SOURCE: U.S. Bureau of the Census 1984a.

Tables

Table 3. Immigrants and refugees granted immigrant status, by country of birth, 1951–1980

Country	1951–60	1961–70	1971–80	1980
Mexico	319,300	444,300	637,200	56,700
Philippines	17,200	101,500	360,200	42,300
Cuba	78,300	256,800	276,800	15,100
Korea	7,000	35,800	272,000	32,300
China	32,700	96,700	202,500	27,700
Vietnam	2,000	4,600	179,700	43,500
India	3,100	31,200	176,800	22,600

SOURCES: U.S. Bureau of the Census 1983a, 1984a.

Table 4. Asian population in the United States, 1980

		Estimated native-born	
	Total	Number	Percent
Chinese	806,040	297,789	36.9
Filipino	774,652	276,390	35.7
Japanese	700,974	512,993	73.2
Asian Indian	361,531	114,606	31.7
Korean	354,593	64,820	18.3
Vietnamese	261,729	23,376	8.9

SOURCES: U.S. Bureau of the Census 1983b, table 38; 1983c, table 161.

Table 5. Immigrants from India admitted to the United States, fiscal year 1981, by classes

Class	Number	Percent	Total
Exempt from numerical limitations			3,319
Parents of U.S. citizens	1,851	8.60	
Spouses of U.S. citizens	802	3.73	
Minor children of U.S. citizens	393	1.83	
Other	273	1.27	
Subject to numerical limitations			18,201
Kinship preferences			
Unmarried sons and daughters (age 21+) of U.S. citizens, and their children (1st preference)	11	.05	
Spouses, unmarried sons and daughters of resident aliens, and their children (2d preference)	6,289	29.22	
Married sons and daughters of U.S. citizens, their spouses and children (4th preference)	94	.44	
Brothers and sisters of U.S. citizens, their spouses and children (5th preference)	8,987	41.76	
Occupational preferences			
Immigrants in professions, their spouses and children (3d preference)	1,920	8.92	
Other workers, their spouses and children (6th preference)	891	4.14	
Nonpreference immigrants	9	.04	
Total		100.00	21,520

SOURCE: U.S. Department of Justice 1981, tables 5–7.

[218]

Table 6. Valleyside Punjabi population, 1954–1980

Year	Population estimates
1954	300
1965	700
1975	4,000
1980	6,000

SOURCES: Jacoby 1954; Wenzel 1966; La Brack 1980:256; Gibson 1983a:31.

Table 7. Occupations of Punjabi Sikh immigrants to Valleyside in 1980, by year of arrival in the United States (in percent)

	1970 and earlier (N = 15)	1971 to 1980 (N = 23)
Farm owner	73.3	0.0
Farm laborer	26.7	69.6
Factory and other	0.0	30.4

SOURCE: Compiled from core sample of thirty-eight Sikh families with children attending twelfth grade at Valleyside High, 1980–1981.

Table 8. Cling peach acreage owned by Punjabi farmers in the Sacramento Valley, 1979–1980

Number of acres	Number of farmers[a]	Percent[b]
1–20	59	31.4
21–40	45	23.9
41–60	37	19.7
61–80	15	7.9
81–100	9	4.8
101–120	7	3.7
121–140	5	2.7
141–160	1	.5
161–180	1	.5
181–200	3	1.6
Above 200	6	3.2

SOURCE: Compiled from records of the Cling Peach Advisory Board, Marysville, Calif., based on data supplied by Bruce La Brack.

[a]It is difficult to compile accurate data on Punjabi landholdings because many farmers own several pieces of land, often in two or even three counties and often in partnership with several other Punjabis. The largest farms, moreover, are frequently held as corporations, rather than in the names of the Punjabi farmers themselves (Personal communication, Bruce La Brack, April 25, 1986).

[b]Because of rounding, figures do not total 100 percent.

Tables

Table 9. Cling peach farmers and acreage available for harvest in the Sacramento Valley, 1975–1985

Season	Number of farmers	Bearing acres
1975–76	504	19,721
1976–77	467	20,009
1977–78	453	18,266
1978–79	434	16,813
1979–80	428	16,792
1980–81	432	17,770
1981–82	406	16,757
1982–83	355	14,438
1983–84	336	12,073
1984–85	289	11,356

SOURCE: "Orchard and Production Surveys" for the period 1975–76 through 1984–85, Cling Peach Advisory Board, San Francisco, Calif.

Table 10. Birthplaces of Valleyside High School students, 1980–1981 (in percent)

Birthplace	Punjabi (N = 230)	Mexican American (N = 215)	Valleysider[a] (N = 185)
California	12.2	62.3	83.2
Other U.S.	—	3.7	16.8
India	77.4	—	—
Pakistan	3.9	—	—
England	4.3	—	—
Fiji	2.2	—	—
Mexico	—	34.0	—

SOURCE: Compiled from school records.
[a]A random sample was taken of Valleysider students, whereas all Punjabis (except one, whose birthplace was not given in school records) and all Mexican Americans were included.

Table 11. Valleyside High School Punjabi students, October 1980, by grade entered U.S. schools (in percent)

	Grade entered	
	K–2	3–12
9th graders (N = 69)	40.6	59.4
10th graders (N = 69)	34.8	65.2
11th graders (N = 47)	34.0	66.0
12th graders (N = 46)	30.4	69.6
Total (N = 231)	35.5	64.5

SOURCE: Compiled from school records.

Table 12. English proficiency of Valleyside High School Punjabi students, 1980–1981, by grade they entered U.S. schools

Grade entered	Total[a]	FEP (in percent)	LEP/NES (in percent)
K–2	71	77.5	22.5
3–4	24	66.7	33.3
5–6	24	12.5	87.5
7–8	29	10.3	89.7
9–10	45	6.7	93.3
11–12	6	0.0	100.0
Total	199	40.2	59.8

SOURCE: Compiled from school records.
[a]Excludes students who had attended schools in England and Fiji.

Table 13. Valleyside High School class of 1984: Instructional track placement on entering ninth grade (in percent)

	Valleysiders (N = 425)	Punjabis* (N = 28)	Mexican Americans* (N = 44)
Mathematics			
ESL and remedial track	37.9	21.4	45.2
Average track	39.8	60.7	42.9
Accelerated track	22.3	17.9	11.9
Science			
ESL and remedial track	28.3	28.6	42.4
Average track	71.7	71.4	57.6
Accelerated track	—	—	—
Social Studies			
ESL and remedial track	27.8	35.7	54.5
Average track	72.2	64.3	45.5
Accelerated track	—	—	—
English			
ESL and remedial track	11.2	25.0	23.8
Average track	41.1	42.9	54.8
Accelerated track	47.7	32.1	21.4

SOURCE: Compiled from school records.
*Includes only students who had entered U.S. schools by second grade.

[221]

Table 14. Percentage of Valleyside High School students taking advanced courses

	Valleysiders[a] Total (N = 1679)	Punjabis[b]		
		Male (N = 27)	Female (N = 22)	Total (N = 49)
English				
English 1	99.0	96.3	99.0	97.9
English 2	99.0	92.6	86.4	89.8
English 3	69.0	55.5	54.5	55.1
English 4	22.0	29.6	9.1	20.4
Mathematics				
Algebra 1	67.0	70.4	63.6	67.3
Geometry	47.0	59.3	36.4	48.9
Algebra 2	26.0	44.4	13.6	30.6
Trig/Math Analysis	10.0	37.0	4.5	22.4
Science				
Intro Phys. Sci.	72.0	66.7	81.8	73.5
Biology 1	52.0	55.6	40.9	48.9
Chemistry	31.0	44.4	13.6	30.6
Biol. 2/Physics	15.0	37.0	9.1	24.5

SOURCE: Compiled from school records.

[a]Includes all those attending Valleyside High School in spring 1981. Percentages are based on my projections of courses students would subsequently take and include students who would eventually drop out or transfer to continuation high school. These projections agreed with those of the high school.

[b]Includes all in the classes of 1981–83 who had entered U.S. schools by second grade, and percentages are based on actual classes taken throughout high school. (Because of the small sample and the rapid growth of Punjabi population, projections were unreliable.) Does not include those who dropped out in ninth or tenth grade, but they were few.

Table 15. Valleyside High School students who passed competency tests on the first try and national comparison (in percent)

Subject	National sample grades 8 and 9	Valleysiders (N = 178)	Punjabis* (N = 78)	Mexican Americans* (N = 157)
Math	45.0	42.6	26.9	14.6
Reading	77.0	81.2	53.8	59.9
Writing	80.0	81.5	64.1	62.4

SOURCE: Compiled from school records.
*Includes only those who had entered U.S. schools by second grade.

Table 16. Punjabi students, Valleyside district, who passed competency tests on first try, by English proficiency (in percent)

Subject	FEP (N = 93)	LEP (N = 79)	NES (N = 43)
Math	26.9	11.4	2.3
Reading	60.2	11.4	2.3
Writing	69.9	16.5	6.9

SOURCE: Compiled from school records.

Table 17. Distribution of competency test scores in Valleyside school district and national comparison (in percent)

Scaled scores	National sample grades 8 and 9 by quartile	Valleysiders (N = 178)	Punjabis* (N = 78)	Mexican Americans* (N = 177)
Mathematics				
171 up	25.0	24.2	10.3	5.7
151–70	25.0	24.2	21.8	14.6
131–50	25.0	28.0	25.6	34.4
100–30	25.0	23.6	42.3	45.2
Writing				
171 up	25.0	17.0	7.7	3.8
156–70	25.0	30.1	20.5	14.6
136–55	25.0	27.3	24.4	34.2
100–35	25.0	25.6	47.4	47.5
Reading				
171 up	25.0	21.1	8.9	5.1
159–70	25.0	25.0	15.2	17.7
137–58	25.0	34.4	29.1	35.4
100–36	25.0	19.4	46.8	41.8

SOURCE: Compiled from school records.
*Includes only those who had entered U.S. schools by second grade.

Table 18. School enrollment in rural Punjab, 1978

Enrollment	Primary Enter grade 1	Primary Finish grade 5	Middle Enter grade 6	Middle Finish grade 8	Secondary Enter grade 9	Secondary Finish grade 10
Total	515,791	215,661	182,048	123,614	80,905	49,337
Male	274,880	125,483	115,795	82,624	54,469	33,647
Female	240,911	90,178	66,253	40,990	26,436	15,690

SOURCE: NCERT 1980.

[223]

Table 19. Percentage of Valleyside High School seniors selecting individualist rather than family orientation

| | Valleysiders (N = 41) | Punjabis | |
		Raised in U.S.[a] (N = 15)	Recent arrivals[b] (N = 19)
Female	78.1	66.7	35.0
Male	62.9	50.0	24.1

SOURCE: Compiled from student questionnaires.
[a]Students born in the United States or who arrived during elementary school.
[b]Students who arrived during junior or senior high school.

Table 20. Ethnic relations at Valleyside High (in percent)

	Punjabi students (N = 36)	High school faculty (N = 51)	Valleysider students (N = 39)
In your opinion, how are relations between Punjabis and non-Punjabis at the high school?			
Very good (needs no improvement)	8.3	1.9	0.0
Good (needs little improvement)	19.4	3.9	0.0
Fair (needs some improvement)	27.8	52.9	23.1
Poor (needs lots of improvement)	44.4	41.2	76.9

SOURCE: Compiled from student and faculty questionnaires.

References

Akbar, M. J. 1985. *India: The Siege Within.* New York: Penguin.

Allen, Sheila. 1971. *New Minorities, Old Conflicts: Asian and West Indian Migrants in Britain.* New York: Random House.

Anisef, Paul. 1975. Consequences of Ethnicity for Educational Plans among Grade 12 Students. In *Education of Immigrant Students*, ed. A. Wolfgang, pp. 122–36. Toronto: Ontario Institute for Studies in Education.

Anwar, Muhammad. 1979. *The Myth of Return: Pakistanis in Britain.* London: Heinemann.

Au, Kathryn H., and Cathie Jordan. 1981. Teaching Reading to Hawaiian Children: Finding a Culturally Appropriate Solution. In *Culture and the Bilingual Classroom: Studies in Classroom Ethnography*, ed. Henry Trueba, Grace P. Guthrie, and Kathryn H. Au, pp. 216–42. Rowley, Mass.: Newbury House.

Bachu, Amara. 1983. Socioeconomic, Demographic, and Linguistic Characteristics of Asian Indian Migrants in the United States. Paper presented at the annual meeting, Mid-Atlantic Region of the Association for Asian Studies, University of Pennsylvania, Philadelphia.

———. 1984. South Asian Immigrant Women in the United States: A Statistical Overview. In *South Asian Women at Home and Abroad: A Guide to Resources*, ed. Jyotsna Vaid, Barbara D. Miller, and Janice Hyde, pp. 8–14. Syracuse: Syracuse University, Metropolitan Studies Program.

Ballard, Roger. 1983. The Context and Consequences of Migration: Jullundur and Mirpur Compared. *New Community* 11(1/2): 117–36.

———. 1984. The Bitter Drama of the Sikhs. *New Society*, 21 June, pp. 464–66.

———. 1985. Punjab's Uneasy Calm. *New Society*, 20 Sept., pp. 405–6.

———. 1986. Differentiation and Disjunction amongst the Sikhs in Britain. Paper presented at conference, The Sikh Diaspora. University of Michigan, Ann Arbor, 11–12 Dec.

Ballard, Roger, and Catherine Ballard. 1977. The Sikhs: The Development of South Asian Settlements in Britain. In *Between Two Cultures: Migrants and Minorities in Britain*, ed. James L. Watson, pp. 21–56. Oxford: Basil Blackwell.

References

Ballard, Roger, and Selma Vellins. 1985. South Asian Entrants to British Universities: A Comparative Note. *New Community* 12(2):260–65.

Banga, Indu. 1978. *Agrarian System of the Sikhs.* New Delhi: Manohar.

Banton, Michael. 1983. *Racial and Ethnic Competition.* New York: Cambridge University Press.

Barnhardt, Ray, ed. 1982. *Cross-Cultural Issues in Alaskan Education.* Vol. 2. Fairbanks: University of Alaska, Center for Cross-Cultural Studies.

Beetham, David. 1970. *Transport and Turbans.* New York: Oxford University Press.

Benedict, Burton. 1968. Family Firms and Economic Development. *Southwestern Journal of Anthropology* 24:1–19.

Ben-Tovin, Gideon, and John Gabriel. 1982. The Politics of Race in Britain, 1962–79: A Review of the Major Trends and of Recent Debates. In *'Race' in Britain: Continuity and Change,* ed. Charles Husband, pp. 145–71. London: Hutchinson.

Berreman, Gerald D. 1972. Race, Caste, and Other Invidious Distinctions in Social Stratification. *Race* 13(4):385–414.

Bhachu, Parminder. 1985a. *Twice Migrants: East African Sikh Settlers in Britain.* London: Tavistock.

———. 1985b. Parental Educational Strategies: The Case of Punjabi Sikhs in Britain. Research Paper 3, Centre for Research in Ethnic Relations, University of Warwick.

Blakely, Mary M. 1983. Southeast Asian Refugee Parents: An Inquiry into Home-School Communication and Understanding. *Anthropology and Education Quarterly* 14(1):43–68.

Boissevain, Jeremy, and Hanneke Grotenbreg. 1986. Culture, Structure and Ethnic Enterprise: The Surinamese of Amsterdam. *Ethnic and Racial Studies* 9(1):1–23.

Bonacich, Edna. 1973. A Theory of Middleman Minorities. *American Sociological Review* 38:583–94.

Bonacich, Edna, Ivan H. Light, and Charles C. Wong. 1977. Koreans in Business. *Society* 14(6):54–59.

Bonacich, Edna, and John Modell. 1980. *The Economic Basis of Ethnic Solidarity: Small Business in the Japanese American Community.* Berkeley: University of California Press.

Bourdieu, Pierre. 1974. The School as a Conservative Force: Scholastic and Cultural Inequalities. In *Contemporary Research in the Sociology of Education,* ed. J. Eggleston. London: Methuen. Reprinted in *Knowledge and Values in Social and Educational Research,* ed. E. Bredo and W. Feinberg, pp. 391–407. Philadelphia: Temple University Press, 1982.

Bowles, Samuel, and Herbert Gintis. 1976. *Schooling in Capitalist America.* New York: Basic Books.

Bradfield, Helen Haynes. 1971. The East Indians of Yuba City: A Study in Acculturation. M.A. thesis, Sacramento State College.

Brake, Mike. 1980. *The Sociology of Youth Culture and Youth Subcultures.* London: Routledge and Kegan Paul.

[226]

Brooks, Dennis, and Karamjit Singh. 1979. Ethnic Commitment versus Structural Reality: South Asian Immigrant Workers in Britain. *New Community* 7(1):19–30.

Brown, Colin. 1984. *Black and White Britain: The Third PSI Survey.* London: Heinemann.

Brown, George H., et al. [1980]. *The Condition of Education for Hispanic Americans.* Washington, D.C.: National Center for Education Statistics.

Buchignani, Norman, and Doreen Indra. 1980. Inter-group Conflict and Community Solidarity: Sikhs and South Asian Fijians in Vancouver. *Canadian Journal of Anthropology* 1(2):149–57.

———. 1985. *Continuous Journey: A Social History of South Asians in Canada.* Toronto: McClelland and Stewart.

Byers, Paul, and Happie Byers. 1972. Nonverbal Communication and the Education of Children. In *Functions of Language in the Classroom*, ed. C. Cazden, V. John, and D. Hymes, pp. 3–31. New York: Teachers College Press. Reprinted by Waveland Press, 1985.

California Postsecondary Education Commission. 1985. Eligibility of California's 1983 High School Graduates for Admission to the State's Public Universities. Sacramento.

California State Department of Education. 1983. *Basic Principles for the Education of Language-Minority Students: An Overview.* Sacramento: State Department of Education, Office of Bilingual, Bicultural Education.

Castile, George Pierre. 1981. Issues in the Analysis of Enduring Cultural Systems. In *Persistent Peoples: Cultural Enclaves in Perspective*, ed. G. P. Castile and G. Kushner, pp. xv–xxii. Tucson: University of Arizona Press.

Castles, Stephen. 1984. *Here for Good.* London: Pluto Press.

Caudill, William, and George De Vos. 1956. Achievement, Culture and Personality: The Case of the Japanese Americans. *American Anthropologist* 58:1102–26.

Cazden, Courtney. 1982. Four Comments. In *Children in and out of School*, ed. Perry Gilmore and Allan A. Glatthorn, pp. 209–26. Washington, D.C.: Center for Applied Linguistics.

Center for South and Southeast Asia Studies. 1988. *South Asians in North America: An Annotated and Selected Bibliography.* Berkeley: University of California, Center for South and Southeast Asia Studies.

Chadney, James G. 1976. The Vancouver Sikhs: An Ethnic Community in Canada. Ph.D. diss., Michigan State University.

———. 1980. Sikh Family Patterns and Ethnic Adaptation in Vancouver. *Amerasia* 7(1):31–50.

Chancellor, Winston Kenneth. 1983. Job-Barriers for Asian Indian Immigrants in the United States. Ph.D. diss. United States International University.

Chiswick, Barry R. 1979. The Economic Progress of Immigrants: Some Apparently Universal Patterns. In *Contemporary Economic Problems*. William Fellner, Project Director. Washington, D.C.: American Enterprise Institute.

Chun, Ki-Taek. 1980. The Myth of Asian American Success and Its Educational Ramifications. *IRCD Bulletin* 15(1–2).

[227]

References

Clearinghouse on Urban Education. 1981. Complying with Title IX Regulations. ERIC/CUE Fact Sheet no. 2 (March). New York.

Cling Peach Advisory Board. 1976–1985. Orchard and Production Surveys (for 1975–76 through 1984–85). San Francisco.

Cohen, Abner. 1969. *Custom and Politics in Urban Africa*. Berkeley: University of California Press.

Cohen, David K. 1970. Immigrants and the Schools. *Review of Educational Research* 40(1/2):13–27.

Coleman, James S., et al. 1966. *Equality of Educational Opportunity*. Washington, D.C.: U.S. Government Printing Office.

Collins, Randall. 1979. *The Credential Society: An Historical Sociology of Education and Stratification*. New York: Academic Press.

Cordasco, Francesco. 1976. *Immigrant Children in American Schools*. Fairfield, N.J.: Augustus M. Kelley.

Covello, Leonard. 1967. *The Social Background of the Italo-American Child: A Study of the Southern Italian Family Mores and Their Effect on the School Situation in Italy and America*. F. Cordasco, ed. Leiden, The Netherlands: E. J. Brill.

Cubberley, Ellwood P. 1909. *Changing Conceptions of Education*. Boston: Houghton Mifflin.

Cummins, Jim. 1981. The Role of Primary Language Development in Promoting Educational Success for Language Minority Students. In *School and Language Minority Students: A Theoretical Framework*, pp. 3–49. Sacramento: California State Department of Education, Office of Bilingual, Bicultural Education.

———. 1984. *Bilingualism and Special Education*. Clevedon, Avon: Multilingual Matters.

———. 1986. Empowering Minority Students: A Framework for Intervention. *Harvard Educational Review* 56(1):18–36.

Desai, Rashmi. 1963. *Indian Immigrants in Britain*. London: Oxford University Press.

De Vos, George. 1975. Ethnic Pluralism: Conflict and Accommodation. In *Ethnic Identity: Cultural Continuities and Change*, ed. George De Vos and Lola Romanucci-Ross, pp. 5–41. Palo Alto, Calif.: Mayfield.

———. 1982. Adaptive Strategies in U.S. Minorities. In *Minority Mental Health*, ed. Enrico E. Jones and Sheldon J. Korchin, pp. 74–117. New York: Praeger.

———. 1983. Achievement Motivation and Intra-family Attitudes in Immigrant Koreans. *Journal of Psychoanalytic Anthropology* 6(1):25–71.

Dirks, Robert. 1975. Ethnicity and Ethnic Group Relations in the British Virgin Islands. In *The New Ethnicity*, ed. John W. Bennett, pp. 95–109. St. Paul: West.

Dumon, W. A. 1974. Educational Adaptation of Permanent Migrants. *International Migration* 12(1/2):270–300.

———. 1979. The Situation of Children of Migrants and Their Adaptation and Integration in the Host Society, and Their Situation in the Country of Origin. *International Migration* 17 (1/2):59–75.

Dumont, Robert V., Jr. 1972. Learning English and How to Be Silent: Studies in Sioux and Cherokee Classrooms. In *Functions of Language in the Classroom*, ed. C. Cazden, V. John, and D. Hymes, pp. 344–69. New York: Teachers College Press. Reprinted by Waveland Press, 1985.

Dworkin, Rosalind J. 1980. Differential Processes in Acculturation: The Case of Asiatic Indians in the United States. *Plural Societies* 11(2):43–57.

Erickson, Frederick. 1984. School Literacy, Reasoning, and Civility: An Anthropoligist's Perspective. *Review of Educational Research* 54(4):525–46.

Erickson, Frederick, and Gerald Mohatt. 1982. Cultural Organization of Participation Structures in Two Classrooms of Indian Students. In *Doing the Ethnography of Schooling: Educational Anthropology in Action*, ed. George Spindler, pp. 136–74. New York: Holt, Rinehart and Winston.

Erickson, Frederick, and Jeffrey Schultz. 1982. *The Counselor as Gatekeeper*. New York: Academic Press.

Fisher, Maxine P. 1980. *The Indians of New York City*. Columbia, Mo.: South Asia Books.

Foner, Nancy. 1983. Jamaican Migrants: A Compartive Analysis of the New York and London Experience. Occasional Paper no. 36. New York: New York University, Center for Latin American and Caribbean Studies.

Fordham, Signithia. 1984. Afro-Caribbean and Native Black American School Performance in Washington, D.C.: Learning to Be or Not to Be a Native. Unpublished manuscript, Department of Anthropology, American University, Washington, D.C.

Fordham, Signithia, and John Ogbu. 1987. Black Students' School Success: Coping with the "Burden of Acting White." *Urban Review* 18(3):1–31.

Fox, Richard G. 1985. *Lions of the Punjab*. Berkeley: University of California Press.

Gardner, Robert W., Bryant Robey, and Peter C. Smith. 1985. Asian Americans: Growth, Change, and Diversity. *Population Bulletin* 40(4).

Gay, John, and Michael Cole. 1967. *The New Mathematics and an Old Culture: A Study of Learning among the Kpelle of Liberia*. New York: Holt, Rinehart and Winston.

Ghosh, B. N. 1979. Some Economic Aspects of India's Brain Drain into the U.S.A. *International Migration* 17(3/4):280–89.

Ghuman, Paul A. S. 1980. Bhattra Sikhs in Cardiff: Family and Kinship Organisation. *New Community* 8(2):308–16.

Gibson, Margaret A. 1976. Ethnicity and Schooling: A Caribbean Case Study. Ph.D. diss., University of Pittsburgh.

———. 1980. Home-School-Community Linkages: A Study of Educational Equity for Punjabi Youth. Proposal submitted to the National Institute of Education, Washington, D.C.

———. 1982. Reputation and Respectability: How Competing Cultural Systems Affect Students' Performance in School. *Anthropology and Education Quarterly* 13(1):3–27.

———. 1983a. *Home-School-Community Linkages: A Study of Educational Oppor-*

tunity for Punjabi Youth. National Institute of Education, Washington, D.C. Also in ERIC: ED 236 276.

———. 1983b. Appendices, Home-School-Community Linkages: A Study of Educational Opportunity for Punjabi Youth. National Institute of Education, Washington, D.C.

———. 1983c. Ethnicity and Schooling: West Indian Immigrants in the United States Virgin Islands. *Ethnic Groups* 5(3):173–98.

———. 1985. Collaborative Educational Ethnography: Problems and Profits. *Anthropology and Education Quarterly* 16(2):124–48.

Gibson, Margaret A., and Parminder Bhachu. 1986. Community Forces and School Performance: Punjabi Sikhs in Rural California and Urban Britain. *New Community* 13(1):27–39.

Giroux, Henry. 1983. Theories of Reproduction and Resistance in the New Sociology of Education: A Critical Analysis. *Harvard Educational Review* 53(3):257–93.

Goodenough, Ward. 1971. *Culture, Language, and Society.* A McCabe Module in Anthropology. Reading, Mass.: Addison-Wesley.

———. 1976. Multiculturalism as the Normal Human Experience. *Anthropology and Education Quarterly* 7(4):4–6.

Gupte, Pranay. 1985. *Vengeance: India after the Assassination of Indira Gandhi.* New York: W. W. Norton.

Guthrie, Grace Pung. 1985. *A School Divided: An Ethnography of Bilingual Education in a Chinese Community.* Hillsdale, N.J.: Lawrence Erlbaum.

Haviland, William A. 1985. *Anthropology.* New York: Holt, Rinehart and Winston.

Heath, Shirley Brice. 1982. Questioning at Home and at School. In *Doing the Ethnography of Schooling: Educational Anthropology in Action,* ed. George Spindler, pp. 105–31. New York: Holt, Rinehart and Winston.

Helweg, Arthur W. 1979. *Sikhs in England: The Development of a Migrant Community.* Delhi, India: Oxford University Press.

———. 1983. Emigrant Remittances: Their Nature and Impact on a Punjabi Village. *New Community* 10(3):435–43.

———. 1986. Sikh Politics in India: The Emigrant Factor. Paper presented at the Conference, The Sikh Diaspora. University of Michigan, Ann Arbor, 11–12 Dec.

Hess, Gary R. 1982. The Asian Indian Immigrants in the United States: The Early Phase, 1900–65. *Population Review* 25(1/2):29–34.

Hewett, Edgar L. 1905. Ethnic Factors in Education. *American Anthropologist* 7(1). Reprinted in *Educational Patterns and Cultural Configurations,* ed. J. Roberts and S. Akinsanya, pp. 27–36. New York: David McKay, 1976.

Hirschman, Charles, and Morrison G. Wong. 1981. Trends in Socioeconomic Achievement among Immigrant and Native-Born Asian-Americans. *Sociological Quarterly* 22(4):495–514.

———. 1984. Socioeconomic Gains of Asian Americans, Blacks, and Hispanics. *American Journal of Sociology* 90(3):584–607.

——. 1986. The Extraordinary Educational Attainment of Asian-Americans: A Search for Historical Evidence and Explanations. *Social Forces* 65(1):1–27.

Hossain, Mokerrom. 1982. South Asians in Southern California: A Sociological Study of Immigrants from India, Pakistan and Bangladesh. *South Asia Bulletin* 2(1):74–83.

Hurh, Won Moo, and Kwang Chung Kim. 1984. Adhesive Sociocultural Adaptation of Korean Immigrants in the U.S.: An Alternative Strategy of Minority Adaptation. *International Migration Review* 18:188–216.

Inglis, Christine. 1986. Policy Issues in the Education of Minorities in Australia. *Education and Urban Society* 18(4):423–36.

Inglis, Christine, and Lenore Manderson. n.d. Education and Reproduction among Turkish Families in Sydney. Unpublished manuscript, Department of Education, University of Sydney.

Jacoby, Harold S. 1954. Why So Few East Indians? A Study in Social Renitency. Unpublished manuscript. Berkeley: University of California, South/Southeast Asia Library.

——. 1956. A Half-Century Appraisal of East Indians in the United States. Sixth Annual Faculty Research Lecture. Stockton, Calif.: College of the Pacific.

——. 1958. More Thind against Than Sinning. *Pacific Historian* 2(4):1–2, 8.

Jensen, Joan M. In press. *Passage from India: Asian Indians in North America.* New Haven: Yale University Press.

Johnston, Hugh. 1979. *The Voyage of the Komagata Maru: The Sikh Challenge to Canada's Colour Bar.* Delhi: Oxford University Press.

Jordan, Cathie. 1984. Cultural Compatibility and the Education of Hawaiian Children: Implications for Mainland Educators. *Educational Research Quarterly* 8(4):59–71.

——. 1985. Translating Culture: From Ethnographic Information to Educational Program. *Anthropology and Education Quarterly* 16(2):105–23.

Jordan, Cathie, Roland G. Tharp, and Lynn Vogt. 1986. Differing Domains: Is Truly Bicultural Education Possible? Working paper, Kamehameha Center for Development of Early Education, Honolulu.

Joy, Annamma. 1982. Accommodation and Cultural Persistence: The Case of the Sikhs and the Portugese in the Okanagan Valley of British Columbia. Ph.D. diss., University of British Columbia.

Juergensmeyer, Mark. 1982. The Gadar Syndrome: Ethnic Anger and Nationalist Pride. *Population Review* 25(1/2):48–58.

Juergensmeyer, Mark, and N. Gerald Barrier, eds. 1979. *Sikh Studies: Comparative Perspectives on a Changing Tradition.* Berkeley: Graduate Theological Union.

Kapur, Rajiv A. 1986. *Sikh Separatism: The Politics of Faith.* Boston: Allen and Unwin.

Kessinger, Tom G. 1974. *Vilyatpur, 1948–1968: Social and Economic Change in a North Indian Village.* Berkeley: University of California Press.

Kim, E. H. 1975. Yellow English. *Asian American Review* 2:44–63.

References

Kim, Kwang Chung, and Won Moo Hurh. 1983. Korean Americans and the "Success" Image: A Critique. *Amerasia* 10(2):3–21.
——. 1985. Ethnic Resources Utilization of Korean Immigrant Entrepreneurs in the Chicago Minority Area. *International Migration Review* 19(1):82–111.
Kleinfeld, Judith S. 1979. *Eskimo School and the Andreafsky: A Study of Effective Bicultural Education*. New York: Praeger.
——. 1983. First Do No Harm: A Reply to Courtney Cazden. *Anthropology and Education Quarterly* 14(4):282–87.
Kramer, Betty Jo. 1983. The Dismal R ⁻cord Continues: The Ute Indian Tribe and the School System. *Ethnic Groups* 5(3):151–71.
Kurokawa, M. 1970. *Minority Responses: Comparative Views of Reactions to Subordination*. New York: Random House.
La Brack, Bruce. 1980. The Sikhs of Northern California: A Socio-Historical Study. Ph.D. diss., Syracuse University.
——. 1982a. Immigration Law and the Revitalization Process: The Case of the California Sikhs. *Population Review* 25(1/2):59–66.
——. 1982b. Occupational Specialization among Rural California Sikhs: The Interplay of Culture and Economics. *Amerasia* 9(2):29–56.
La Brack, Bruce, and Karen Leonard. 1984. Conflict and Compatibility in Punjabi-Mexican Immigrant Families in Rural California, 1915–1965. *Journal of Marriage and the Family* 46(3):527–37.
Lambert, Wallace E. 1975. Culture and Language as Factors in Learning and Education. In *Education of Immigrants*, ed. Aaron Wolfgang, pp. 55–83. Toronto: Ontario Institute for Studies in Education.
Leacock, Eleanor Burke. 1968. *Teaching and Learning in City Schools: A Comparative Study*. New York: Basic Books.
——. 1982. The Influence of Teacher Attitudes on Children's Classroom Performance: Case Studies. In *The Social Life of Children in a Changing Society*, ed. K. Borman, pp. 47–64. Hillsdale, N.J.: Lawrence Erlbaum Association.
Leaf, Murray J. 1984. *Song of Hope: The Green Revolution in a Punjab Village*. New Brunswick, N.J.: Rutgers University Press.
——. 1985. The Punjab Crisis. *Asian Survey* 25(5):475–98.
Lee, Yongsook. 1984. A Comparative Study of East Asian American and Anglo American Academic Achievement: An Ethnographic Study. Ph.D. diss., Northwestern University.
Leonard, Karen. 1985. Punjabi Farmers and California's Alien Land Law. *Agricultural History* 59(4):549–62.
Leonhard-Spark, Philip J., and Parmatma Saran. 1980. The Indian Immigrant in America: A Demographic Profile. In *The New Ethnics: Asian Indians in the United States*. ed. P. Saran and E. Eames, pp. 136–62. New York: Praeger.
Lepervanche, Marie M. de. 1984. *Indians in a White Australia*. Sydney: George Allen and Unwin.
Lieberson, Stanley. 1980. *A Piece of the Pie: Black and White Immigrants since 1880*. Berkeley: University of California Press.

———. 1985. Unhyphenated Whites in the United States. In *Ethnicity and Race in the U.S.A.*, ed. Richard D. Alba, pp. 159–80. Boston: Routledge and Kegan Paul.

Light, Ivan H. 1972. *Ethnic Enterprise in America: Business and Welfare among Chinese, Japanese, and Blacks.* Berkeley: University of California Press.

———. 1984. Immigrant and Ethnic Enterprise in North America. *Ethnic and Racial Studies* 7(2):195–216.

———. 1985. Immigrant Entrepreneurs in America: Koreans in Los Angeles. In *Clamor at the Gates*, ed. N. Glazer, pp. 161–78. San Francisco: Institute for Contemporary Studies.

Little, A., C. Mabey, and G. Whitaker. 1968. The Education of Immigrant Pupils in Inner-London Primary Schools. *Race* 9:439–52.

McDermott, R. P. 1974. Achieving School Failure: An Anthropological Approach to Illiteracy and Social Stratification. In *Education and Cultural Process*, ed. George D. Spindler, pp. 82–118. New York: Holt, Rinehart and Winston.

———. 1977. Social Relations as Contexts for Learning in School. *Harvard Educational Review* 47(2):198–213.

McDermott, R. P., and Kenneth Gospodinoff. 1979. Social Contexts for Ethnic Borders and School Failure. In *Non-verbal Behavior: Applications and Cultural Implications*, ed. A. Wolfgang, pp. 175–96. New York: Academic Press.

McFee, Malcolm. 1968. The 150% Man, a Product of Blackfeet Acculturation. *American Anthropologist* 70(6):1096–107.

Marjoribanks, Kevin. 1980. *Ethnic Families and Children's Achievements.* Sydney: George Allen and Unwin.

Martin, Jean I., and P. Meade. 1979. *The Educational Experience of Sydney High School Students.* Report no. 1. Canberra: Australian Government Publishing Service.

Masemann, Vandra. 1975. Immigrant Students' Perceptions of Occupational Programs. In *Education of Immigrant Students*, ed. A. Wolfgang, pp. 107–21. Toronto: Ontario Institute for Studies in Education.

Matute-Bianchi, Maria Eugenia. 1986. Ethnic Identities and Patterns of School Success and Failure among Mexican-Descent and Japanese-American Students in a California High School: An Ethnographic Analysis. *American Journal of Education* 95(1):233–55.

Mayer, Adrian C. 1959. A Report on the East Indian Community in Vancouver. Vancouver: Institute of Social and Economic Research, University of British Columbia.

Mehan, Hugh. 1978. Structuring School Structure. *Harvard Educational Review* 48(1):32–64.

Mehan, H., A. Hertweck, and J. L. Meihls. 1986. *Handicapping the Handicapped.* Stanford: Stanford University Press.

Mehrlander, Ursula. 1986. The Second Generation of Migrant Workers in Germany: The Transition from School to Work. In *Education and the Integration of Ethnic Minorities*, ed. Dietmar Rothermund and John Simon, pp. 12–24. New York: St. Martin's Press.

[233]

References

Mercer, Jane R. 1973. *Labeling the Mentally Retarded*. Berkeley: University of California Press.

Metha, H. 1926. A History of the Growth and Development of Western Education in the Punjab, 1846–1884. Punjab Government Record Office, Monograph no. 5. Languages Department, Punjab.

Miller, Allan P. 1950. An Ethnographic Report on the Sikh (East) Indians of the Sacramento Valley. Unpublished manuscript. Berkeley: University of California, South and Southeast Asia Library.

Min, Pyong-Gap. 1984. A Structural Analysis of Korean Business in the United States. *Ethnic Groups* 6(1):1–25.

Minocha, Urmil. 1984. Indian Immigrants in the United States: Demographic Trends, Economic Assimilation in the Host Society, and Impact on the Sending Society. Unpublished manuscript, Honolulu: East-West Population Institute.

Model, Suzanne. 1985. A Comparative Perspective on the Ethnic Enclave: Blacks, Italians, and Jews in New York City. *International Migration Review* 19(1):64–81.

Mullard, Chris. 1982. Multiracial Education in Britain: From Assimilation to Cultural Pluralism. In *Race, Migration and Schooling*, ed. John Tierney, pp. 120–33. London: Holt, Rinehart and Winston.

Nandi, Proshanta K. 1980. *The Quality of Life of Asian Americans: An Exploratory Study in a Middle-Size Community*. Monograph Series no. 2. Chicago. Asian American Mental Health Research Center.

National Commission on Excellence in Education. 1983. *A Nation at Risk: The Imperative for Educational Reform*. Washington, D.C.: United States Department of Education.

National Commission on Secondary Education for Hispanics. 1984. *Make Something Happen*. Washington, D.C.: Hispanic Policy Development Project.

Nayar, Kuldip, and Khushwant Singh. 1984. *Tragedy of Punjab: Operation Bluestar & After*. New Delhi: Vision Books.

NCERT (National Council of Educational Research and Training). 1980. Fourth All-India Educational Survey: Some Statistics on School Education. New Delhi.

Nee, Victor, and Jimy Sanders. 1985. The Road to Parity: Determinants of the Socioeconomic Achievements of Asian Americans. *Ethnic and Racial Studies* 8(1):75–93.

Nee, Victor, and Herbert Y. Wong. 1985. Asian American Socioeconomic Achievement: The Strength of the Family Bond. *Sociological Perspectives* 28(3):281–306.

Ogbu, John U. 1974. *The Next Generation*. New York: Academic Press.

——. 1978. *Minority Education and Caste: The American System in Cross-Cultural Perspective*. New York: Academic Press.

——. 1981. *Schooling in the Ghetto: An Ecological Perspective on Community and Home Influences*. National Institute of Education, Washington, D.C. Also in ERIC: ED 252 270.

——. 1982. Cultural Discontinuities and Schooling. *Anthropology and Education Quarterly* 13(4):290–307.

———. 1983. Minority Status and Schooling. *Comparative Education Review* 27(2):168–90.

———. 1984. Understanding Community Forces Affecting Minority Students' Academic Effort. Unpublished manuscript, Achievement Council of California, Mills College, Oakland.

———. 1985. Research Currents: Cultural-Ecological Influences on Minority School Learning. *Language Arts* 62(8):860–69.

Ogbu, John U., and Maria Eugenia Matute-Bianchi. 1986. Understanding Sociocultural Factors: Knowledge, Identity, and School Adjustment. In *Beyond Language: Social and Cultural Factors in Schooling Language Minority Students*, pp. 73–142. Sacramento, Calif.: State Department of Education, Bilingual Education Office.

Parekh, Bhikhu. 1983. Educational Opportunity in Multi-ethnic Britain. In *Ethnic Pluralism and Public Policy*, ed. N. Glazer and Ken Young, pp. 108–23. London: Heinemann.

Paulston, Christina Bratt. 1982. Swedish Research and Debate about Bilingualism. Report to the National Swedish Board of Education. Stockholm.

Peng, Samuel S., et al. 1984. School Experiences and Performance of Asian American High School Students. Paper presented at the annual meeting, American Educational Research Association, New Orleans, La., 23–27 April. Also in ERIC: ED 252 635.

Pettigrew, Joyce. 1977. Socio-Economic Background to the Emigration of Sikhs from Doaba. *Punjab Journal of Politics* 1(1):48–81.

Philips, Susan U. 1972. Participant Structures and Communicative Competence: Warm Springs Children in Community and Classroom. In *Functions of Language in the Classroom*, ed. C. Cazden, V. John, and D. Hymes, pp. 370–94. New York: Teachers College Press. Reprinted by Waveland Press, 1985.

———. 1983. *The Invisible Culture: Communication in Classroom and Community on the Warm Springs Indian Reservation*. New York: Longman.

Polgar, Steven. 1960. Biculturation of Mesquakie Teenage Boys. *American Anthropologist* 62:217–35.

Portes, Alejandro, and Robert L. Bach. 1985. *Latin Journey: Cuban and Mexican Immigrants in the United States*. Berkeley: University of California Press.

Portes, Alejandro, Robert N. Parker, and Jose A. Cobas. 1980. Assimilation or Consciousness: Perceptions of U.S. Society among Recent Latin American Immigrants to the United States. *Social Forces* 59(1):200–24.

Ramakrishna, Jayashree. 1979. Health Behavior and Practices of the Sikh Community of the Yuba City Area of California. Ph.D. diss., University of California, Berkeley.

Ramsey, Craig A., and E. N. Wright, 1974. Age and Second Language Learning. *Journal of Social Psychology* 94:115–21.

Rist, Ray C. 1970. Student Social Class and Teacher Expectations: The Self-Fulfilling Prophecy in Ghetto Education. *Harvard Education Review* 40(3):411–51.

References

Romo, Harriett. 1984. The Mexican Origin Population's Differing Perceptions of Their Children's Schooling. *Social Science Quarterly* 65:635–50.

Rosenfeld, Gerry. 1971. *"Shut Those Thick Lips!": A Study of Slum School Failure.* New York: Holt, Rinehart, and Winston. Reissued by Waveland Press, 1985.

Rosenthal, Erich. 1960. Acculturation without Assimilation? The Jewish Community of Chicago, Illinois. *American Journal of Sociology* 66(3):275–88.

Rosenthal, Robert, and Lenore Jacobson. 1968. *Pygmalion in the Classroom: Teacher Expectation and Pupils' Intellectual Development.* New York: Holt, Rinehart and Winston.

Rutter, M., et al. 1974. The Children of West-Indian Migrants. *New Society* 27:597, 630–33.

Sacramento Bee, 13 Dec. 1984, 31 March, 11 Aug., 22 Sept., 1 Oct., 4 Dec. 1985, 16 Jan., 21 Feb. 1986, 11 Jan. 1987.

Sanday, Peggy R., A. E. Boardman, and O. A. Davis. 1976. The Cultural Context of American Education. In *Anthropology and the Public Interest*, ed. P. R. Sanday, pp. 75–94. New York: Academic Press.

Santry, Patricia Josephine. 1982. An Historical Perspective on the Factors Preventing Sikh Assimilation in California, 1906–1946. M.A. thesis, California State University, Fullerton.

Saran, Parmatma. 1985. *The Asian Indian Experience in the United States.* Cambridge, Mass.: Schenkman.

Saran, Parmatma, and Edwin Eames, eds. 1980. *The New Ethnics: Asian Indians in the United States.* New York: Praeger.

Schermerhorn, R. A. 1970. *Comparative Ethnic Relations.* New York: Random House.

Schwartz, Audrey J. 1971. The Culturally Advantaged: A Study of Japanese-American Pupils. *Sociology and Social Research* 55(3):341–53.

Scollon, Ron, and Suzanne B. K. Scollon. 1981. *Narrative, Literacy and Face in Interethnic Communication.* Norwood, N.J.: Ablex.

Scully, Malcolm G. 1985. Riots over Affirmative Action Dramatize Continuing Role of India's Caste System. *Chronicle of Higher Education*, 8 May, pp. 31–32.

Sharma, T. R. 1981. Some Political Implications of the Green Revolution. Paper presented at seminar, Changing Trends in Punjabi Politics, 30 Jan.–1 Feb. Chandigarh, Punjab: Indian Council of Social Science Research—North Western Regional Centre, Punjab University.

Sieber, Timothy R. 1978. Schooling, Socialization, and Group Boundaries: A Study of Informal Social Relations in the Public Domain. *Urban Anthropology* 7:67–98.

Singh, Amrik. 1985a. *Punjab in Indian Politics.* Delhi: Ajanta.

——. 1985b. The Delhi Carnage and After. In *Punjab in Indian Politics*, ed. A. Singh, pp. 314–30. Delhi: Ajanta.

Singh, Gopal. 1984. Socio-Economic Bases of the Punjab Crisis. *Economic and Political Weekly*, 7 Jan., pp. 42–47.

Singh, K. P. 1979. Economic Development and Female Labor Force Participation in Punjab. Paper presented at seminar, Regional Development: Socio-Economic Aspects, 4–6 March. Chandigarh, Punjab: Indian Council of Social Science Research—North Western Regional Centre, Punjab University.

Singh, Khushwant. 1953. *The Sikhs*. London: Allen and Unwin.

——. 1966a. *A History of the Sikhs*. vol. 1. *1469–1839*. Princeton: Princeton University Press.

——. 1966b. *A History of the Sikhs*. vol. 2. *1839–1964*. Princeton: Princeton University Press.

——. 1976. *The Sikhs Today: Their Religion, History, Culture, Customs and Way of Life*. New Delhi: Sangam Books.

Singh, Patwant, and Harji Malik, eds. 1985. *Punjab: The Fatal Miscalculation*. New Delhi: Patwant Singh.

Skutnabb-Kangas, Tove. 1979. Language in the Process of Cultural Assimilation and Structural Incorporation of Linguistic Minorities. In *Dialectology and Sociolinguistics: Essays in Honor of Karl-Hampus Dahlstedt*, published in Sweden in 1977 and reproduced by the National Clearinghouse for Bilingual Education, Rosslyn, Va.

——. 1981. Guest Worker or Immigrant—Different Ways of Reproducing an Underclass. *Journal of Multilingual and Multicultural Development* 2(2):89–115.

Sowell, Thomas. 1986. Assumptions versus History in Ethnic Education. In *Education: Assumptions versus History*, ed. T. Sowell, pp. 39–75. Stanford, Calif.: Hoover Institution Press. Reprinted from *Teachers College Record*, Fall 1981.

Spicer, Edward H. 1971. Persistent Cultural Systems: A Comparative Study of Identity Systems That Can Adapt to Contrasting Environments. *Science* 174:795–800.

——. 1980. *The Yaquis: A Cultural History*. Tucson: University of Arizona Press.

Steinberg, Laurence, Patricia Lin Blinde, and Kenyon S. Chan. 1984. Dropping Out among Language Minority Youth. *Review of Educational Research* 54(1):113–32.

Suarez-Orozco, Marcelo M. 1986. In Pursuit of a Dream: New Hispanic Immigrants in American Schools. Ph.D. diss., University of California, Berkeley.

Sue, Stanley, and Derald Sue. 1971. Chinese-American Personality and Mental Health. *Amerasia* 1(2):36–49.

Sung, Betty Lee. 1979. Transplanted Chinese Children. Report to the Administration for Children, Youth and Family, Department of Health, Education and Welfare, Washington, D.C.

Suzuki, Bob H. 1977. Education and the Socialization of Asian Americans. *Amerasia* 4(2):23–51.

——. 1983. The Education of Asian and Pacific Americans: An Introductory Overview. In *The Education of Asian and Pacific Americans*, ed. D. Nakanishi and M. Hirano-Nakanishi, pp. 1–13. Phoenix, Ariz.: Oryx Press.

Swann Committee Report. 1985. *Education for All*. Report of the Committee of Inquiry into the Education of Children from Ethnic Minority Groups. Cmnd. 9453. London: Her Majesty's Stationery Office.

Taft, Ronald. 1983. The Social and Ideological Context of Multicultural Education in Immigrant Countries. In *Multicultural and Multilingual Education in Immigrant Countries*, ed. T. Husen and S. Opper, pp. 1–14. Oxford: Pergamon Press.

Taft, Ronald, and Desmond Cahill. 1981. Education of Immigrants in Australia. In *Educating Immigrants*, ed. Joti Bhatnagar, pp. 16–46. New York: St. Martin's Press.

Taylor, Daniel E. 1981. Education, On-the-Job Training, and the Black-White Pay Gap. *Monthly Labor Review* 104(4):28–34.

Taylor, Monica J. 1981. *Caught Between: A Review of Research into the Education of Pupils of West Indian Origin*. Windsor: NFER-Nelson.

Taylor, Monica, and Seamus Hegarty. 1985. *The Best of Both Worlds . . . ? A Review of Research into the Education of Pupils of South Asian Origin*. Windsor: NFER-Nelson.

Tinker, Hugh. 1977. *The Banyan Tree: Overseas Emigrants from India, Pakistan, and Bangladesh*. Oxford: Oxford University Press.

Tomlinson, Sally. 1983. *Ethnic Minorities in British Schools*. London: Heinemann.

Troike, Rudolph C. 1981. Synthesis of Research on Bilingual Education. *Educational Leadership* 38(6):498–504.

———. 1984. SCALP: Social and Cultural Aspects of Language Proficiency. In *Language Proficiency and Academic Achievement*, ed. Charlene Rivera, pp. 44–54. Clevedon, Avon: Multilingual Matters.

Troyna, Barry. 1978. Differential Commitment to Ethnic Identity by Black Youths in Britain. *New Community* 7(3):406–14.

Tsang, Sau-Lim, and Linda C. Wing. 1985. Beyond Angel Island: The Education of Asian Americans. ERIC/CUE Urban Diversity Series, no. 90.

Tully, Mark, and Satish Jacob. 1985. *Amritsar: Mrs. Gandhi's Last Battle*. London: Jonathan Cape.

Turner, Jonathan H., and Edna Bonacich. 1980. Toward a Composite Theory of Middleman Minorities. *Ethnicity* 7:144–58.

Turner, Wallace. 1981. Bright Asian Students Restive at Berkeley. *Sacramento Bee*, 12 April.

Tyack, David B. 1974. *The One Best System: A History of American Urban Education*. Cambridge: Harvard University Press.

United States Bureau of the Census. 1970. *Statistical Abstract of the United States, 1970* (table 127). Washington, D.C.

———. 1975. *Historical Statistics of the United States, Colonial Times to 1970*, pt. 1. Washington, D.C.

———. 1983a. *Statistical Abstract of the United States, 1984* (table 126). Washington, D.C.

———. 1983b. *1980 Census of Population*. Vol. 1: *Characteristics of the Population*, chap. B: General Population Characteristics, pt. 1: U.S. Summary, PC80–1–B1 (tables 38 and 69). Washington, D.C.

———. 1983c. *1980 Census of Population*. vol. 1: *Characteristics of the Population*, chap. C: General Social and Economic Characteristics, pt. 1: U.S. Summary, PC80–1–C1 (tables 123, 128, 133, 161, 164, 166). Washington, D.C.

——. 1984a. *Statistical Abstract of the United States, 1985* (table 125). Washington, D.C.

——. 1984b. *1980 Census of Population*. Vol. 1: *Characteristics of the Population*, chap. D: Detailed Population Characteristics, pt. 1: U.S. Summary, PC80–1–D1–A (tables 254, 255, 256, 262). Washington, D.C.

——. 1984c. *1980 Census of Population*. Vol. 2: *Subject Reports, Earnings by Occupation and Education*, PC80–2–8B (tables 3, 4, 5, 6, 7). Washington, D.C.

——. 1985. *Statistical Abstract of the United States, 1986* (table 128). Washington, D.C.

United States Commission on Civil Rights. 1980. Success of Asian Americans: Fact and Fiction. Clearinghouse Publication 64.

United States Department of Justice. 1981. Statistical Yearbook of the Immigration and Naturalization Service. Washington, D.C.

United States Department of State. 1981. Statistics on Immigrant Visa Issuances during Fiscal Year 1981. Bureau of Consular Affairs, Immigrant Visa Control and Reporting Division (A–627). Washington, D.C.

——. 1984. Immigrant Numbers for January 1984. Bureau of Consular Affairs, Visa Office, no. 47(5), p. 2. Washington, D.C.

Valverde, Sylvia A. 1987. A Comparative Study of Hispanic High School Dropouts and Graduates: Why Do Some Leave School Early and Some Finish? *Education and Urban Society* 19(3):320–29.

Vellins, Selma. 1982. South Asian Students in British Universities: A Statistical Note. *New Community* 10(2):206–12.

Vernon, Philip E. 1982. *The Abilities and Achievements of Orientals in North America*. New York: Academic Press.

Vialet, Joyce. 1980. A Brief History of U.S. Immigration Policy. Congressional Research Service, Report no. 80–223 EPW. Library of Congress, Washington, D.C.

Vincent, Joan. 1974. The Structuring of Ethnicity. *Human Organization* 33(4):375–79.

Wallace, Paul. 1986. The Sikhs as a "Minority" in a Sikh Majority State in India. *Asian Survey* 26(3):363–77.

Wenzel, Lawrence. 1966. The Identification and Analysis of Certain Value Orientations of Two Generations of East Indians in California. Ph.D. diss., University of the Pacific.

Willis, Paul E. 1977. *Learning to Labour: How Working Class Kids Get Working Class Jobs*. Westmead: Saxon House.

Wilson, Kenneth L., and Alejandro Portes. 1980. Immigrant Enclaves: An Analysis of the Labor Market Experiences of Cubans in Miami. *American Journal of Sociology* 86(2):295–319.

Wilson, Peter. 1983. Ethnic Minority Business and Bank Finance. *New Community* 11 (1/2):63–73.

Wolfgang, Aaron, ed. 1975. *Education of Immigrant Students*. Toronto: Ontario Institute for Studies in Education.

Wong, Eugene F. 1985. Asian American Middleman Minority Theory: The Framework of an American Myth. *Journal of Ethnic Studies* 13(1):51–88.

References

Wong, Morrison G. 1980. Model Students? Teachers' Perceptions and Expectations of their Asian and White Students. *Sociology of Education* 53(4):236–46.

Yoshiwara, Florence M. 1983. Shattering Myths: Japanese-American Educational Issues. In *The Education of Asian and Pacific Americans*, ed. Don T. Nakanishi and Marsha Hirano-Nakanishi, pp. 15–37. Phoenix, Ariz.: Oryx Press.

Young, Anne McDougall. 1983. Youth Labor Force Marked Turning Point in 1982. *Monthly Labor Review* 106(8):29–34.

Index

Index

[242]

Library of Congress Cataloging-in-Publication Data

Gibson, Margaret A.
Accommodation without assimilation.

(Anthropology of contemporary issues)
Bibliography: p.
Includes index.
1. Sikhs—United States—Cultural assimilation—Case studies. 2. Sikhs—United States—Ethnic identity—Case studies. 3. East Indian students—United States—Social conditions—Case studies. 4. Minorities—Education (Secondary)—United States—Case studies. 5. Discrimination in education—United States—Case studies. 6. Home and school—United States—Case studies. I. Title. II. Series.
E184.S55G53   1988   305.6'946'073   87–47861
ISBN 0-8014-2122-5 (alk. paper)
ISBN 0-8014-9503-2 (pbk.: alk. paper)